Measuring the Effectivity of Environmental Law

PETER LANG

Normandy Peace Chair Collection

The aim of this collection is to promote the work carried out by the Normandy Chair for Peace, which conducts research on the rights of future generations and peace with the Earth. Resolutely open to the international scene and committed to multidisciplinarity, the Normandy Chair for Peace will publish here the works it has coordinated in fields as varied as :

Process of change in fundamental rights and legal systems
Good Stories
Climate justice and international jurisdictions
Indigenous Peoples' Rights and the Renewal of the Law through the Lens of Indigenous Knowledge
Education on the rights and duties of future generations
Environmental ethics for lawyers
Bioethics/Biological rights
Transitional justice and environmental peace building
Legal indicators of the SDGs
Economics and law of conservation, protection and restoration of nature
Representation and defense of future generations

This collection aspires to be coherent in order to weave together the various transformations currently underway in international, regional and national legal systems in order to establish a sustainable protection of the environment, environmental rights and the future. The collection also explores the protection of the future human condition as well as the bio-ethical issues that constantly renew the legitimate fields of law.

Drawing from the immemorial wisdom of Humanity, this collection intends to promote all types of works illustrating the civilization imperative according to which: "We will have peace on Earth when we live in Peace with the Earth".

Measuring the Effectivity of Environmental Law

Legal Indicators for Sustainable Development

Michel Prieur
President of the International Centre for Comparative Environmental Law (CIDCE)
Professor Emeritus of Law
Scientific director of CRIDEAU, University of Limoges (France)
Graduate of Sciences Po, Paris

and

Christophe Bastin
President of the Société Ingénierie et Conseil de Nouvelle Aquitaine
Consulting Engineer

With assistance from Mohamed Ali Mekouar
Former Law Professor at the University of Casablanca,
Vice-President of the International Centre for
Comparative Environmental Law

Preface by Alfredo Pena-Vega
Research Lecturer
Scientific Director
Global Youth Climate Pact
Institut interdisciplinaire d'anthropologie du contemporain
Edgar Morin Centre / EHESS-CNRS

Normandy Chair for Peace Collection
Vol. 3

With the support of
The International Center for Comparative Environmental Law and the Normandy Chair for Peace

Cover design: Anne Lacherez

1 avenue Maurice, B-1050 Brussels, Belgium
brussels@peterlang.com; www.peterlang.com

ISSN 2736–3279
ISBN 978-2-8076-1975-3
ePDF 978-2-8076-1972-2
ePUB 978-2-8076-1977-7
DOI 10.3726/b18559
D/2021/5678/48

Bibliographic information published by "Die Deutsche Nationalbibliothek".

"Die Deutsche National Bibliothek" lists this publication in the "Deutsche Nationalbibliografie"; detailed bibliographic data is available on the Internet at <http://dnb.de>.

“Our knowledge of legal facts, in the same way as economic facts, relies upon the methodical collection of precise numerical data”[1].

“Not everything that counts can be counted and not everything that can be counted counts”[2].

“If you cannot measure it, you cannot improve it”[3].

“Evaluating the effectiveness of environmental law is a Herculean task”[4].

1 H. Lévy-Bruhl, “Note sur la statistique et le droit”, in *La statistique, ses applications, les problèmes qu'elle soulève* (Paris, Presses universitaires de France, 1935) pp. 141–147: *“Notre connaissance des faits juridiques ne saurait, pas plus que celle des faits économiques, se passer de données numériques précises et méthodiquement établies”.*

2 Attributed to Albert Einstein.

3 Attributed to Lord Kelvin, 19th century British Physicist.

4 Chris McGrath, *Does Environmental Law Work? How to Evaluate the Effectiveness of an Environmental Legal System* (Riga, Lambert Academic Publishing, 2010) p. 13.

Contents

Acknowledgments

This publication has benefited from much advice and valuable contributions from the members of the Normandy Chair for Peace group that focuses on Legal Indicators in the Law of Future Generations. Special thanks go to: Alexandra Aragão (Professor, University of Coimbra, Portugal), Boris Barraud (Research Lecturer, Aix-Marseille University), Julien Bétaille (Associate Professor, Toulouse 1 University), Odeline Billant (Ph.D. student, LEMAR), Marie Bonnin (Researcher, LEMAR), Pierre Brunet (Professor, University of Paris 1), Fernanda Cavendon-Capdeville (Postdoctoral Fellow, Federal University of Santa Catarina, Brazil), Guillaume Chapron (Associate Professor, Department of Ecology, Swedish University of Agricultural Sciences), Leïla Chikhaoui-Mahdaoui (Professor, University of Carthage, Tunisia), Jérôme Fromageau (Associate Researcher, Institute for Political Social Sciences, ISP Paris-Saclay), Émilie Gaillard (Co-Director of the MRSH Risk Centre, University of Caen, MRSH Caen), José Juste Ruiz (Professor, University of Valencia, Spain) and Alfredo Pena-Vega (Research Fellow, Edgar Morin Centre IIAC/EHESS).

This publication was made possible thanks to Pascal Buléon, Director of the Maison de la Recherche en Sciences Humaines (MRSH) in Caen, and Émilie Gaillard, General Coordinator of the Normandy Chair for Peace.

In addition, documentary support was provided by Vanessa René Galvan at the Georgia State University College of Law in Atlanta, USA.

We would also like to thank the partners of the Normandy Chair for Peace: the Normandy Region, the University of Caen and the CNRS, Professor Nicholas A. Robinson, Chairman Emeritus of the Normandy Chair for Peace, as well as Antonio Oposa Jr., Chair Leader of the Normandy Chair for Peace.

Foreword

In February 2018, the methodological principles for the legal indicators described in this publication received approval during a symposium held in Yaoundé, entitled "Effectiveness and judicial education of environmental law in Francophone Africa". It was organized by the Institut de la Francophonie pour le développement durable (IFDD, Institute of La Francophonie for Sustainable Development), with the participation of UNEP[5], IUCN[6], ECOWAS[7], OIF[8] and CIDCE[9].

Following this, IFDD released the following publication: *Les indicateurs juridiques. Outils d'évaluation de l'effectivité du droit de l'environnement* (Legal Indicators. Tools for assessing the effectivity of environmental law),[10] which describes best practice in measuring the effectivity of environmental law.

This work aims to shed new light on the implementation and use of legal indicators, following two years of experience and exchange.

Environmental indicators are the subject of numerous publications. Yet these publications contain no mention of legal indicators to measure the processes of application of environmental law, and therefore its effectivity. They merely report on the performance of environmental law within current development models.

But beyond this survey of indicators, what have been their achievements? Which indicators have been used repeatedly? Who are they used by? Is there consensus?

Despite differences in methods, their frequent lack of transparency and disagreements between experts, there is one point of consensus for most environmental indicators. That is the link between what is required from the measurements and what is required by governance, particularly with regards to the Sustainable Development Goals (SDGs) and international environmental conventions.

In face of the global challenge of environmental protection, there is a clear need for clarification and harmonization of legal indicators. Moreover, it appears to be vital in order to meet the governance requirements that this challenge poses to the international community.

---

5 United Nations Environment Programme.

6 International Union for Conservation of Nature.

7 Economic Community of West African States.

8 International Organisation of La Francophonie.

9 International Centre for Comparative Environmental Law.

10 https://moged.ifdd.francophonie.org/index.php/fr/publications/download/14/187/19?method=view

Readers may question the usefulness of legal indicators. The answer can be found in Principle 11 of the 1992 Rio Declaration on Environment and Development, which called on States to "enact **effective** environmental legislation".

There are of course a wealth of indicators that measure impacts on the environment. References to the measurement of environmental law in these indicators only mention legal outcomes (number of court rulings, number of offenses, budgets, staffing, etc.).

Measurements of the effectivity of the law are missing. The creation of legal indicators to complement existing environmental, economic and social indicators, is something that is long overdue.

The goal of this publication is to make a real contribution towards meeting the challenges of environmental protection; in particular, achieving the SDGs and ensuring the effective application of international environmental conventions.

We have endeavored to illustrate how legal indicators can be used as innovative tools to better manage reforms and avoid regressions in environmental law, as well as to explain the methodology behind their creation.

We hope to provide readers with a method that is accessible, can be applied easily and that responds to the needs of decision-makers and civil society.

Michel Prieur
Creator of the legal method
Professor Emeritus at the University of Limoges
Scientific Director of CRIDEAU
Honorary Dean of the Faculty of Law and Economic Sciences of Limoges
President of the International Centre for Comparative Environmental Law

Christophe Bastin
Creator of the scientific method
Engineer
Founding President of the Société Ingénierie et Conseil de Nouvelle Aquitaine

Preface

Challenges in the creation of legal indicators for the environment

This publication aims to contribute to a cognitive innovation. To bring scientific rationale to legal indicators[11] used to determine the feasibility of law in the assessment of the Sustainable Development Goals and environmental preservation. A careful balance is sought between the scope of national and international environmental law, and the extent to which the effective application of the law is identified and measured. This approach therefore serves as a powerful tool that can be used in a variety of contexts, from environmental policy management to global ocean governance.

Generally speaking, legal indicators for the environment can be used to identify and measure the effective application of environmental law, reflecting in a variety of ways the impact that a given human activity can have on the environment. For example, biodiversity conservation is a complex issue, full of uncertainty. This fact, combined with a lack of action from political leaders and budget constraints, means that States and international bodies struggle (perhaps willingly) to enforce environmental policies. This calls for forms of monitoring in the broad sense, with the introduction of assessment tools such as indicators. Although this publication does not offer a ready-made solution, it does constitute a significant scientific contribution to the search for legal tools for environmental rehabilitation.

This publication is important for several reasons. Given the current ecological crisis, there are both political and practical reasons to support legal indicators that are scientifically feasible on a local (domestic law) and global (international law) scale, and that protect the biosphere. The current context of global change and growing environmental uncertainty due to human activity is leaving behind a trail of irreversible ecological disasters. Policy makers are putting enormous pressure on legislators to relax environmental standards, ignoring ecological limits and focusing solely on the cult of economic growth. The goal of legal indicators is to offer to every government, international institution and civil society, a tool for assessing the effectivity of the law. In addition, in attempting

11 Eric Angel and others, "An indicator framework to support comprehensive approaches to sustainable fisheries management," *Ecology and Society*, Vol. 24, No. 4 (2019).

to outline recommendations for legal indicators, this will push the boundaries of our knowledge and lead to a better appreciation of the real contributions of environmental law, provided that legal measures based on the Sustainable Development Goals (SDGs) are introduced. It must be noted however that sustainable development is a somewhat ambiguous concept. It must be rethought in terms of sustainability, a concept which takes into account both the biosphere, that is, environmental and living conditions, as well as the future, that is, what might happen to future generations.

This publication comes after two decades in which sustainability indicators have multiplied in the scientific community. One example is the Millennium Development Goals (MDGs), which combined different areas of concern into a set of quantitative indicators that measured progress towards global sustainable development. But while it is important to assess the progress of social, economic and ethical indicators for sustainable development, if it is not possible to report on the effectivity of the law, then this assessment is not only insufficient but also politically misleading.

At last, the scientific community and policy makers working towards finding solutions for environmental sustainability are showing a greater interest in knowledge exchange between science and politics. The impact of this may not be seen for some time as causal links are difficult to detect. Conventional ways of assessing the impact of indicators can be insufficient both scientifically, given the complexity of the science involved, and in terms of decision-making, given the complexity of the real world. This work is not directed towards any specific scientific community of legal theorists or practitioners. In fact the reflections and methodology presented here transcend disciplinary boundaries. As a result, this publication facilitates collaboration between researchers, decision-makers and practitioners. This could contribute to a better understanding of how legal indicators are agreed upon and utilized in policymaking[12].

In the future, it will no longer be possible to ignore the absence of the law when evaluating the state of the environment. Policy makers and public opinion will not be able to underestimate nor deny the weight of the law and its usefulness.

---

12 Stephen Posnera and Christopher Cvitanovic, "Evaluating the impacts of boundary-spanning activities at the interface of environmental science and policy: A review of progress and future research needs," *Environmental Science and Policy*, No. 92 (2019), pp. 141–151.

It remains to be seen what impact this publication will have in terms of essential learning and feedback between the different actors involved.

Alfredo Pena-Vega
Research Lecturer
Scientific Director
Global Youth Climate Pact
Institut interdisciplinaire d'anthropologie du contemporain

Abstract

1. The United Nations General Assembly resolution of 25 September 2015 on the Sustainable Development Goals (SDGs)[13] revealed an apparent willingness among States to better assess the progress of sustainable development. This will lead to greater awareness of the value of environmental law, provided that legal indicators to assess the SDGs are introduced.

2. This publication aims to demonstrate to both States and civil society that legal indicators can be used as a new tool to evaluate environmental policies. To date there has been no scientific work carried out anywhere in the world that focuses on the creation and use of such indicators to assess the effectivity of environmental law.

   The function of legal indicators is to show whether or not environmental law is being applied and why it is misapplied. This will allow the underlying performance and progress of a country to be analyzed. Unlike existing indicators, the goal is not to compare States in a ranking. The aim is to enable urgent necessary legal reforms to be easily identified in order to improve the effectivity of environmental law.

3. As environmental law is both national and transnational, legal indicators are also approached from both of these perspectives, acknowledging that concepts, processes and methods of interpretation may differ in each case when assessing effectivity.

4. The purpose of this publication is to provide empirical guidance to stakeholders by proposing a set of model legal indicators that can be used in both international and comparative law.

5. At present, official assessments of environmental policies, in the form of reports and studies on the state of the environment, do not report on the existence nor effectivity of environmental legislation. Whether these assessments are national, regional or global, only scientific, economic and social indicators can be found. There is no mention of legal indicators for the simple reason that they do not yet exist[14]. The fact that the law is completely missing from

---

13 "Transforming our world: the 2030 Agenda for Sustainable Development," United Nations General Assembly, Resolution 70/1, 25 September 2015 (A/RES/70/1).

14 In the lists of environmental and sustainable development indicators drawn up by the United Nations, the European Environment Agency, the European Union and individual States, there are no qualitative legal indicators.

assessments of the state of the environment means that policy makers and public opinion tend to ignore, underestimate or deny the weight of the law and its usefulness. In reality, due to this lack of data regarding which legislation is applicable and which is actually applied, decision-makers are forced to act almost blindly.

6. Therefore the creation of scientifically based legal indicators for the environment will make it possible to identify and measure the effective application of environmental law. It is clear that legal indicators do not constitute a miracle solution to fill the gaps in the application of environmental law, which are common in all countries to varying extents. Nevertheless they should be seen as a new way to:

   - Clarify and raise awareness of the position and role of the law in environmental policies;
   - Demonstrate the usefulness of environmental law when it is challenged through simplification or derogation;
   - Draw the attention of elected officials and the general public to gaps and regressions in environmental law;
   - Enable both the public and officials charged with applying and monitoring the law to be better informed about the role that environmental law can play in the success or failure of environmental policies;
   - Provide the public with a clear idea of what the effective application of existing environmental law consists of;
   - Provide policy makers, parliaments and governments with assessment criteria for the effective application of international agreements and national laws on the environment with a view to preparing reforms;
   - Enable the outcomes of legal indicators to be aggregated with scientific indicators at a later stage in order to assess effectiveness of environmental policies, that is, the balance between the objectives pursued and the results achieved.

The benefits derived from the creation of legal indicators measuring the effectivity of environmental law are even greater when taking into account the considerable cost of non-compliance with existing laws. In the European Union this cost is estimated to be at around a staggering €55 billion per year[15].

---

15 According to the report by the European Union Network for the Implementation and Enforcement of Environmental Law (IMPEL), *Challenges in the Practical Implementation of European Union Environmental Law and How IMPEL Could Help Overcome Them*, 23 March 2015, p. 11.

7. In his Ph.D. thesis, Julien Bétaille[16] identified 127 theoretical legal indicators, which should be tested and validated in order to be given a value at a later stage. Similar questions arise at each stage of evaluation of the implementation processes of legal norms, for both international and domestic law. These stages are the legal components of effectivity represented by legal indicators related to the following observations:

   - Existence of the rule;
   - Validity of the rule;
   - Entry into force of the rule;
   - Justiciability of the rule;
   - Awareness of the rule;
   - Substance of the rule;
   - Progress or regression of the rule;
   - Clarity of the rule;
   - Administrative review of the rule;
   - Judicial review of the rule;
   - Sanctioning of the rule;
   - Application of sanctions.

8. In support of our proposal to create legal indicators, we have carried out a systematic review of existing environmental indicators, examining the role of environmental law in each case. These indicators were created by international organisations, countries, universities, foundations and NGOs. We have learned the following:

   - Environmental assessment is equivalent to the search for the Holy Grail: it is a never-ending and frustrating pursuit.
   - Jurists who have studied the effectiveness of environmental law have never dared to seriously consider actually measuring the conditions of application of the law.
   - Environmental texts refer to effectiveness, efficiency and efficacy often interchangeably. Confusion is often worsened by inconsistency in translations[17]. In this publication we deliberately use the term "effectivity"

16 Julien Bétaille, *Les conditions juridiques de l'effectivité de la norme en droit public interne: illustrations en droit de l'urbanisme et de l'environnement*, thesis supervised by Michel Prieur, University of Limoges, 2012.

17 The terms effectiveness and efficiency are false friends in French, therefore while effectiveness should be translated as *efficacité* it is often mistranslated as *effectivité*. The same is true for efficiency or efficacy which should be translated as *effectivité* but are often

to make a clear distinction in meaning and avoid confusion between other, similar terms[18].

- Aside from the environment, legal indicators have been used in studies and experiments within two other areas at the United Nations. These are human rights and the rule of law.
- While it is generally agreed that environmental indicators are a necessity, legal indicators have only been regarded as such in exceptional circumstances, for instance at the 1993 Vienna Conference and in the 2012 guide for measuring human rights indicators.
- The term "legal indicator" has actually only been used by three entities: Inter-American Commission on Human Rights, International Labour Organization, The Access Initiative.
- The most relevant assessments successfully incorporate all three complementary levels: international, regional and national.
- Where statistics are available on legal matters, they reflect the number of proceedings, the sanctions imposed and events relating to those proceedings, but never the processes and conditions of application of the existing rules.
- Some institutions seem more open than others to integrate legal data directly into their environmental reviews. These include: the EU Network for the Implementation and Enforcement of Environmental Law (IMPEL); the International Network for Environmental Compliance and Enforcement (INECE); the United Nations Environment Programme (UNEP); the Organisation for Economic Co-operation and Development (OECD); the UN and the 2030 SDGs; the European Union; the Barcelona Convention on the Mediterranean.
- Legal indicators should be treated separately at international and national levels by expanding the practices relating to the reporting system at the international level.

---

translated as *efficacité*. The same confusion occurs in translations from French into English.

18 For the purposes of this study, the notion of effectivity refers to the ability of legal, administrative and jurisdictional processes to achieve the desired result of a legal rule. Effectiveness on the other hand refers directly to the end result, whether that be economic, social or environmental. Efficiency, or sometimes efficacy, have the connotation of getting the best result possible with the resources available.

- Legal indicators of effectivity can only be relevant if they are complemented by institutional, cultural and social data regarding the conduct of actors involved with the application of environmental law.

9. As a practical example, we put forward a total of 17 model indicators, 8 of which relate to international law and 9 to national law. These indicators have been tested by one individual legal expert in four African countries: Benin, Cameroon, Madagascar and Tunisia. These tests have made it possible to experiment with a mathematical method of ad hoc measurement.
   The legal indicators cover international treaty law, international law connected to the 2030 Sustainable Development Goals and national law.
   In international law, two global and three regional conventions were selected to examine the effectivity of national implementation.
   In national law, we have retained five general principles and two specific fields: protected areas and impact assessments. Legal indicators were also tested in four countries covering three continents. In Europe: France and Portugal; in Africa: Tunisia; in South America: Brazil. This involved an assessment of one protected area and the implementation of SDG 14 regarding oceans.

10. The legal indicators seek to address six criteria for the implementation of the legal rule, as follows:

    - Existential indicators: whether the law exists and what its sources are;
    - Indicators of applicability: legality and implementing legislation;
    - Institutional indicators: relevant authorities, environmental control bodies and financial resources;
    - Substantive indicators concerning the content of the law applied;
    - Procedural indicators and indicators of citizen's and jurisdictional control enabling the exercise of rights;
    - Non-legal indicators that affect, to some extent, the effective application of the law.

    In each case, an assessment of effectivity is carried out. There is a formal assessment of the legal text, as well as an evaluation of the practical application, or material assessment, of the implementation process. There is no evaluation of the outcome, that is to say there is no monitoring of the causal link between the legal text and the level of pollution observed. This would require a different, complementary and multidisciplinary study. The evaluation of outcomes is a study of effectiveness, not effectivity. This could take place at a later stage with help from mathematicians and statisticians.

11. The operational set up of national legal indicators in a limited area of environmental law could be achieved in around 24 months. It would require a project manager, a leader and a coordinator; a team of 5 to 10 legal researchers, depending on the number of areas studied; and 2 experts, a mathematician and a statistician, to decide on the methodology to be used to measure the data that will produce the legal indicators.
    The method for measuring legal indicators should be finalized with the support of mathematicians and statisticians who have experience working with environmental or sustainable development indicators.

Introduction

This publication does not outline all of the tools associated with the assessment of effectiveness in environmental law that are usually linked to mechanisms of public policy analysis. This has already been studied in detail in the fields of law, political science and political sociology.

Instead it focuses solely on the recommended method of use of a new tool: legal indicators. During two seminars held in Abidjan in 2013 and Rabat in 2016, African environmental lawyers particularly stressed the need for such a tool in the future. To date there has been no extensive research carried out anywhere in the world that focuses on the creation and use of such indicators to assess the effectivity of environmental law. The first state of the play was published in 2018 by IFDD (Institute of La Francophonie for Sustainable Development) with the support of IUCN (International Union for Conservation of Nature), UN Environment (United Nations Environment Programme), ECOWAS (Economic Community of West African States) and CIDCE (International Centre for Comparative Environmental Law)[19]. It was based on a theoretical study which was limited to a trial of questionnaires with a national expert in the following four French-speaking countries: Benin, Cameroon, Madagascar and Tunisia.

Since 2019, legal indicators have been included in the Normandy Chair for Peace program within the area of Law for Future Generations. A research seminar led by Emilie Gaillard, Senior Lecturer at Sciences Po, Rennes, undertook to extend basic research in order to produce practical outcomes for decision-makers and experts that could be reproduced both internationally and nationally. This research seminar was held at the University of Caen, at the Maison de la Recherche en Sciences Humaines (MRSH) and at the CNRS. Within this context, and with support from the Normandy region, a group of researchers has worked towards developing and testing a scientific method for the creation of legal indicators.

The goal is to be able to offer a tool to every government, international institution and civil society that will allow for an evaluation of the effectivity of both international and national environmental law. Once it has been tested in Europe (France and Portugal), Africa (Tunisia) and South America (Brazil), it will be

19 *Les indicateurs juridiques, outils d'évaluation de l'effectivité du droit de l'environnement*, Quebec, IFDD, OIF, CIDCE, UNEP, IUCN, ECOWAS, 2018, www.ifdd.francophonie.org/media/docs/publications/733_indicateur-juridique_web.pdf.

possible to apply this assessment tool not only to environmental law, but also towards strengthening and measuring achievement of the 2030 Sustainable Development Goals through the effective use of existing legal instruments. The proposed method could then be extended to other regions of the world and even be applied to other rights such as human rights.

As environmental law is both national and transnational, we will approach the issue of legal indicators from both of these perspectives, fully aware that the concepts, processes and methods of interpretation differ.

Given the innovative nature of this topic and its broad scope, encompassing both environmental and sustainable development law, as well as the fact that environmental policies must take into account international, regional and national law, it was agreed that in the first instance legal indicators will only be considered in the context of limited geographical and thematic areas.

The purpose of this publication is to inform both researchers and governments of the value of using such indicators, and to present a method of measurement using legal indicators that can assess progress and better understand any problems encountered. The resulting legal indicators will subsequently have to undergo two complementary processes before becoming operational:

a) Their legal and societal relevance will have to be verified by way of a peer review carried out by environmental jurists in each specific area.
b) Following validation, the legal indicators will have to be "measured" in order to mathematically represent their respective importance in relation to optimal effectivity in environmental law. The selected data will then be quantified and qualified. At a later stage, it will be possible to aggregate these data to report on all areas of environmental law.

Recommending specific indicators that can report on the effectivity of environmental law is an acknowledgment of their significance in the evaluation of one of the public policies that the survival and future of humanity most depends upon.

This need for indicators to accurately assess effectivity when monitoring the implementation of environmental law was recognized by Professor Stéphane Doumbé-Billé at the Environmental Law Network symposium, held by the Agence Universitaire de la Francophonie (AUF) in Yaoundé, from 14 to 15 June 2001. He called for monitoring "in the broad sense, which implies the establishment of evaluation instruments such as indicators, that are reliable and acceptable to all"[20].

---

20 Stéphane Doumbé-Billé, "La mise en œuvre et le suivi du droit international de

Until that time, effectivity in law had only been studied by legal philosophers and theorists, who posed the question as to what the purpose of the law really was. Specialists in legal sociology sought to answer the same question by using behavioral studies that too often relied solely on subjective assessments[21]. Many countries have created more ad hoc bodies such as public policy evaluation committees and councils, in order to evaluate the effects of legislation. Environment ministry general inspectorates have also assessed legislation and regulations using reports from their territorial services. All of these studies and experiments focus only on specific aspects of environmental policies and particular stages of application of the law. But there is no comprehensive overview of all the legal stages involved in the implementation of legislation. Assessments that do exist lack suitable tools to assess not just the general effects of the law, but its legal effectivity, that is, the legal conditions of its application process that lead to compliance.

The creation of legal indicators will make it possible to design a scientific instrument for identifying and measuring the effective application of environmental law, and not just its assumed application through reading the legal text.

We will not enter here into the doctrinal debate occurring among certain lawyers and legal philosophers regarding the relevance of measuring the law[22]. The goal of legal indicators, as with all indicators, is to produce quantified measurements that will make it possible to visualize and classify raw data. These legal indicators are a source of information that can aid decision-making. However, under no circumstances would they be legally binding before a decision-maker or a judge. This is not in any way an attempt to advocate governance through figures.

---

l'environnement. Rapport général", in AUF, *La mise en œuvre nationale du droit international de l'environnement dans les pays francophones* (Limoges, PULIM, 2003), p. 498. Professor Doumbé-Billé passed away in early 2020. A tribute was paid to him in Lyon on 13 February 2020 on the occasion of the posthumous release of a collection of essays in his honor entitled *Droit, humanité et environnement* (Brussels, Bruylant, 2020), 1247 pages.

21 Theoretical questioning surrounding effectivity in law is something recent. See the following theses: V. Richard, *Le droit et l'effectivité, contribution à l'étude d'une notion*, Paris II, 2003; and Y. Leroy, *L'effectivité du droit au travers d'un questionnement en droit du travail*, Nancy, LGDJ, 2011.

22 Alain Supiot, *La gouvernance par les nombres* (Paris, Fayard, 2015); Isabelle Pariente-Butterlin, *Le droit, la norme et le réel* (Paris, PUF, 2005).

There will be no blissful admiration of numbers nor blind belief in the potential merits of applying performance benchmarking to law, having previously been used in the fields of trade and finance. We believe that legal indicators will make it possible in the future to return the law to its rightful place as one of the key drivers affecting the outcome of environmental policy.

Legal philosopher Henri Lévy-Bruhl was quite right in his observation: "Our knowledge of legal facts, in the same way as economic facts, cannot do without precise and methodically established numerical data"[23]. According to the philosopher, mathematician and politician Condorcet, progress of quantification should go hand in hand with the design of a uniform and universal legal system, and it should be possible to calculate the legal rules applicable to all humankind[24]. Indeed, environmental law is characterized precisely by its strongly universalist character in that it applies to humanity as a whole.

This interest in reassessing environmental law comes at a time when, in many countries, the vast array of texts on the subject has led some to criticize what they call a "punitive" ecology, and advocate for the suppression or simplification of texts. This is leading to a regression in the contributions and ambitions of the environmental policies of the 1970s through the 1990s[25]. In order to measure this threat of regression in environmental law, the successes and progress of these laws must be made visible.

Perhaps more than any other area of law, environmental law often displays a clear intent and concern for effectivity, as though its implementation were a collective necessity as a result of ecological urgency. There are many examples of international and national texts that express a desire to be effective. This demand a priori for effectivity of norms can also be found in the field of human rights.

At present, official assessments of environmental policies, through reports and studies on the state of the environment, do not account for the existence

23 H. Lévy-Bruhl, "Note sur la statistique et le droit," in *La statistique, ses applications, les problèmes qu'elle soulève* (Paris, PUF, 1935), pp. 141–147.

24 Condorcet, *Observations sur le 29° livre de* L'esprit des lois, quoted by A. Supiot, *La gouvernance par les nombres, op. cit.*, p. 153.

25 On the principle of non-regression as an obstacle to setbacks in law: M. Prieur and G. Sozzo (dir.), *La non régression en droit de l'environnement* (Brussels, Bruylant, 2012); M. Prieur, "The principle of non regression," in L. Krämer and E. Orlando (eds.), *Principles of Environmental Law*, Elgar Encyclopedia of Environmental Law series, vol 6 (Edward Elgar Publishing, 2018), p. 251.

nor effectivity of environmental legislation[26]. Indeed, whether they be national, regional or international assessments, only scientific, economic and social indicators can be found. There is no mention of legal indicators for the simple reason that they do not yet exist[27]. Rarely is there a mention of any legal element. If there is, there is no qualitative or quantitative assessment. The fact that the law is completely missing from assessments of the state of the environment means that policy makers and public opinion tend to underestimate or deny the weight of the law and its usefulness. In reality, due to this lack of data regarding which legislation is applicable, decision-makers are acting blindly. That is why the creation of legal indicators for environmental law can be seen as an essential contribution to the rigorous and documented evaluation of environmental policies. In turn, this assessment will help decision-makers draw the attention of elected officials and the general public to gaps and regressions in the law. Finally, in more general terms, legal indicators will enable both the public and officials responsible for applying the law to be better informed about the role that environmental law can play in the success or failure of environmental policies.

It is encouraging to note that during the meeting of environment ministers at the G7 summit in Bologna on 11 and 12 June 2017, the value of environmental indicators was highlighted through a commitment to develop measurement and monitoring capacities, identify gaps and develop new global, regional and national indicators. Given this fact, our proposal for new indicators of a legal nature is timed appropriately and should find support within the G7[28].

It is clear that legal indicators are no miracle solution for filling the gaps in the application of environmental law that are sadly common in all countries, to varying degrees. Nevertheless they should be considered as a way to:

- Clarify and raise awareness of the position and role of the law in environmental policies;
- Demonstrate the usefulness of environmental law when it is called into question;

---

26 See the OECD "State Environmental Performance Reviews" from 1992 onwards, where environmental law is mentioned but is not subject to any in-depth assessment or measurement.

27 The legal indicators that we advocate for do not appear in the lists of environmental and sustainable development indicators from the United Nations, the European Environment Agency, the European Union and several States.

28 G7 Bologna Environment Ministers' Meeting, *Communiqué*, 11–12 June 2017, annex "5-year Bologna roadmap," p. 13.

- Evaluate compliance with environmental law according to relevant indicators, either quantitatively or qualitatively;
- Give the public a clear idea of effective application of existing environmental law in order to gain trust in public authorities;
- Provide policy makers, parliaments and governments with assessment criteria for the effective application of international agreements and national laws on the environment with a view to preparing reforms;
- Enable the outcomes of legal indicators to be aggregated with scientific indicators at a later stage in order to assess effectiveness of environmental policies; that is, the balance between the objectives pursued and the results achieved.

The benefits arising from the creation of legal indicators measuring the effectivity of environmental law are even greater when taking into account the cost of non-application of existing law. In the European Union this is estimated to be at around a staggering €55 billion per year[29].

Since the United Nations General Assembly resolution of 25 September 2015 on the SDGs, the willingness of States to better take into account the assessment of progress in sustainable development may mean that the contributions of environmental law will be given more consideration. The tendency to increase the number of categories of indicators should make it possible, on the basis of our proposals, to measure the effectivity of environmental law. The World Bank could then be encouraged to enrich its 2017 SDG Atlas, measuring sustainable development indicators, by including the law. In the same way as it was able to begin measurement of business law with the development of the theory of law and economics. The new list of sustainable development indicators proposed in 2017 by the Committee of Experts at the United Nations Economic and Social Council can only serve to encourage an increase in research towards the creation of legal indicators, which has so far been neglected[30]. Our proposals should also contribute to the work of the United Nations Statistical Commission and the Inter-Agency and Expert Group on Sustainable Development Goal Indicators (IAEG-SDGs), by convincing them that it is no longer possible to assess progress

29 According to the European Union IMPEL network report *Challenges in the Practical Implementation of European Union Environmental Law and How IMPEL Could Help Overcome Them*, 23 March 2015, p. 11. See also: COWI and Eunomia, *Study: The costs of not implementing EU environmental law. Final Report* (Brussels, European Commission, 2019).

30 Report in E/CN.3/2017/2, annex III.

in sustainable development without the presence and contribution of environmental law. The meetings of these two bodies continue to ignore legal environmental indicators, thus reinforcing the goal of our project to introduce new indicators that reflect both the existence and usefulness of environmental law[31]. However, it is interesting to note that this expert group has now allowed for the inclusion of a "human rights dimension" within the indicators[32]. Introducing the environment and sustainable development into statistical tools is well recognized among the fundamental principles of official statistics[33]. This should be continued with the introduction of environmental law, given that where there is society, there is law.

This publication is divided into six sections:

- The need for effectivity in environmental law;
- Acknowledgment that truly legal indicators do not exist;
- Sustainable Development Goal indicators;
- Why create legal indicators for the environment?
- How to create legal indicators based on criteria of effectivity in environmental law;
- How to measure and represent legal indicators.

31 IAEG-SDGs, 5th meeting, Ottawa, 28–31 March 2017 (ESA/STAT/AC.333/L/3); UN Statistical Commission, 48th session, 7–10 March 2017 (E/2017/24-E/CN.3/2017/35).

32 Outcome of the Expert Group Meeting on the indicator framework for the post-2015 development agenda, New York, 25–26 February 2015: proposal endorsed by the UN Statistical Commission at its 46th session, Decision 1, 6 March 2015.

33 United Nations General Assembly resolution of 29 January 2014 (A/RES/68/261).

I. The need for effectivity in environmental law

It is important to clarify the notion of effectivity, given that it does not appear in dictionaries as a noun. Effectivity is intended to denote what is effective, that is, what is done, what produces real and concrete effects, what exists in reality. In order for a law to be effective, one might say that it must be put into effect in practice. In other words, effectivity in law is its practical application. However, it is not a question of the primacy of fact over law but of the translation of law into fact. It is the feasible law, that is, the law that is practically applicable and applied. In other words, it is the law that is applied and which should produce effects. Alongside the law on paper, or formal law, we are concerned with the law that is applied, or real law. Effectivity could be considered, in its legal sense, as the meeting point between law and fact, ideally leading to unity between the two. A living law is one that is effectively applied. A dead law is inadequate and therefore obsolete, ignored or violated. Living law is that which is still in force, because it is endowed with the legal means allowing for its application, monitoring and potential sanctioning. Thus, effectivity in law requires a sequence of components that will allow to go from the law (the text), to fact (its application). Effectivity in law is ultimately quite an obvious and simple requirement: law is created in order to be applied. That said, effectivity in law implies most importantly that the rule exists, that it is legally applicable, that it is legal, known, understood, respected, used, enforced and that potential offenders can be sanctioned by the public authorities or by the courts.

First we will make a distinction between effectivity in international law and in domestic law, and then between effectivity and effectiveness. We will then comment on the growing interest in effectiveness in law, and finally outline the legal components of effectivity in relation to non-effectivity.

A. Effectivity in international and domestic law

The previously mentioned thesis by Julien Bétaille, defended at the University of Limoges in 2012, can be used as a basis for domestic law. In international law, reference will be made to the thesis written by Florian Couveinhes-Matsumoto, defended at the University of Paris II in 2011[34], and to the course given at The

34 Florian Couveinhes-Matsumoto, *L'effectivité en droit international* (Brussels, Bruylant, 2014). Thesis supervised by Denis Alland.

Hague Academy of International Law by Professor R. Wolfrum in 1998[35]. It is important to stress that the notion of effectivity carries a considerably different meaning in domestic and international law. In domestic law it could be said to be a non-legal concept questioning the conditions of application of the law. In international law, it is a legal criterion affecting the application of international law by identifying the subjects of the law and the appropriation of territories. The aim here is to clarify the concept of effectivity, specifying the legal content that will lead to the development of legal indicators which will reflect both domestic and international law.

The Ministerial Declaration on SDGs of the High Level Political Forum on Sustainable Development, 19 July 2017, mentions the words effective and effectiveness on 16 occasions[36]. In 2018, the declaration adopted by this Forum also contains a dozen mentions of these terms[37]. This concern for effectiveness is also increasingly reflected in the voluntary national review summaries submitted by States to the same Forum, with 13 mentions in 2016[38], 18 in 2017[39], 29 in 2018[40] and 31 in 2019[41]. This confirms the current concern for a real application of the Sustainable Development Goals, which itself entails adequate and effectively applied legal instruments.

It is obvious that the legal conditions and the socio-political context in the application of domestic law differ from that of public international law. It is therefore not surprising that effectivity does not have the same meaning in these two fields of law. Nevertheless, we will attempt to make adjustments in order to apply the effectivity criteria identified in domestic law to international law. Ultimately, however, it will be necessary to identify the dual effectivity of international law: that which is assessed within the framework of international law by the bodies of an international convention or by an international judge;

---

35 R. Wolfrum, "Means of ensuring compliance with and enforcement of international environmental law," *Recueil des cours de l'Académie de droit international*, Vol. 272 (1999).

36 E/HLS/2017/1.

37 E/HLS/2018/1.

38 DESA, *Synthesis of Voluntary National Reviews 2016* (New York, 2016).

39 High-level Political Forum on Sustainable Development, *2017 Voluntary National Reviews Synthesis Report* (New York, DESA, 2017).

40 High-level Political Forum on Sustainable Development, *2018 Voluntary National Reviews Synthesis Report* (New York, DESA, 2018).

41 High-level Political Forum on Sustainable Development, *2019 Voluntary National Reviews Synthesis Report* (New York, DESA, 2019).

and that which is assessed within the framework of domestic law by national institutions and by a national judge. This distinction leads us to consider four types of evaluations of effectivity, and so four categories of indicators:

- Assessment of the application of international law in terms of the requirements of international law;
- Assessment of the application of international law in terms of its transposition into national law;
- Assessment of the application of national law in terms of the requirements of international law;
- Assessment of the application of national law in terms of the requirements of national law.

On the topic of effectiveness, Julien Bétaille made an interesting distinction between "state effectiveness" and "action effectiveness"[42]. He explains that state effectiveness is what exists in reality and action effectiveness is what produces an effect on reality. State effectiveness corresponds to the historical definition of the term "effectiveness", according to international law, that is, the observation and legal assessment of a fact such as the occupation of a territory or a maritime blockade. International law observes a fact and deduces its effectiveness, which then leads to a legal qualification or legal consequence. In traditional international law, fact creates law.

Action effectiveness on the other hand is the expression of the law in operation, that is, the effects of the law on the ground, manifested through compliance with the law. This would apply to domestic law. In this case, effectiveness "has a practical purpose in that it aims to assess the degree to which the law is applied in society"[43]. For the purposes of this study, we use the term effectivity to denote this type of effectiveness. The gap between law and practice has until now only been measured by sociologists. Our aim is to add a legal measurement with legal indicators, which will aim to capture and numerically measure the degree of application of a legal norm on the basis of purely legal criteria. We recognize that assessing the application of a legal rule involves more than simply observing compliance and violation. Effectivity exists to varying extents and must satisfy the requirements at each of the multiple stages that make up the processes of application of the law. As a consequence, legal indicators will have to take into

---

42 J. Bétaille, *Les conditions juridiques de l'effectivité…*, *op. cit.*, p. 2.

43 F. Rangeon, "Réflexions sur l'effectivité du droit," in CURAPP, *Les usages sociaux du droit* (Paris, PUF, 1989), p. 128, quoted by J. Bétaille, *ibid.*, p. 15.

account the fact that effectivity is always relative and variable, resulting in a scale of effectivity according to the progression within a specific process.

In reality, state effectiveness and action effectiveness are two sides of the same concept. While the first allows the historical forms of effectiveness in international law to be described, it does not exclude action effectiveness as a means of describing international law. The application of both international and national law requires an assessment of the following: the legal tools for implementing international law; the elements relating to compliance or non-compliance with the norm; and the relative effectivity in the application of the norm, which is an application by degree.

Identifying obstacles to the effective application of the law is particularly complex in environmental law, due to its highly technical nature. There is also a psychological factor, in that what is perceived as complicated is easily ignored. This has been pointed out with regard to nature conservation legislation[44].

The same questions relating to legal effectivity can be found in both international and national law. For each question, specific indicators will need to be created. Some of these indicators will be specific to international law and others to domestic law, but the issues are the same. Six key questions will serve as a basis for the formulation of legal indicators in the questionnaires sent out to actors involved with the application of the law:

1. Does the norm exist, in which text and what is its legal value in the hierarchy of norms (constitution, law, regulation in domestic law; treaty, custom, general principles, hard law, soft law in international law)?
2. Is the norm valid (constitutionally and legally) and therefore applicable and what are the legal requirements for its applicability?
3. Does the norm require special institutional mechanisms with appropriate human and budgetary resources?
4. What is the substantive content of the norm, how are each of its provisions implemented?
5. Is the norm applied and monitored, how and by whom (the administration, the judge, the public), and/or is it sanctionable, how and by whom? Are judicial decisions enforced?
6. Non-legal elements will need to be included to complement the legal issues by assessing the social, economic and political obstacles to the implementation of norms, as the law cannot be assessed without taking into account the

44 Lothar Gündling, *Legal obstacles to the application of nature conservation legislation*, Nature and environment No. 89 (Strasbourg, Council of Europe, 1997), p. 11.

> societal context. If where there is society there is law (*ubi societas ibi jus*), then conversely, where there is law there is society. Indeed, as W. Friedmann wrote, one cannot measure the effectiveness of a normative order without addressing questions concerning the political and social reality that reflect the local context of the application of the law[45].

For this reason, in addition to the strictly legal indicators, some non-legal indicators will be proposed, and should be scientifically validated by sociologists and anthropologists. A rule's effectivity inevitably has a social, cultural and geopolitical dimension[46]. Hence, assessments will strive to be more qualitative than quantitative.

Among the non-legal elements of effectivity assessment, it will be important to take into account the role of particularly strong national cultures[47]. In some cases or in certain countries, custom is a source of law just like international law.

Among the non-legal elements of the assessment, one important contributor to effectivity is the influence that the legal norm exerts on behavior as a result of its mere existence and strong legitimacy. F. Couveinhes-Matsumoto writes that "the ability of a norm to influence the behavior of its addressees is usually reinforced by the overall respect it already enjoys, the sustained agreement of its subjects, etc., so that its current effectivity is almost always beneficial for its future effectivity. The habitual and obvious compliance with a legal rule furthermore increases the feeling that it is legitimate, multiplies the expectations of legal subjects with regard to future compliance, increases the fear of informal or legally organized sanctions in the event of violation and thus constitutes a way of guaranteeing future compliance with the rule"[48].

It should be noted that the validity of a rule is part of its effectivity. But unlike the question regarding validity of the rule, which is answered by a simple yes or no in the context of a judge's assessment of its legality, the question of effectivity cannot be judged in this way because of its complex components and its progressive nature. The degree of effectivity in law has been well examined in the

45 W. Friedmann, *Legal Theory* (London, Stevens and Sons, 1967), p. 278, quoted by F. Couveinhes-Matsumoto, *L'effectivité en droit international, op. cit.*, p. 90, note 353.

46 Philippe Auvergnon, "Une approche comparative de la question de l'effectivité du droit du travail," in Philippe Auvergnon (dir.), *L'effectivité du droit du travail, à quelles conditions?* (Bordeaux, Presses universitaires de Bordeaux, 2008), p. 17.

47 On the subject of labour law in relation to the universal ILO standards, see J. M. Servais, "Normes du droit universelles et cultures nationales," in Philippe Auvergnon (dir.), *ibid.*, pp. 363–385.

48 F. Couveinhes-Matsumoto, *L'effectivité en droit international, op. cit.*, p. 102.

work of F. Couveinhes-Matsumoto, which describes the importance of several variables[49]. For example, the assessment of effectivity will not be the same for general and individual acts, for general principles and technical rules, for legal norms and for judicial decisions.

B. Distinction between effectivity and effectiveness

It is important to differentiate between effectivity and effectiveness, as the objectives and methods of evaluation are different. Effectiveness is that which is most commonly sought in a legal rule. A legal rule is considered relevant if it is effective, and vice versa. That is, if it is socially useful in achieving the objective it sets. It is a consideration of the impact that a rule has on society. This means that it must contribute to achieving a result that is outside the legal system. Whereas analysis of the effectivity of the law is within the legal system. Effectiveness is therefore assessed in relation to the aim and purpose of the legal norm. The objective of the norm, for instance to reduce pollution, may be partially or fully achieved. Effectiveness is measured by scientists' assessment of clean up rates.

On the other hand, effectivity will be evaluated with reference to the legal process used to apply the norm. This assessment will be carried out by jurists, actors involved in the legal application of the norm. Effectivity, like effectiveness, will be judged as total or partial. Legislation regarding water or air which sets clean up targets will be effective if the scientifically measured level of clean up is fully or partially achieved. Effectiveness will be considered as being total or relative. Effectivity may also be absolute or relative. With reference to the earlier distinction, we are referring here to state effectiveness: the concrete and material effect of the legal rule assessed on the ground. Effectiveness therefore measures whether or not the legal norm has achieved its objective(s), either wholly or partially. Effectivity, which is the legal measurement of the application of the law, can thus be considered a necessary requirement, but not needed for effectiveness.

Effectiveness indicators are scientific indicators that measure things such as clean up rates in water and air pollution or the number of protected species. In official documents on the state of the environment at the national and international level, there are a series of numerical indicators for levels of pollution, clean up and the state of biodiversity. These are indicators of effectiveness, also known as performance indicators. These measurements are those most commonly given, but they are not the result of the application of a particular legal text. One initial

49 *Ibid.*, p. 78.

step would be to compare pollution clean up figures with legal texts that impose clean up norms. At present this comparison is not carried out. Currently, effectiveness measurement in environmental law does not reflect the way in which the law has been applied, monitored and enforced. Without evaluating the legal process, which may have been respected to a greater or lesser degree, it is only possible to determine either a poor or healthy state of the environment. The purpose of legal indicators is precisely to evaluate this legal process by measuring a set of factors that contribute to the effectivity of a legal rule in a specific area and lead to the achievement of a result, in this case pollution reduction. It is about being able to demonstrate whether or not this is the direct result of a rigorous and effective application of the legal rule.

If a law's usefulness is determined depending on whether or not it has served a purpose, then there must be an assessment of both the effectiveness of the law in relation to its objectives and the effectivity of the law in relation to the stages of its implementation.

Our aim here is to seek only an assessment of effectivity of the environmental legal rule, without regard for the effectiveness of that rule. Indeed, the search for effectiveness implies the use of exact sciences to scientifically measure the levels of pollution or biodiversity loss. In contrast, measuring effectivity requires a detailed legal and socio-legal analysis of the multiple factors that contribute to the process of applying a legal rule. It is up to jurists to be able to identify and break down the different stages of implementation of the law after it is adopted. Given that an assessment of effectivity is an assessment of a process, we will outline all of the procedural, substantive, institutional and financial instruments that enable the law to be effectively applied.

C. The effectiveness of environmental law according to McGrath

In the interesting publication with the thought-provoking title, *Does Environmental Law Work?*[50], the author proposes a method for assessing the effectiveness of environmental law. The method uses the Pressure-State-Response (PSR) method of State of the Environment Reporting, originally developed by the OECD, applied in the context of climate change and its effects on Australia's Great Barrier Reef. It involves a series of successive studies of a causal relationship: human pressures on the natural environment; the state of

50 C. McGrath, *Does Environmental Law Work?, op. cit.*, p. 1.

the environmental elements and the responses provided by the law; policies and funding. This method, selected by the author after reviewing other methods, is actually unsuitable[51]. The Driving Force-Pressure-State-Impact-Response (DPSIR) method, developed by the European Environment Agency and UNEP, does no better in reflecting the role of the law. The goal of these methods is to assess of the state of the environment. This is not presented as the end result of the assessment but as the second or third step in the assessment process. Thus, there is a clear lack of logic in both the PSR and DPSIR methods. One should be selected between two models:

- Either begin with an assessment of the current state of the environment, which is objectively measurable as a baseline; then examine human and natural pressures; and finally assess existing and proposed responses; this would be the SPR model;
- Or begin with the current state of the environment; then examine existing pressures and assess the responses given, in addition to an assessment of the effectivity of the legal responses in relation to a desired environmental state, using goals that have already been or will be set; this would be the SPRG model. The 2030 Sustainable Development Goals (SDGs) make use of this type of assessment to determine whether or not the state of the environment and legal responses will lead to achievement of the goals.

Whichever assessment process is selected, we are most concerned here with the assessment of the response, because this is where environmental law is key. Sadly, although McGrath does mention the need for environmental indicators (pp. 112–116), he does not mention a need for legal indicators. He offers only a description of the legal response, including both international and national law, but without ever addressing the question of how legal effectivity could be measured as an essential element of the response.

In fact, the author's understanding of effectiveness in environmental law is not to do with the way in which it is applicable and applied. He is only concerned with the study of whether or not environmental law contributes to improving the environment[52]. We have already explained that effectiveness can only be considered after having examined the conditions and processes of legal effectivity.

We can nevertheless conclude from McGrath's study that the legal response to reports on the state of the environment is either very weak or even non-existent,

51 *Ibid.*, p. 109.
52 *Ibid.*, p. 16.

because these reports are written by scientists, with no input from jurists[53]. McGrath does not however conclude that if the legal response is non-existent, it is also because there are no instruments to measure the effective application of the law.

D. The growing interest in legal effectivity, particularly in environmental law

It is important to note that the topic of legal effectivity is meeting with growing interest from researchers and decision-makers. There has been a recent trend towards "juridification" in the demand for effectivity in legal rules. This is reflected both in the particular attention paid to specific procedures for monitoring and promoting norms, mechanisms for achieving conformity, and also in the use of words stressing the role of effectiveness, which has become a component of legal discourse[54].

It is surprising that the UNEP program on environmental law has not placed more emphasis on the need for effectivity in law by differentiating it from effectiveness. In the mid-term review of the Fourth Montevideo Programme on environmental law there was some development on effectiveness in environmental law, but there was no distinction made from effectivity, calling for "respect for and an effective enforcement" of environmental law[55].

At the meeting of senior government officials specializing in environmental law, held at the 2nd session of the United Nations Environment Assembly in May 2016, one recommendation was to "develop criteria to assist States in assessing the effectiveness of environmental law"; however neither the nature nor the content of such criteria were specified[56].

The Fifth Montevideo Programme on environmental law, adopted by the 4th session of the United Nations Environment Assembly in Nairobi on 15 March 2019, is much clearer. It aims to provide countries with "best practices and model indicators for the effective development and effective implementation of environmental law"[57].

---

53 *Ibid.*, p. 240.

54 Antoine Jammeaud, "Le concept d'effectivité," in Philippe Auvergnon (dir.), *L'effectivité du droit du travail, op. cit.*, pp. 45–46.

55 *Mid-term review of the Fourth Programme for the Development and Periodic Review of Environmental Law*, UNEP/EA.2/13, 14 March 2016, para. 4.

56 UNEP/EA.2/13, Annex, para. 3-c-iii.

57 Resolution adopting the Fifth Montevideo Programme: UNEP/EA.4/Res.20; text of the Fifth Montevideo Programme: UNEP/EA.4/19, Annex 1, para. 4-a.

The general public and jurists themselves are concerned about the uncontrolled increase of environmental legislation. It is often said that too much legislation ends up defeating the law. Indeed, both in terms of awareness of the rule and its effective application, an increasing amount of legislation is a problem. The result is that new laws are little or poorly applied. In this respect, environmental law is particularly vulnerable, as a new type of law that has very quickly multiplied in number, both internationally and nationally. This excess is clearly detrimental to its proper application. It is therefore not surprising that attention is now focused on the application of environmental law and no longer on its creation, as was the case ten years ago. Having existed for some time now, environmental law must justify its existence, both in terms of its effectivity as well as its effectiveness. The bibliographies of the two theses mentioned above clearly illustrate the large quantity of books and articles now devoted to the topic of effectiveness in law, in particular environmental law[58].

Environmental legislation also expressly refers to the need for effectiveness. While legal texts do not generally refer to the application of rules, aside from provisions on sanctions, several environmental texts do use the word "effectiveness" in order to highlight decision-makers' interest in adopting texts that will be effectively, or genuinely, applied. The terms "effectiveness" and "effective" are explicitly mentioned in the following locations: paragraph 5 of the preamble and paragraphs a) and b) of the 7th guideline in the Declaration on a Programme of Action on the Protection of the Global Environment, September 2, 1991[59]; the objective of part A, the objective and activities b) and d) of part B, the strategy and activity a) ii. of part C of the Programme for the Development and Periodic Review of Environmental Law for the 1990s, adopted on 21 May 1993[60]; in the 1998 Aarhus Convention: "effective remedy" (art. 9.4) and "effective participation" (art. 6.3 and 8.a); in *The future we want*, from Rio+20 in 2012, the word "effective" appears only once, but paragraph 38 recognizes the need for broader "measures of progress" of sustainable development to better inform policy makers and requests that the United Nations Statistical Commission work towards this; in the *2030 Sustainable Development Agenda* it appears twice, and indicators of "progress in sustainable development" are called for on 8 occasions[61]. Decision

58 See the references of 12 publications on the effectiveness of environmental law between 1998 and 2009 in F. Couveinhes-Matsumoto, *L'effectivité en droit international*, *op. cit.*, note 560, p. 154; and the 60 page bibliography in Julien Bétaille's thesis, *op. cit.*

59 *Institute of International Law Yearbook*, Vol. 64, Part II (1991), pp. 409–412.

60 https://wedocs.unep.org/bitstream/handle/20.500.11822/20586/Montevideo-II.pdf?sequence=1&amp%3BisAllowed=.

61 United Nations General Assembly Resolution 70/1, 25 September 2015 (A/RES/70/1).

1/CP21 and the Paris Agreement on Climate Change of 12 December 2015 refer to effectiveness on 21 occasions in the demand for effective implementation. This demand is accompanied by the use of non-legal indicators on 34 occasions, thus showing the extent to which it has become customary to create only scientific and economic indicators[62].

In the 1992 Rio Declaration, Principle 10 refers to "effective access to justice"; Principle 11 reads "States shall enact effective environmental legislation"; and Principle 15 regarding precaution refers to "effective measures". It should be noted that, in Agenda 21 adopted in Rio in 1992, effectiveness is a frequently recurring theme. The adjective "effective" and the nouns "effectiveness" and "efficacy" are used 231 times across 349 pages. That is to say, in practically every paragraph. "Indicators" are also referred to 34 times, particularly in chapters 8 and 39, but "legal" indicators are ignored. Examples include paragraph 8.6: "develop systems for monitoring and evaluation of progress … by adopting indicators"; paragraph 8.17(a): "making laws and regulations more effective"; paragraph 8.21: "maximize compliance with its laws and regulations … conducting periodic evaluations of the effectiveness of compliance and enforcement programmes"; paragraph 8.44.a: "support … the utilization of sustainable development indicators"; paragraph 39.2: "to evaluate and promote the efficacy of that law"; paragraph 39.3.b: "enhancing the efficacy of international law"; paragraph 39.5: "assess … the effectiveness of existing international agreements".

On a linguistic note, in the French translation of Agenda 21, both the words effectiveness and efficacy are translated using the same word: "*efficacité*".

The World Declaration on the Environmental Rule of Law was adopted in Rio de Janeiro on 29 April 2016 by the IUCN World Congress at the initiative of its World Commission on Environmental Law. It demonstrates that judges and environmental jurists are now convinced that the future of environmental law depends on its effectivity. In this declaration, the effective application of the law is called for on 7 occasions in the text, which is 4 pages in length. In addition to effective application of laws and regulations, it calls for the recognition of "innovative legal tools for effective compliance and enforcement at all governance levels". Legal indicators are an ideal response to this call.

The Ministerial Declaration of the High Level Political Forum on Sustainable Development, 19 July 2017, mentions the words effective and effectiveness on 16

62 Conference of the Parties, 21st session, *Adoption of the Paris Agreement* (FCCC/CP/2015/L.9).

occasions[63]. This further underlines the current concern for a true application of the Sustainable Development Goals, which will only be possible through the use of adequate and effectively applied legal instruments.

Florian Couveinhes-Matsumoto quite rightly points out the following paradox: very often, it is the least binding texts that demand effectiveness, whereas treaties, which are by their very nature binding, rarely do so. Including effectivity as an objective in law would help to reveal those fields of law that are seeking to bring change to the non-compliance and ignorance that is so common[64]. This is the case in environmental law and human rights law.

The European Court of Human Rights in Strasbourg reiterates consistently that its role is to "guarantee not rights that are theoretical or illusory but rights that are practical and effective"[65]. The European Social Charter of 1961, amended in 1996, which has the legal status of an international treaty, insists in each of its articles on the commitment of States to ensure that the various rights concerned are "effectively realized". The word "effective" is used 31 times, in each of the 31 articles of the Charter. This should also be the case for the right to the environment, which has now also become a human right.

In the absence of an international environmental court to embody this message, our proposal for legal indicators for the environment functions to uphold the aim of the European Court of Human Rights to achieve concrete, effective environmental rights.

Following the French draft of the Global Pact for the Environment, the UN Secretary-General's report on the gaps in international environmental law of December 2018 refers to the need for effectiveness, highlighting existing gaps in the implementation and efficacy of international environmental law[66]. This report rightly emphasizes the importance of monitoring compliance with the law and the effective implementation of international environmental law (paras. 86, 92 and 100). Implementation is mentioned one hundred times. The recommendation of the ad hoc working group on the draft Global Pact is even more emphatic on the issue of the effective application of both national and international law.

---

63 Ministerial Declaration of the High Level Political Forum on Sustainable Development organized in 2017 under the auspices of the Economic and Social Council on the theme "Eradicating poverty and promoting prosperity in a changing world," E/2017/L.29-E/HLPF/2017/L.2.

64 F. Couveinhes-Matsumoto, *L'effectivité en droit international*, *op. cit.*, p. 156 and note 570.

65 ECHR, *Airey v. Republic of Ireland*, October 7, 1979.

66 A/73/419, 10 December 2018, paras. 85 *et seq.*

This recommendation, adopted by the United Nations General Assembly resolution 73/333 of 30 August 2019, particularly stresses the need to strengthen the effective application of environmental law. In only 2 pages, the word effective is used twice, and the need to "strengthen" or "promote" the "implementation" of international environmental law and applicable texts, is mentioned on 15 occasions[67].

E. Effectivity in relation to non-effectivity

In measuring the effectivity of the law, its non-effectivity is also clearly measured. When the law is not applied or is applied incorrectly, it is often considered as worthless. However, while the failure to apply the law is a clear sign of non-effectivity, it does not necessarily render the law totally useless. How many times must a rule be ignored or broken in order for it to be considered ineffective? Non-effectivity in a law does not mean that it does not exist, that it is useless nor that it is non-legal in character. Rules that cannot be applied or that are misapplied may still be useful, if only because of their existence, as opposed to cases of nonexistence. It is their degree of effectivity or non-effectivity that is called into question. Even partially ineffective legal norms form part of the foundations of the rule of law. They serve as a moral safeguard, given that their purpose is to be utilized. Ineffective rules can help to play a symbolic role and fulfill certain social functions[68].

Professor Maurice Kamto, a pioneer in environmental law in Africa, has made some harsh yet realistic observations. He considers that environmental law as a whole in Africa is "dormant" and that weaknesses surrounding the concept of law in Africa "results in weakness of legal rules and therefore, their non-effectivity"[69]. Nevertheless, this respected author does add that "it is better to have unenforced rules than a lawless world. The expression of the democratic process under way on the African continent has shown how a dormant law comes to life when a community realizes the need for norms to regulate social relations[70]".

The creation of legal indicators of effectivity in environmental law could be an important contributing factor to the awakening of this dormant law. Indeed,

67 A/RES/73/333, Follow-up to the report of the ad hoc open-ended working group, 5 September 2019, in particular paras. 3, 4, 6, 7, 8, 10, 14, 15, 16, 17 and 18.

68 F. Couveinhes-Matsumoto, *L'effectivité en droit international, op. cit.*, p. 183.

69 Maurice Kamto, *Droit de l'environnement en Afrique* (Paris, AUPELF-UREF, EDICEF, 1996), p. 18. Preface by Michel Prieur.

70 *Ibid.*

this new type of indicator will offer a tool to the various stakeholders in society that can reveal the level of non-effectivity and the failures in implementation of existing law. For this reason, we will attempt to identify indicators that will be both signs of effectivity and non-effectivity, according to their interpretation and the comparisons made. For example, the fact that there is one environmental inspector for every 1,000 polluting firms may be seen a positive indicator of the effectivity of monitoring capacities within a State. However this will be considered as an indicator of non-effectivity in comparison with other countries such as France, where there is one inspector for every 320 facilities[71].

There are numerous legal components in assessments of effectivity. It is possible to compile a list, which must then be submitted to a panel of experienced jurists and legal practitioners for completion or amendment. Once finalized, the next step will be to award a weighting to each of these components by giving them a numerical value in the form of a percentage. A combination of quantitative and qualitative values should be introduced, with the help of mathematicians, before possibly arriving to a model.

On the basis of Julien Bétaille's above-mentioned thesis, 127 theoretical legal indicators have been identified. These will need to be checked and then validated before being given a value. As mentioned previously, when assessing the implementation processes of legal norms, similar questions arise at each stage for both international and domestic law. These stages are the legal components of effectivity, represented by legal indicators linked to a series of criteria, each representing a stage in the complex process that leads to the application of a legal text and, at the same time, one of the legal conditions of effectivity. The processes involved in the effective implementation of a legal text can thus be broken down into several elements, each of which serving as legal indicators, namely:

- Existence of the rule;
- Validity of the rule;
- Entry into force of the rule;
- Justiciability of the rule;
- Knowledge of the rule;
- Substance of the rule;
- Progress or regression of the rule;

71 M. Prieur and others, *Droit de l'environnement*, 8th ed. (Paris, Dalloz, 2019), p. 716.

- Clarity of the rule;
- Administrative review of the rule;
- Judicial review of the rule;
- Sanctioning of the rule;
- Application of sanctions.

II. Acknowledgment that truly legal indicators do not exist

According to labor lawyer Antoine Jeammaud, indicators "are data, mathematical variables, used to identify or measure a phenomenon, or to predict its occurrence". Indicators "provide a systematic and stylized account of what legal instruments do or have done"[72]. This author is thus referring to indicators related to the impact of labor law, or effectivity indicators. He also mentions effectivity in labor law by looking at implementation and compliance. The biggest challenge will always be to make clear this distinction between the two categories of indicators: effectiveness and effectivity. The author goes on to clarify the following: "Jurists believe that the main objectives of legal sociology are as follows: measuring the effectivity of legal rules; explaining their possible and often too frequent non-effectivity and seeking ways of ensuring greater effectivity". We can deduce from this observation that the time has come for jurists to take up the question of effectivity by seeking indicators of a legal nature. This same author also reflects upon effectivity in law in terms of the content of norms: "The concept of effectivity of a legal rule is deceptively simple. Legal rules, in contrast with traditional definitions, are not ultimately all requirements for or prohibitions of a particular conduct, to be obeyed by adopting or refraining from certain behaviors. Moreover, the degree to which behavior, situations, operations and other areas conform to the ideal models provided by legal rules only partially reveals their impact on actions".[73]

It makes more sense to focus on actor's use of the provisions and to find out what they actually achieve in practice[74]. This last point reinforces the view that legal indicators alone cannot account for the full effectivity of the law. They must be supplemented by social indicators that reflect those behaviors and uses that facilitate or hinder the application of a rule. These will be referred to as non-legal indicators.

---

72 Antoine Jeammaud, *Le concept d'impact des normes sociales européennes, quels indicateurs?* (CRDS (IETL), Université de Lyon 2, study for the European Commission, 2005), p. 60.

73 *Ibid.*, p. 63.

74 *Ibid.*, p. 70.

Many authors, especially those writing in the English language, have reflected upon the question of whether it is possible to measure the law[75]. Can we measure the unmeasurable? Mathias M. Siems argues that, aside from performance indicators, or benchmarking, three types of indicators can be combined: functional indicators for issues to be considered in a comparative law perspective; indicators measuring the quality of institutions or judicial systems; and indicators to survey perceptions of the conditions of law enforcement. The latter involves gathering perceptions of businesses, the public and the authorities. But the level of law enforcement would require both performance calculations and data regarding perceptions. For this reason, numerical comparative law as an approach has now become unavoidable[76].

Does positive law mention legal indicators? There are very few pieces of environmental legislation that mention the need for indicators. In international environmental law, article 18.4 of the 2008 Protocol on Integrated Coastal Zone Management in the Mediterranean requires States to define "indicators" in order to assess the effectiveness of strategies, plans and programs. As it is not specified, these indicators could well be scientific or legal. The International Tropical Timber Agreement of 27 January 2006 mentions, in its preamble (para. g), the need to "promote and apply comparable criteria and indicators for sustainable forest management as important tools for all members to assess, monitor and promote progress toward sustainable management of their forests"[77]. Here again, the door is open to scientific, economic and/or legal indicators, but the drafters of the text have considered only non-legal indicators. In reality, as we have already stated above, existing indicators are all measures of effectiveness and not effectivity.

At present, legal indicators to express effective processes in the application of law do not exist, neither in doctrine nor in practice. However, it appears also that many of the examples given do in fact utilize the law as an indicator through the occasional reference to legal texts. But the mere mention of a legal text within a

75 See the bibliography in Mathias M. Siems, "Measuring the immeasurable: How to turn law into numbers", in M. Faure and J. Smits (eds.), *Does Law Matter? On Law and Economic Growth* (Cambridge, Intersentia, 2011), p. 115.

76 Mathias M. Siems claims to have coined the term numerical comparative law in the following article: "Numerical comparative law: Do we need statistical evidence in order to reduce complexity?", *Cardozo Journal of International and Comparative Law*, Vol. 13 (2005), p. 521.

77 https://www.itto.int/direct/topics/topics_pdf_download/topics_id=3363&no=1&disp=inline.

set of indicators does not constitute a truly legal indicator. Indeed, the law covers only quantitative matters, such as the quantity of environmental acts that exists and the amount of environmental treaties that have been ratified. This does not constitute an assessment of the application of these texts, but only their theoretical existence on paper.

We will critically evaluate the indicators proposed by doctrine and by certain institutions, in relation to our recommendations. We will first examine those that occasionally address the environment, and afterwards those that focus specifically on the environment. Finally, we will look at the more developed human rights indicators. In each case, it will become clear that if the law appears as an indicator, it is never to assess its effectivity as a complex legal process, but only as raw, statistical data.

A. Indicators that occasionally address the environment

There are an increasing amount of indicators that relate directly or indirectly to legal issues, such as business law, the rule of law, governance and justice. They may occasionally deal with environmental issues, but these are not legal indicators.

1. Indicators related to the economic weight of the law: Doing Business Index (Law and Economics)

The classic and well-documented matter of indicators for investors based on business law must be excluded from this study from the outset[78]. Initiated by the International Finance Corporation of the World Bank Group and applicable to business law, this approach consists of measuring the cost of law. This economic analysis of the law aims to demonstrate that the law is an instrument for highlighting economic calculation in order to serve neoliberal competitiveness. This work has been the subject of a critical analysis by the *Mission Droit et Justice* (Law and Justice Mission) at the French Ministry of Justice[79]. A similar methodology could be considered for environmental law, but that is not the aim here,

78 For example, Tor Krever, "Quantifying law: Legal indicator projects and the reproduction of neoliberal common sense", *Third World Quarterly*, Vol. 34, No. 1 (2013), pp. 131–150; R. Cooter and T. Ulen, *Law and Economics*, 6th ed. (Boston, Addison Wesley Longman, 2012).

79 Bertrand du Marais (dir.), *Des indicateurs pour mesurer le droit? Les limites méthodologiques des rapports* Doing Business (Paris, La Documentation française, 2006).

and it would involve work in the field of economic science[80]. We could describe our research on legal indicators as *Law and Ecology*, in contrast to this work and by paraphrasing its title, *Law and Economics.*

2. Indicators to assess the psychological perception of the law

We will also discard work that uses psychometric methods to measure people's psychological perception of law and justice. For instance, with reference to SDGs 16.3 and 16.6, one 2018 study measured the perception and attitudes of a population towards civil justice on the basis of 35 questions submitted to a panel of 1061 adults[81]. This methodology can help to understand non-effectivity of the law by revealing people's psychological and behavioral reasoning, but it ignores analysis of the content of the rule and its legal mechanisms of implementation.

3. Indicators related to governance: Worldwide Governance Indicators

The indicators developed by the World Bank since 1996 on global governance (Worldwide Governance Indicators or WGI) include environmental and legal elements that are interesting in terms of the data and criteria used. They refer to the rule of law, government effectiveness, regulatory quality, control of corruption, political stability and the absence of violence, and accountability. With regards to government effectiveness, there are indicators for drinking water, sanitation and the management of waste disposal sites. On the rule of law, there is access to water in agriculture. Finally, on regulatory quality, one of the indicators is entitled "stringency of environmental regulations". This method does not claim to report factual elements on governance, but to translate into figures the perception surrounding the issue in question. While the authors of this work are well aware of the need to distinguish between the law as it is written and the law as it is applied, they only evaluate perception of the application of the law, and not the legal modalities of its application. It relies upon information gathered from 30 specialist organizations, responses to hundreds of questions put to businesses, citizens and experts. Some questions reflect only very general perceptions. For instance: are civil liberties and political rights respected? Is the judicial process fair? Is it easy to start a new business? Is the judiciary

80 M. Faure, *Analyse économique du droit de l'environnement* (Brussels, Bruylant, 2006). Preface by Michel Prieur.

81 P. Pleasance and N. Balmer, "Measuring the Accessibility and Equality of Civil Justice", *Hague Journal on the Rule of Law*, Vol. 10 (2018), pp. 255–294.

independent?[82] It is important to note that these indicators are a measure of an obvious subjectivity, whereas the legal indicators that we propose aim to reflect the actual role of each stage in the application of the law in terms of effectivity of the rule. The 2019 report covers more than 200 countries and territories[83]. The methodology used is summarized in a 2010 report[84].

Governance indicators have been the subject of general analysis and critical study by Christiane Arndt[85]. She is critical of the indicators for their lack of transparency, lack of a comparison across time, sampling bias, subjective perception, failure to take into account errors in measurement and failure to make survey data available to the public.

4. The Natural Resource Governance Index

In 2017 the Natural Resource Governance Institute (NRGI) published a list of indicators in French measuring the quality and effectiveness of governance in the field of oil, gas and mineral exploitation[86]. 150 experts answered 149 questions and data was collated from 10,000 documents. A score was given out of 100, following which the 81 countries studied were grouped into performance bands: good for a score greater than 74, satisfactory for between 60 and 74, insufficient for between 45 and 59, poor for between 30 and 44 and failing if less than 30. The index is divided into three component groups: value realization, which has an environmental sub-component; revenue management; and general conditions of governance. The sub-components of governance directly incorporate legal elements, using the qualifiers and methodology of the Worldwide Governance Indicators mentioned previously. Here again, the willingness to measure the implementation of existing legal frameworks is hampered by the absence of real indicators measuring the effectivity of the law applied.

---

82 World Bank, *A decade of measuring the quality of governance: governance matters* 2007. *Worldwide governance indicators 1996–2007* (Washington, D.C., 2007), p. 16.

83 *Worldwide Governance Indicators 2019*, https://info.worldbank.org/gouvernance/wgi.

84 D. Kaufman, A. Kraay and M. Mastruzzi, *The Worldwide Governance Indicators: Methodology and Analytical Issues*, Policy Research Paper 5430 (The World Bank, September 2010).

85 Ch. Arndt and Ch. Oman, *Governance Indicators: Uses and Abuses* (Paris, OECD Development Centre, 2006); Ch. Arndt, *Governance Indicators*, Dissertation, Maastricht University, 2009.

86 *2017 Resource Governance Index. Measuring the quality of governance in the oil, gas and mining sectors of 81 countries*, www.resourcegovernanceindex.org.

5. The Ibrahim Index of African Governance Indicators

Since 2007, the Mo Ibrahim Foundation has produced an annual report on indicators that relate exclusively to Africa. The main partners are the African Development Bank, the United Nations Economic Commission for Africa and the African Peer Review Mechanism (APRM), which is an agency of the African Union. The foundation's headquarters are in London and it has an office in Dakar. It has published 11 annual reports, the most recent of which was in 2018, highlighting developments and setbacks over the past 11 years in 54 African countries. This index is composed of 102 indicators, with 14 sub-categories in four areas: security and rule of law; participation and human rights; sustainable economic development; and human development. Although they do not directly address the topic of the environment, these reports nevertheless represent an interesting contribution to our research because they take into account legal elements by way of the rule of law, participation and human rights. The 2007 report included an indicator for ecological vulnerability, under the category of "sustainable economic development". This indicator disappeared in 2016. Now under "infrastructure", there is only mention of "access to water". Under the heading "social protection" in 2016, both "environmental sustainability" and "environmental policy" are mentioned. But environmental law is never specifically addressed as such.

An inventory of governance indicators was carried out in 2003. It contained 47 references to measurements of governance around the world that use indicators, including 6 in Africa[87]:

- *Africa Competitiveness Report*, by the World Economic Forum;
- *Afro-Barometer: Population Attitudes to Democracy*, by the Institute for Democracy in South Africa;
- Centre for Studies and Research on International Development (CERDI), University of Auvergne;
- International Development and Integration Index (IDIA), for 7 African States and Madagascar;
- *Nationwide Study Monitoring Progress toward Good Governance in Ghana* (Ghana and 13 other African States);
- United Nations Economic Commission for Africa, *Striving for Good Governance in Africa*.

87 Marie Besançon, *Good Governance Rankings: The Art of Measurement* (Somerville, World Peace Foundation, 2003).

Of these 47 references, the only measurement of good governance that addressed environmental issues was the *Compendium of Sustainable Development Indicators*, developed by the International Institute for Sustainable Development (IISD)[88].

In 2019, the Ibrahim Foundation published the *African Governance Report* which summarized the goals set by the United Nations in 2015 for the 2030 SDGs, in parallel with Agenda 2063, approved by the African Union in 2013 on the occasion of the 50th anniversary of the Organization of African Unity[89].

6. The Praia Group Governance Indicators

The African State of Cape Verde showed great initiative in creating the so-called Praia Group, within the United Nations Economic and Social Council[90]. It was launched in 2014 to study statistical instruments related to governance. Its work does not directly include the environment. However, it does relate to fields concerning the environment, in particular legal issues such as the quality of democracy, justice and human rights, corruption and access to justice. There is also a plan to include support for SDG 16 on access to justice and effective institutions. In 2015, the Praia Group submitted its first report to the United Nations Economic and Social Council, which was reviewed in March 2016[91]. Here again, the necessity for legal indicators is clear. A 2020 edition of this report is available online[92].

7. The United Nations Rule of Law Indicators: Rule of Law Index

The United Nations published a report in 2012 entitled *The United Nations Rule of Law Indicators: Implementation Guide and Project Tools*[93]. Although it is a subjective assessment of the application of the law, this report does propose an interesting methodology that could be applied in part to an assessment of

---

88 https://www.iisd.org/library/compendium-sustainable-development-indicator-initiatives.

89 Mo Ibrahim Foundation, *African Governance Report 2019. Agendas 2063 and 2030: Is Africa on Track?*, 2019.

90 Economic and Social Council, Statistical Commission, 46th session, *Report of Cabo Verde on governance, peace and security statistics*, E/CN.3/2015/17, 9 December 2014.

91 Economic and Social Council, Statistical Commission, 47th session, *Report of the Praia Group on governance statistics*, E/CN.3/2016/16, 17 December 2015.

92 Praia City Group, *Handbook on Governance Statistics*, 2020, https://paris21.org/news-center/news/new-praia-city-group-handbook-governance-statistics.

93 New York, United Nations, 1st edition, 2012.

legal effectivity. The objective of this model of indicators is nevertheless very well defined. The aim is to monitor changes and the functioning of criminal justice in conflict and post-conflict situations. Most of the proposed indicators are not legal indicators. They aim to measure the effectiveness of three institutions: police, justice and prisons. Although it is wholly based on human rights and criminal justice, the aim is not to measure respect for human rights, but to assess the extent to which each of these three institutions are effective, honest, transparent, accountable and able to act using human and material resources. The questions, which highlight effectiveness rather than effectivity, led to the formulation of 135 indicators grouped into 25 "baskets", each comprised of between 2 and 9 indicators. They are given a rating of between 1 and 4, 4 being the highest. These ratings are the result of surveys carried out among the public and experts. For each question, respondents must choose one of the following responses, as appropriate: "very effective" (4), "effective" (3), "ineffective" (2), "very ineffective" (1); or "fully agree", "partly agree", "disagree", "strongly disagree".

Other results are given in percentages to allow for comparisons to be drawn, for example, between the number of prisoners and the number of doctors in prisons. While most of the proposed indicators reflect the content of a legal norm, they do not directly reflect the process of application of the rule. They only reflect the institutional and social reality and the respective roles of the three institutions assessed. This reinforces the view that the development of legal indicators will need to be complemented by non-legal indicators, as they are a prerequisite for the effective application of the law.

Following this publication, the United Nations Secretary-General submitted a report to the General Assembly on 16 March 2012 entitled *Delivering justice: program of action to strengthen the rule of law at the national and international levels.* According to this report: "Member States may also wish to consider how progress in the attainment of rule of law goals, once agreed upon, can be effectively monitored"[94]. Following this, on 24 September 2012 the United Nations General Assembly approved the Declaration of the High-level Meeting of the General Assembly on the Rule of Law at the National and International Levels, addressing the rule of law in general terms, but without referring to indicators to assess respect for the rule of law[95].

---

94 A/66/749, para. 56.

95 A/RES/67/1.

8. Global Rule of Law indicators: World Justice Project

This rule of law index has existed since 2006. It originated as an initiative of the American Bar Association, which has become an independent NGO located in Washington, D.C., as part of the World Justice Project[96]. The 2016 edition ranked 113 countries by assessing their performance in terms of respect for the principles of the rule of law. The aim is not to measure the written rule, but how the legal rule and the practice are perceived by the general public and by legal professionals in particular, through surveys (1000 people per country) and questionnaires completed by legal experts (24 per country). The survey includes questions based on "perception" (123) and "experience" (213). The selected indicators are divided into 9 factors, which are then subdivided, resulting in a total of 47 performance indicators. The 9 factors are: Constraints on Government Power; Absence of Corruption; Open Government; Fundamental Rights; Order and Security; Regulatory Enforcement; Civil Justice; Criminal Justice; Informal Justice.

The 2020 edition covers 128 countries, includes 53 indicators and uses the same criteria as the previous edition[97]. Questionnaire responses were gathered from 130,000 households and 4,000 legal experts.

We are mostly concerned with those indicators relating to open governance, information and participation, fundamental rights and, above all, regulatory enforcement. This last factor is divided into 5 very general indicators: effective enforcement of regulations; enforcement of regulations without improper influence (such as corruption); administrative proceedings without unreasonable delay; respect in proceedings; and no expropriation without compensation. Environmental protection is mentioned as an area of application in some questions on effectiveness and respect for proceedings, but no specific indicator determines the legal conditions for the application of environmental law. Two examples can be given.

5.1. Are government regulations effectively enforced? On this point, the 5 questions related to environmental indicators are as follows:

- What is the general situation? a) companies are respecting the law (either voluntarily or as a result of court orders, fines or other sanctions); b) companies

96 *World Justice Project*, www.worldjusticeproject.org; Juan Botero and Alejandro Ponce, "Measuring the Law", World Justice Project, Working Paper Series 1, November 2011.

97 *WJP Rule of Law Index 2020*, https://worldjusticeproject.org/our-work/research-and-data/wjp-rule-law-index-2020.

are paying bribes or influencing the authorities to hide violations of the law; c) absolutely nothing is happening;

- How likely is it that a medium-sized company would be inspected by environmental protection authorities following a complaint from the neighborhood about pollution? very likely (1); likely (0.667); unlikely (0.333); very unlikely (0);
- How likely is it that a medium-sized company would be regularly inspected by environmental protection authorities? very likely (1); likely (0.667); unlikely (0.333); very unlikely (0);
- What is the likelihood that environmental authorities will impose sanctions if violations are detected? (same multiple choice);
- If environmental protection authorities notified an industrialist that they were polluting a river beyond authorized levels, what would happen? Would the company comply with the law? Would the company pay a bribe or influence authorities so that the violation is ignored? Or would nothing happen?

5.2. Are government regulations implemented and enforced without improper influence? On this point, there are three questions related to the environment. Interestingly they follow the same format, which is not always suited to the specific nature of environmental issues.

Despite the comparative value of this index, between countries and over time, it does not contribute to our goal in this study for several reasons. As well as relying only on qualitative and subjective data, which is always disputable, it ignores the following: the impact of international law; the role of institutional mechanisms and available resources; the creation of new law, by considering only the law that is already applied; and the legal processes that lead to effectivity in law. Environmental law is only considered in a very anecdotal way, looking at industrial pollution alone. Nevertheless, elements of the methodology used and general conclusions on the rule of law are of some use to our proposals. It should be noted that the four States included in the 2018 publication are among the States surveyed: Benin, Cameroon, Madagascar and Tunisia.[98]

9. The Rule of Law Checklist of the Venice Commission, Council of Europe

The European Commission for Democracy through Law, or the Venice Commission, established within the Council of Europe, approved a list of criteria

98 See note 19 above.

that could be considered as indicators of a legal nature, on 18 March 2016[99]. They propose criteria for each of the elements relating to the rule of law: legality, legal certainty, prevention of abuse of powers, equality before the law and non-discrimination, and access to justice. To respond to the questions in each criterion, they rely on both hard and soft international law. Although it does not address environmental issues, and although it only includes passive criteria (depending on the text), this list is indicative of what real legal indicators could look like. The criteria could be considered as legal indicators, in particular those points concerning legality and access to justice. This list was adopted by Resolution 2187 of the Parliamentary Assembly of the Council of Europe on 11 October 2017, and was used to assess the rule of law crisis in Poland and Hungary.

The European Commission for the Efficiency of Justice within the Council of Europe has assessed the efficiency of various judicial systems using indicators[100].

10. The perception of justice in Brazil

There is an interesting national experiment related to assessment of the rule of law, concerned with the perception of justice in Brazil. The work was carried out by the G. Vargas Foundation, focusing on the Justice Confidence Index, which measures public perception of the administration of justice[101].

11. The Justice Indicators of the Vera Institute of Justice

Located in New York, with the support of the World Justice Project and the American Bar Association, this institute studies the rule of law in the United States using justice indicators. In 2008, it conducted a pilot test on the rule of law in 4 cities in India, Nigeria, Chile and in New York, using 60 indicators. The methodology incorporated the World Justice Project indicators described previously[102]. Since then, this institute has focused on the human rights of migrants, prisoners and victims of the Novel Coronavirus (Covid-19).

---

99 https://www.coe.int/fr/web/portal/rule-of-law.

100 European Commission for the Efficiency of Justice, *European Judicial System: Efficiency and Quality of Justice*, CEPEL Studies 11 (Strasbourg, Council of Europe, 2008).

101 Luciana Gross Cunha, Fabiana Luci de Oliveira and Rubens Eduardo Glezer, "Brazilian Justice Confidence Index. Measuring Public Perception on Judicial Performance in Brazil", *Revista Colombiana de Derecho Internacional*, No. 25 (2014), pp. 445–472.

102 J. Parsons and others, *Developing Indicators to Measure the Rule of Law: A Global Approach* (Vera Institute of Justice and Altus Global Alliance, 2008).

12. Indicators measuring access to justice

The Tilburg Institute in Antwerp has developed an interesting method for measuring the cost and quality of access to justice[103]. It is a measure of litigants' perceptions of their judicial experience. Users of the justice system are questioned using three basic indicators: the cost of the proceedings, the quality of the proceedings and the outcome of the proceedings. Each basic indicator is divided into several sub-indicators in order to specify people's material, legal and psychological perceptions. The 2016 *Justice Index* contains 112 indicators[104]. The method is explained in depth. It could be applied to justice in general or to a specific sector[105]. We could employ this index with reference to access to justice in environmental matters.

Since 2014, Canada has applied this method to the area of access to administrative justice, with a non-linear weighting system for a variety of indicators. It is based on 3 assessments with a value of 1, 5 or 10, depending on the perceived importance of the question asked[106].

On 25 February 2020, Peter Chapman, on behalf of the NGO Open Society Justice Initiative, put forward a proposal to the UN Statistical Commission for a complementary indicator to SDG 16 regarding access to justice. It addresses "the proportion of the population that has gone through legal proceedings in the last two years and were able to resolve their problem formally or informally"[107]. The same indicator could be applied to legal disputes related to the environment.

13. UNDP Human Development Report indicators

Since 1990, the UNDP has presented an annual report looking at the past and the future, accompanied by a series of indicators designed to rank States using a Human Development Index (HDI). This index aims to measure and aggregate

---

103 A. Gramatikov and others, *A Handbook for Measuring the Cost and Quality of Access to Justice* (Antwerpen, Maklu and Tilburg Institute for Interdisciplinary Studies of Civil Law and Conflict Resolution Systems, 2009).

104 *The Justice Index 2016*, https://justiceindex.org.

105 https://justiceindex.org/methodology/general-methodology/#site-navigation.

106 Susan McDonald, "Development of an Access to Justice Index for Canada's Federal Administrative Bodies in Canada", 2017, www.justice.gc.ca.

107 This became indicator 16.3.3 at the 51st session of the Statistical Commission: *Tier Classification for Global SDG Indicators as of 17 April 2020*, p. 37, https://unstats.un.org/sdgs/files/Tier%20Classification%20of%20SDG%20Indicators_17%20April%20 2020_web.pdf.

three areas of data: health, knowledge and a decent standard of living. Each year a specific theme is chosen based on current international issues. Since 1992 the environment and sustainable development have of course been a part of these reports. It should be noted, however, that their inclusion has been quite limited and haphazard.

Each year the statistical tables retain a varying number of environmental factors, but environmental law is almost always ignored due to a lack of legal indicators. The UNDP relies solely on existing statistics and data. However, it is striking that in the report itself, the UNDP does not hesitate to refer to the role of certain laws. The 2004 report (table 30) mentions human rights texts, but does not draw any conclusions in terms of indicators. In particular, chapter 5 ("Rising to the Policy Challenges", pp. 81–98) of the 2011 report entitled "Sustainability and Equity", dedicates several pages to the constitutional recognition of the right to a healthy environment as a way of promoting equity, and mentions "explicit environmental rights"[108]. It is a pity that these data are not then used to measure the reality of these rights in the form of legal indicators.

The same 2011 report states that "global norms" reflect "good practice", thus recognizing their usefulness, and that sustainability can be measured "in a normative manner" (p. 41). On environmental migration, the report goes so far as to argue that "legal constraints on movement make migration riskier" (p. 58). The law is therefore not absent. Surprisingly, however, the only mention of law in a table of indicators is in the indicator index of the 2004 report, with a reference to customs duties. The UNDP nevertheless devoted table 15 in the 2016 and 2018 reports to "the status of fundamental human rights treaties". Although it only gives the year that each country ratified 11 different international human rights conventions. The 2004 report includes an indicator based on the ratification of 4 international environmental conventions (table 21). This constitutes a first step. What is actually needed is a table containing all of the universal and regional environmental conventions with indicators for their national implementation, rather than this static vision, which only contains the ratification status and ignores the effective implementation of the conventions beyond their formal ratification.

Examples of environmental indicators adopted by the UNDP in the annual Human Development Reports include the following:

108 UNDP, *Human Development Report. Sustainability and equity: a better future for all* (New York, 2011).

- In 2004[109], table 7, "Water, sanitation and nutritional status" (p. 160), and table 21, "Energy and the environment" (p. 207): carbon dioxide emissions;
- In 2011, there is evidence of real progress in environmental integration. It is the focus of 3 out of 11 tables: table 6, "Environmental sustainability", with indicators such as ecological footprint, environmental performance, carbon dioxide and endangered species; table 7, "Human development effects of environmental threats", including natural disasters and deaths due to pollution; table 8, "Perceptions about well-being and the environment", with the results of a global survey concerning global warming, participation in an active environmental group, and satisfaction with water and air quality and with actions to preserve the environment;
- In 2014[110], 2 out of 16 tables are devoted to the environment: table 14 entitled "Environment" includes fossil fuels supply, electrification rate, carbon dioxide emissions per capita, depletion of natural resources, forest area, fresh water withdrawals, population living on degraded land and impact of natural disasters; table 16 captures surveys on the perception of well-being and the environment;
- In 2016[111], 2 out of 15 tables concern the environment: table 14, on the perception of well-being, and dashboard 2, on sustainable development, which includes 3 groups of indicators on economic sustainability, social sustainability and environmental sustainability. This perspective limits the environment to dealing only with renewables, carbon dioxide emissions, forest area and fresh water withdrawals;
- In 2018[112], "Environmental sustainability" groups together statistical data including percentages of fossil and renewable energy consumed, carbon emissions, forest area and mortality rates attributed to air and water pollution. Table 14 on perceptions of well-being (pp. 74–77) indicates the percentage of people in each country who are satisfied with State actions to preserve the environment. The general conclusion is as follows: "the degradation of the

---

109 UNDP, *Human Development Report 2004. Cultural Liberty in Today's Diverse World* (New York, 2004).

110 UNDP, *Human Development Report 2014. Sustaining human progress: reducing vulnerabilities and building resilience* (New York, 2014).

111 UNDP, *Human Development Report 2016. Human Development for All* (New York, 2016).

112 UNDP, *Human Development Indices and Indicators 2018. Statistical Update* (New York, 2018).

environment and atmosphere, coupled with significant declines in biodiversity, threatens the human development of current and future generations" (p. 11);

- In 2019[113], Chapter 5 entitled "Climate change and inequalities in the Anthropocene" offers a particularly detailed and well presented explanation of the manifestations of the environmental crisis, including the development of disasters (pp. 175–196). Dashboard 4 on environmental sustainability (p. 338) provides a country overview.

One of the UNDP Human Development Reports focusing specifically on Africa is centered on gender parity[114].

In none of these reports is the effectivity of environmental law really addressed.

14. International Labour Organization indicators[115]

Labor law has often been assessed in terms of effectiveness, using a combination of effectivity indicators and performance indicators based on State reports. Each year, the ILO Committee on the Application of Standards (conventions and recommendations) publishes a report. In the report of 16 June 2017, the word "indicator" appears only twice[116]. Convention 169 on Indigenous and Tribal Peoples, which is largely concerned with the environment, is based on the application of fundamental rights. However in its implementation guidance there is no mention of evaluation methods. Nevertheless, a lot of ILO's work is based on what they describe as legal indicators, in combination with performance indicators. These include the 2012 report on *Decent Work Indicators in Africa*; the 2015 report on *Employment Protection Legislation: Summary Indicators*; the 2012 report entitled *Legal Framework Indicators*; and the 2010 report, *Table on Legal Indicators for "Combining work, family and personal life" by country and region*. The 2016 report, *Labour inspection and other compliance mechanisms in the domestic work sector. Introductory guide*, states that "the effectiveness of legislation on domestic work may increase with the establishment of indicators and legal presumptions" (p. 25). The ILO provides a link to the SDGs and contributes

113 UNDP, *Human Development Report 2019. Beyond Incomes, beyond averages, beyond today: Inequalities in human development in the 21st century* (New York, 2019).

114 UNDP, *African Human Development Report 2016. Accelerating progress towards gender equality and the empowerment of women in Africa* (New York, 2016).

115 ILO, www.ilo.org.

116 ILO, Conference Committee on the Application of Standards, *Extract from the record of proceedings*, Geneva, 2017, paras. 35 and 105.

to the approval of special indicators under SDG 8, which are then validated by the UN Inter-Agency and Expert Group on SDG indicators[117].

The ILO is increasingly introducing legal requirements in its indicators. The 19th Conference of Labour Statisticians stressed the "need to interpret the statistical indicators of social dialog within the national legal framework"[118]. Yet this has not resulted in the establishment of real legal indicators of effectivity. Nevertheless, since 2013, in addition to purely statistical quantitative indicators, qualitative indicators called "legal framework indicators" have been included. There are 21, and they have been established in relation to the decent work indicators[119]. These legal framework indicators are based on applicable national law and international legal standards. They relate to, for example: labor law administration, child labor, forced labor, freedom of association, the right to collective bargaining, tripartite consultation, and the legal minimum wage. For each of these 21 legal indicators, in addition to references to texts and a description of their content, there is a section entitled "ratification of ILO conventions", which is purely descriptive. There is also a section on "evidence of implementation effectiveness", which refers to complaints and comments from bodies that monitor compliance with international conventions. This is a clear effort to assess the effectivity of the law, but which ignores the national legal process of application or non-application.

The environment is not ignored. In the ILO's Programme and Budget for 2018–2019, even though the indicators are still quantitative, they appear to be weighted by more qualitative elements. For example, Indicator 3.1, "Number of member States that have adopted … social protection strategies … or legal frameworks to extend coverage", is accompanied by 4 criteria for success, of which criterion 3.1.4 is to take into account "environmental sustainability or climate change" (p. 22). In the same document, Indicator 8.2 covering protection against "unacceptable

117 ILO, Resolution concerning the methodology of SDG indicator 8.8.2 on labour rights, 20th International Conference of Labour Statisticians, Geneva, 2018; Proposed methodology for SDG indicator 8.b.1: "Existence of a developed and operationalized national strategy for youth employment, as a distinct strategy or as part of a national employment strategy", 20th International Conference of Labour Statisticians, Geneva, 2018.

118 19th International Conference of Labour Statisticians, General Report of the Conference, Geneva, 11 October 2013, para. 56.

119 ILO, *Decent work indicators: guidelines for producers and users of statistical and legal framework indicators*, ILO Manual, 2nd version (Geneva, 2013).

forms of work" is supplemented by the success criterion: protect workers "that are affected by environmental degradation or disasters" (p. 40).

In the future, the ILO wishes to further integrate the environment as one of its four cross-cutting labor policy drivers, under the title: "Just transition to environmental sustainability", as a contribution to the implementation of the SDGs. "Environmental sustainability is a precondition for sustainable development, decent jobs and social justice. Progress towards the SDGs with decent work for all requires societies to move towards sustainable consumption and production patterns and safeguard the natural environment"[120].

15. The transparency indicators of the Global Transparency Initiative

The Global Transparency Initiative (GTI)[121] is a network of civil society organizations created to promote transparency in international financial institutions such as the World Bank, IMF, EBRD and regional development banks. Its secretariat is located in South Africa, at the Institute for Democracy in South Africa (Cape Town). Members of this network include the Center for Law and Democracy in Halifax, Canada, and the Access to Information Network (ATIN) based in the Philippines. In 2007, it launched the "Transparency Charter for International Financial Institutions: Claiming our Right to Know"[122]. Based on Article 19 of the Universal Declaration of Human Rights, this document contains 9 principles. While it does not refer to the environment, it was nevertheless reviewed in 2017 in light of the principles of the Aarhus Convention on Access to Information, Public Participation in Decision-making and Access to Justice in Environmental Matters, based on transparency indicators relating to the right of access, automatic disclosure, access to decision-making, the right to request information, and limitation of exceptions and appeals.

16. Corruption and Transparency International

The Transparency International network has regularly published corruption-related indicators since 1995[123]. The 2019 Corruption Perceptions Index[124] ranks

---

120 ILO, *Programme and Budget for the Biennium 2018–19* (Geneva, 2017), para. 189, p. 51.
121 https://eyeonglobaltransparency.net/global-transparency-initiatiive-archive.
122 http://www.freedominfo.org/wp-content/uploads/GTI-charter.pdf.
123 www.transparency.org.
124 https://transparency-france.org/actu/indice-de-la-perception-de-la-corruption-2019-de-transparency-international-il-y-a-urgence-pour-la-france-a-relancer-la-lutte-contre-la-corruption/#.Xt-2piOF5T4.

180 countries on a scale of 0–100, comparing progress in the fight against corruption across States. It deals specifically with election financing and the public decision-making process, but does not address the environment. The ranking is based on 13 data sources and 12 independent institutes. It takes into account possible laws on conflicts of interest, access to information and whistleblowers. A regional barometer on corruption, published in 2019, covers Africa, Latin America and the Caribbean, the Middle East and North Africa. This barometer is based on surveys and interviews. Transparency International has however, since 2020, been working on corruption in the fight against climate change, which should encourage it to take into account related law. A special report on Brazil, published in 2019, took stock of recent setbacks in the legal and institutional fight against corruption. This was based on surveys and interviews and made no reference to indicators.

B. Indicators focusing specifically on the environment

It should be stressed that there is a great deal of literature on the topic of environmental indicators. The majority of these indicators are scientific or economic, especially those related to the Millennium Development Goals (MDGs) and subsequently the Sustainable Development Goals. While the latter are universal and so involve commitment from every country in the world, the 8 MDGs were only relevant to developing countries, and contained only 21 targets, measured against only 60 indicators[125]. The UN resolution approving the SDGs in 2015 does not specify the nature of the indicators to be put in place, but it is clearly stated that the SDG targets will be reviewed using global indicators, complemented by regional and national indicators (para. 75). In addition, States and national parliaments are encouraged "to conduct regular and inclusive country-led and country-owned reviews of progress" (para. 79). Several experiments highlight to different extents the legal data that is essential for environmental policies.

We will not address here the documents which, in some States, list all the measures taken to monitor the activity of polluting companies. These are not

125 United Nations, *Millennium Development Goals. Report 2015* (New York, 2015). The official list of MDG-related indicators, which does not include strictly speaking legal indicators: http://mdgs.un.org/unsd/mdg/Resources/Attach/Indicators/OfficialList2008_fr.pdf.

indicators, but nevertheless they are statistics that are useful for assessing effectivity in law[126].

Some States place strong emphasis on environmental indicators and ensure they are easily accessible. One example is Spain, where the Ministry of Agriculture and the Environment has a "Public Bank of Environmental Indicators". It is composed of 16 themes and 68 indicators[127], but none refer directly to the law. After reviewing the indicators within the European Union, we will go on to describe a series of indicators that take into account environmental issues to varying extents.

1. European Union indicators

a) *From the 7th Action Programme for monitoring compliance with environmental law*

In its 7th Environment Action Programme to 2020, in force since 2014, the European Union notes that EU legislation is insufficiently implemented and calls for progress to be assessed using indicators[128]. The Commission's project included indicators to monitor the implementation of environmental legislation[129], thus adding further justification to this publication.

The European Union has several sets of indicators related to the environment: structural indicators, indicators related to the Europe 2020 Strategy, Euro-indicators and sustainable development indicators.

The Lisbon European Council called for a set of structural indicators to be used to underpin the analysis in the annual Spring Report assessing progress. These indicators were adopted in 2002 and cover six areas, one of which is the environment. They address the issues of climate change, environmentally sustainable transport, public health risks and natural resource management, through the following six indicators: greenhouse gas emissions; energy intensity of the economy; volume of transport relative to GDP; distribution by mode of

126 For example, the EPA's (US Environmental Protection Agency) ECHO (Enforcement and Compliance History Online) website contains records of permits granted, violations identified, monitoring requirements and penalties imposed for 800,000 companies.

127 Gobierno de España, Ministerio de Agricultura y Pesca, Alimentación y Medio Ambiente, *Calidad y Evaluación Ambiental*, http://origin.magrama.gob.es/es/calidad-y-evaluacionambiental/temas.

128 Decision No. 1386 of 20 November 2013, Annex, para. 6.

129 Proposal for a Decision of 29 November 2012, COM (2012) 710 final, para. 102.

transport; ambient air quality; municipal waste; and share of renewable energy. The list of indicators changes every year[130]. In 2004, out of 14 indicators, only one addressed the environment: greenhouse gas emissions. The following indicators were subsequently developed: consumption of toxic chemicals, healthy life expectancy, biodiversity index, resource productivity, recycling rate of certain materials, and generation of hazardous waste[131].

The Europe 2020 Strategy, adopted by the European Council on 17 June 2010, identifies 9 key indicators. Only one refers to the environment: climate change and energy. In 2015, the French Economic, Social and Environmental Council criticized this situation by calling for a diversification of environmental indicators (p. 27) and a healthy environment index (p. 30)[132]. A review was published in 2019[133].

Euro-indicators do not directly address the environment. They are the main European economic indicators, supplemented by labor market indicators.

The EU sustainable development indicators were agreed upon in a 2016 communication outlining the next steps for a sustainable European future[134]. They are regularly updated[135].

There is no doubt that the European Union, which has a large body of environmental law at its disposal, has not yet realized the urgent need for an assessment of the effectivity of applicable law that goes beyond just the reporting system. As this has become quite comprehensive, it could have been used to design legal indicators to evaluate the implementation of European Union directives.

The European Commission has long conducted systematic reviews of Member States' implementation of each directive concerning the environment. Reports on "monitoring implementation" for each country are then published as

---

130 Communication from the Commission, *Structural Indicators*, COM (2002) 551 final, 16 October 2002.

131 Communication from the Commission, *Structural Indicators*, COM (2003) 585 final, 8 October 2003.

132 A. Delmas, *Perspectives pour la révision de la stratégie Europe 2020*, Conseil économique, social et environnemental, *JORF*, 6 July 2015.

133 Eurostat, *Smarter, greener, more inclusive? Indicators to support the Europe 2020 strategy*, 2019 edition, European Union, September 2019.

134 Communication from the Commission, *Next steps for a sustainable European future*, COM (2016) 739 final, 22 November 2016.

135 Eurostat, *EU SDG Indicators set 2020. Result of the review in preparation of the 2020 edition of the EU SDG monitoring report*, European Commission, Final version of 16 January 2020.

Commission Staff Working Documents. These are followed by summaries of the entire environmental policy.

The concern for greater effectiveness in European environmental law is present in all documents relating to its implementation in 2007 and 2008[136]. The 2008 report on environmental law called for studies on effective compliance with EU standards. In the Better Regulation Guidelines for 2015, there are numerous references to indicators to measure performance and progress and to measure transposition, implementation and the effective application of Community law[137].

Since 2017, the Commission has put in place a new procedure for monitoring the effective application of Community law. In the communication "COM (2016) 316 final", a new tool was launched to identify the causes for poor implementation of environmental law and to propose solutions, retaining the possibility to initiate infringement procedures if necessary. This procedure works in parallel to potential sanctions, and is entitled: "Environmental Implementation Review" or EIR[138]. Each State must report every two years on how it has applied the law and the difficulties it has encountered. This results in an information exchange between the Commission and the Member States, a presentation of good practice from experts in several countries, and finally the provision of necessary support to States. The first implementation review report was published on 3 February 2017[139]. It included the national reports and the Commission's summary, along with 17 proposed actions to remedy the causes of ineffectiveness in law. The second report was published on 4 April 2019[140]. Annexed to this report was a list of priority actions for each environmental sector with a view to better implementation of environmental policies. These priority actions are to do with practical management, but do not emphasize direct links to specific legal obligations. It resulted in a mixture of tangible, economic, practical, institutional and legal advice. In order to motivate States to better apply standards, meetings

136 Communications from the Commission, *A Europe of results – Applying Community law*, COM (2007) 502 final, 5 September 2007; *Applying Community environmental law*, COM (2008) 773 final, 18 November 2008.

137 Commission Staff Working Document, *Better Regulations Guidelines*, SWD (2015) 111 final, 7 July 2017, pp. 22, 30, 47.

138 Communication from the Commission, *Delivering environmental benefits from EU environmental policies through regular review of implementation*, COM (2016) 316 final, 27 May 2016.

139 COM (2017) 63 final.

140 COM (2019) 149 final.

and exchanges between experts are regularly organized. Their aim is to explore together how environmental law can be better and more effectively enforced.

At the same time, a new policy was put in place in 2018, providing public authorities with the means to promote, monitor and enforce environmental law. The various aspects of the Environmental Compliance Assurance monitoring policy[141] are set out in Annex 4 of the document. They are as follows: compliance promotion by communicating to stakeholders the importance of respecting the law to protect the environment and human health, by providing guidance on how to comply with relevant obligations, and by encouraging self-monitoring and audits; compliance monitoring by identifying the causes of non-compliance and contributing to compliance enforcement by organizing planned and periodic site-inspections; and follow-up action and enforcement by putting an end to non-compliance, drawing up reports, launching proceedings, publishing cases of non-compliance in the press and applying the polluter-pays principle. The program focuses on the training of inspectors, the role and use of administrative and criminal sanctions, with emphasis on the concept of environmental crime, particularly in relation to waste. Access to environmental justice is also addressed, with actions related to the Aarhus Convention. An action plan was adopted to this end, with the establishment of an expert group: the Environmental Compliance and Governance Forum[142]. The program of work for 2020–2021, issued on 4 February 2020, takes into account the new European Green Deal.

These educational efforts are commendable. However, observations surrounding poor application of the rules are superficial without real scientific instruments for measuring failings. While the need and urgency to better apply the rules is definitely on the agenda, the Commission has not yet expressed the need to accompany its new strategy with tools to better understand the barriers to effectivity of the law.

In Istanbul there was a call for academic experts to produce concrete evidence-based data using new environmental indicators capable of promoting quality governance and improving the democratic process[143]. This is encouraging for the promotion of legal indicators.

141 Commission Staff Working Document, *Environmental Compliance Assurance – scope, concept and need for EU actions*, SWD (2018) 10 final, 18 January 2018.

142 Communication from the Commission, *EU actions to improve compliance with environmental legislation and environmental governance*, COM (2018) 10 final, 18 January 2018.

143 European Commission, OECD, UNDP and World Bank, 2nd OECD Global Forum on Statistics, Knowledge and Policy, Istanbul, 2007.

b) *European Environment Agency indicators*

The European Environment Agency has only limited involvement with the field of law. As a result, it employs many scientific and economic indicators, but no legal indicators. A large number of indicators can be identified in the annual "Environmental signals" reports, as well as in specific reports and studies[144]. The Agency uses 122 indicators covering 13 areas of the environment. Each field of environmental science employs its own indicators. According to the Agency, an indicator is a generally quantitative measurement that serves to illustrate and communicate complex environmental phenomena in a simple way, showing trends and progress. The indicators are divided into five categories: type A, descriptive indicators; type B, performance indicators – are objectives being achieved, is progress being measured?; type C, efficiency indicators, expressing the relationship between driving forces and pressures as percentages; type D, policy effectiveness indicators; type E, indicators of wellbeing – do we feel better?[145]. This distinction in English between the terms efficiency and effectiveness could have led to taking into account legal measures in order to assess legal effectivity, but this was not the case. An example of a type D indicator is the production and consumption of ozone-depleting substances or the use of cleaner fuel. Where a selected indicator is able to rely on a legal text concerning for example marine protected areas, it only reports on their number and surface area.

It is unfortunate that the evaluation capacity of the Agency is not directed towards ensuring compliance with all of the environmental directives and international environmental agreements signed by the European Union.

c) *The network of environmental agencies*[146]

The European Environment Agency established a Network of the Heads of European Environment Protection Agencies in Copenhagen in 2003. In 2008 this network approved the Oslo statement, *Improving the Effectiveness of European Union Environmental Regulation: A Future Vision*, which focused on effectiveness in environmental law. Its approach to effectiveness is directed more towards the creation of law than its enforcement. There is a working group called the

144 European Environment Agency, *Europe's Environment – State and Outlook 2020; Environmental Indicators Report*, EEA, No 19 (2018).

145 European Environmental Agency, *Digest of Environmental European Agency Indicators*, Technical Report No. 8, 2014.

146 European Environmental Agency, *PBE and Enviro Windows*, http://pbe.eea.europa.eu.

Better Regulation Programme that aims to make improvements to regulation. Nevertheless, in a January 2007 report entitled *Barriers to Good Environmental Regulation*, the network did express the need for effective monitoring of the implementation of the law in one question which specifically referred to indicators: "Have indicators for measuring implementation been included and are they adequate?". The report concluded that if the answer is no then monitoring would be necessary, but did not specify exactly how that would be done.

d) *The IMPEL European network*[147]

The network for the Implementation and Enforcement of Environmental Law, or IMPEL, was created in 1992. In 2020 it had 55 members in 37 countries, including the 27 EU Member States. Its members include the European Commission and representatives of the national control and inspection authorities of Member States and candidate countries. The secretariat is operated by the Directorate-General for Environment in Brussels. It is an informal network promoting information exchange, good practice and reflection on the effective application of environmental law in the European Union. The aim is therefore to improve compliance with applicable law. This instrument, which promotes effective implementation of environmental law, was expected to lead to the creation of legal indicators. However, its direct aim was not the systematic and critical review and evaluation of the conditions for compliance with the law, but rather an assessment of adequacy of technical and administrative control mechanisms. It is nevertheless surprising that environmental jurists have so little to do with the work of the network, which remains essentially the domain of scientific experts and engineers. Also there is very little legal work among the many projects carried out or financed by IMPEL[148]. IMPEL was behind the inspection manual for environmental controls, which gave rise to the European authorities official recommendation of 4 April 2001 (2001/331/EC, OJ, L.118/41).

---

147 European Union Network for the Implementation and Enforcement of Environmental Law, IMPEL, www.impel.eu.

148 With the exception of *The criminal law aspects of the application of environmental law in the European Union* (December 2000) and the report entrusted to the European Council of Environmental Law (ECDE) chaired by A. Kiss on *Citizens' remedies and access to justice in environmental matters* (May 2000). This study was resumed and completed under the direction of J. Ebbeson, *Access to Justice in Environmental Matters in the EU*, Kluwer Law International, 2002.

IMPEL published a report in 2006 on the creation of a checklist of elements that could be used to assess the practicability and enforceability of environmental legislation.

The applicability criteria include: the definition of terms used in the texts, the deadlines given for applying the texts, and the resources required. The proposed enforceability criteria are the capacity to use existing legal instruments, the level of sanctions, and inspection and control. It is clear that these reports have a long way to go before making serious legal assessments of effectivity, that are based on both appropriate legal vocabulary and a satisfactory and comprehensive use of existing procedures.

The network's 2016–2020 program of work refers to a study carried out in March 2015, entitled *Challenges in the Practical Implementation of EU Environmental Law and How IMPEL Could Overcome Them*. At last, this document makes a first reference to the need to develop "self-assessment tools and indicators … to measure progress with implementation [of the law]" (p. 18). It is therefore possible to assume that IMPEL would be interested in legal indicators.

Given that IMPEL's objective is to help bridge the implementation gap in environmental law, the creation of legal indicators can only facilitate monitoring.

In this same 2015 study, a questionnaire was sent to IMPEL members. One of the questions asked was: "What are the main underlying reasons and causes of the problems in achieving the requirements of relevant environmental legislation?" There were 6 responses to choose from, but none directly addressed effectivity in law. 60 % of responses identified insufficient capacity in regulatory institutions. This is by no means an assessment of the complex causes of non-compliance with the law, although it does also highlight the number of infringement cases against Community environmental law: 481 in 2008; 334 in 2013; 276 in 2015; 269 in 2016. Although significant, this number does not reflect effectivity in the application of the law, as non-compliance is always greater than the number of infringements actually detected.

2. OECD Indicators: Environmental Indicators, Environmental Indicators for Agriculture and Welfare Indicators

The OECD has long undertaken extensive work on environmental indicators[149]. The Working Party on Environmental Information (WPEI) is responsible for

149 *Environmental Indicators, Pilot Study*, OECD, 1991; *Key Environmental Indicators*, OECD, 2008; *OECD Environmental Outlook to 2050: The Consequences of Inaction*, OECD, 2012; *Environment at a Glance: OECD indicators*, OECD, 2015.

the coordination and dissemination of environmental statistics and indicators. As early as 1991, the OECD advocated for more environmental indicators, yet it did not establish a link between the law and indicators[150]. The most relevant studies that include a section on environmental law are devoted to a country's environmental performance review. This consists of a systematic evaluation of State policies, using environmental statistics and field assessments by third party experts. But this type of evaluation remains traditional and subjective, and does not include legal indicators. It should be noted that one African nation has been the subject of an evaluation of this type, that is South Africa in 2013. In 2014, the Green Growth Indicators were published through green growth in action[151].

The OECD publishes three sets of environmental data: 10–13 Key Environmental Indicators; 40–50 Main Environmental Indicators; and sectoral environmental indicators. The law is almost never mentioned. The objectives of these indicators are to monitor progress and review performance.

The OECD has in effect sought to develop performance indicators for the environment, some of which are based more or less directly on a legal analysis. One 2005 document is worthy of note in relation to this point: *Funding Environmental Compliance Assurance: Lessons Learned from International Experience.*

The report *Ensuring Environmental Compliance: Trends and Good Practices*[152] is a key document for our study[153]. This report on compliance with environmental standards directly addresses the issue of enforcement of environmental law as an integral part of regulation. It noted the lack of interest among States in assessing compliance with legal provisions related to the environment, and pointed out disparities between countries in the application of the law. To improve effectiveness, it called for the development of indicators "that could be used for international benchmarking" (p. 15).

The compliance instruments are divided into three pillars which function as useful sequences for the design of different indicators (p. 24):

- Compliance promotion through encouragement, without the use of sanctions (through information dissemination, technical assistance, and financial incentives);

150 OECD Recommendation on Environmental Indicators and Information, C(90) 165/final, 31 January 1991.

151 OECD, *Green Growth Indicators*, Paris, 2014.

152 OECD, 2009.

153 It was taken over and developed by Ana Barreira, *Environmental Rule of Law: An Analysis of Data Availability* (Green Growth Knowledge Platform, 2019).

- Compliance monitoring by collecting data (through inspections, audits, self-monitoring and citizen monitoring);
- Response to non-compliance by triggering action on the part of public authorities and/or the general public to enforce compliance through sanctions (reports, records, objections, official complaints).

This 2009 report does not yet specifically mention the need for truly legal indicators of effectivity. It does however suggest the use of compliance assessment tools and the development of a limited list of performance indicators, developing data on the way monitoring authorities operate. Nevertheless this report remains limited in its scope, since it does not deal with all environmental law, but only with the regulatory framework for pollution prevention and reduction in the industrial sector. Moreover, it is limited to matters concerning the application of national law and does not address the application of international law in States. This report was followed by two complementary publications[154].

As a result of the OECD Green Growth Programme, two 2015 publications, *Towards Green Growth* and *Green Growth Indicators for Agriculture*, dedicated 1 indicator out of 25 to "regulation and management practices". Unfortunately, this indicator is described as "still to be developed"[155]. In the publications entitled *Green Growth Indicators* (2017) and *Environment at a Glance* (2020), there is absolutely no mention of the role of law in environmental policies.

In 2014, the OECD published a compendium of agri-environmental indicators. Based on 18 statistical indicators, it aims to outline the environmental performance of 35 Member States. Water, air, soil, biodiversity and landscapes were taken into account, with figures on agricultural production and organic farming, nitrogen and phosphorus balances, pesticide sales, energy, erosion, water withdrawals, ammonia and greenhouse gas emissions, and bird populations. But these quantitative data are not related to legal and political realities. Although there is mention of the Pressure-State-Response approach, which is the causal link between public action, agricultural factors, environmental effects and impact on human well-being, this causal chain is not analyzed with reference to the law. No indicator seeks to measure the relationship between applicable law, the actual conditions of its application and its effects on the environment.

---

154 *Outcome Performance Measures of Environmental Compliance Assurance: Current Practices, Constraints and Ways Forward*, OECD, 2010; *Environmental Enforcement in Decentralized Governance Systems: Towards a Nationwide Level Playing Field*, OECD, 2011.

155 *Green Growth Indicators for Agriculture*, OECD, 2015, p. 24.

Environmental indicators for agriculture have been developed since 1999 in three publications[156]. The OECD has since made available a database on *Environmental Indicators for Agriculture*, which facilitates online searches for statistical data from 1990 onwards[157].

Since 2011, every two years the OECD has released a well-being indicator. In the 2017 French edition the following themes were addressed: inequalities, immigrants, governance[158]. In the 2020 English edition, alongside health, housing and quality of work, there is a chapter on environmental quality which offers statistics in three areas: air pollution, access to recreational green spaces in urban areas, and environmental inequalities[159].

3. Indicators to combat wildlife and forest crime

The International Consortium on Combating Wildlife Crime (ICCWC) aims to combat crimes committed against wildlife and forests. It brings together the CITES Secretariat, Interpol, the United Nations Office on Drugs and Crime (UNODC), the World Bank and the World Customs Organization. In 2016, it published a framework of indicators for combating crime related to wildlife species and forests[160], the aim of which was to analyze the effectiveness of current legal and administrative responses in the battle against wildlife crime at the national level. It assessed the capacity and effectiveness of existing legal and institutional responses, with a view to suggesting reforms and adjustments. 50 indicators were put forward, divided into 8 outcomes. This methodology combined performance indicators with indicators of legal effectiveness. Two-thirds of the indicators are based on an expert self-assessment which provides a qualitative answer scale with 4 options scored between 0 and 3. Other responses are based on raw data (number of infringements) or on whether or not texts or ad hoc procedures exist.

---

156 OECD, *Environmental Indicators for Agriculture: Volume 1, Concepts and Framework* (Paris, 1999); *OECD, Environmental Indicators for Agriculture: Volume 2, Issues and Design – "The York Workshop"* (1999); OECD, *Environmental Indicators for Agriculture: Volume 3, Methods and Results* (Paris, 2001).

157 http://www.oecd.org/fr/croissanceverte/agriculture-durable/indicateurs-agro-environnementaux.htm.

158 OECD, *Comment va la vie? Mesurer le bien-être* (Paris, 2017).

159 OECD, *How's life? 2020. Measuring Well-being* (Paris, 2020).

160 *ICCWC Indicator Framework for Combating Wildlife and Forest Crime. A self-assessment framework for national use. Assessment Guidelines*, July 2016.

4. The Environmental Performance Index

The Environmental Performance Index (EPI) is a set of 32 performance indicators for 180 countries, covering 11 environmental sectors: health, air, drinking water and sanitation, water resources, agriculture, forests, fisheries, biodiversity and habitat, climate and energy, ecosystem services, and heavy metals[161]. The results for 2016 can be compared with the evolution of scores since 1950. Much of this work is being carried out by the Center for Environmental Law and Policy at Yale University in the United States, the International Center for Earth Science Information at Columbia University and the World Economic Forum in Davos.

The 2016 report refers in some places to the presence of the law, but in a static manner and formulates quantitative rather than specific indicators, such as the number of protected areas. The conventions on biological diversity, the law of the sea and fisheries law are also mentioned[162]. It is regrettable that such an exercise, led by two American environmental law centers, did not give greater value to the contribution of law and its effectivity for environmental quality. The 2018 report groups the data around two policy objectives: environmental health, weighted at 40 %, and ecosystem vitality at 60 %[163]. The same percentages are applied in the 2020 report[164].

5. The International Finance Corporation Performance Standards

On 1 January 2012, the International Finance Corporation, the private sector investment arm of the World Bank Group, approved a set of performance standards for environmental and social sustainability which are imposed upon clients in loan agreements. In addition to the obligation to comply with applicable national and international environmental law, recipient companies must also comply with these performance standards, which also function as guidelines for good practice. Compliance with these standards is monitored.

Although they do not formally appear as such, each of these performance standards actually functions as an indicator. It would therefore make sense for them to be described in this way. This document does seek to ensure effectiveness

---

161 https://epi.yale.edu.

162 EPI, *Environmental Performance Index, 2018 Release*, https://sedac.ciesin.columbia.edu/data/set/epi-environmental-performance-index-2018.

163 EPI, *Environmental Performance Index 2020. Global metrics for the environment: Ranking country performance on sustainability issues*, https://epi.yale.edu/downloads/epipolicymakersummaryr9.pdf.

164 EPI, *Global Metrics for the Environment*, 2016, https://epi.envirocenter.yale.edu.

in environmental law, but it is not clear exactly how. References to respect for human rights are missing. Among the 8 performance standards, the following should be highlighted:

- Standard 1: Assessment and Management of Environmental and Social Risks and Impacts;
- Standard 3: Resource Efficiency and Pollution Prevention;
- Standard 6: Biodiversity Conservation and Sustainable Management of Living Natural Resources;
- Standard 8: Cultural Heritage.

6. UNEP and indicators

The UNEP Scientific Committee on Problems of the Environment undertook to develop global quantitative indicators. *Towards a green economy*, published in 2011, repeatedly mentioned essentially scientific and economic indicators, completely ignoring the existence of environmental law[165]. In table 1 on potential indicators for measuring progress towards green agriculture, a distinction is made between action indicators and outcome indicators. The first action indicator is the "number of enacted and implemented policy measures". Here, it would have been more appropriate to write "number of legal texts on…". UNEP acknowledges that "information on regulation is of a qualitative nature and not always easy to evaluate"[166]. This affirmation reinforces the usefulness and urgency surrounding the creation of legal indicators.

UNEP has supported the IFDD initiative through its contribution to the publication of our 2018 study on legal indicators, as well as the seminar on assessment of effectiveness in environmental law, held in Yaoundé in February 2018[167].

In the 2019 publication, *Environmental Rule of Law*[168], UNEP argues that in the future there should be a regular assessment of the effectiveness of environmental law by means of indicators, referring to the before-mentioned work by M. Prieur on legal indicators (p. 236). It is clear that there is a call for future indicators to assess the reality of the rule of law.

165 UNEP, *Towards a green economy: Pathways to sustainable development and poverty eradication* (Nairobi, 2011).

166 UNEP, *Measuring Progress towards an Inclusive Green Economy* (Nairobi, 2012), p. 25.

167 M. Prieur, *Les indicateurs juridiques…, op. cit.*

168 UNEP, *Environmental Rule of Law. First Global Report*, 2019.

7. Indicators from the Barcelona Convention for the Mediterranean

The Mediterranean Strategy for Sustainable Development (MSSD), developed by the Mediterranean Commission on Sustainable Development (MCSD) and approved by the Parties to the Barcelona Convention and its Protocols, includes a table of monitoring indicators[169]. 49 indicators were put forward by the 17th meeting of the MCSD in Athens in July 2017, to monitor the MSSD 2016–2025 as a follow-up to the work of Plan Bleu[170]. Since 2005, the MSSD had relied on 34 indicators. In 2017, of the 49 indicators proposed, it is interesting to note 7 legal indicators. Some are factual (number of protected areas, number of threatened species in legal documents, number of ratifications); others include a variety of factors and data that have not yet been collated (level of compliance, public participation mechanisms). A compendium of "indicator factsheets" is being uploaded to the sustainable development indicator website, to enable monitoring of MSSD implementation[171]. In these factsheets, there are several references to legal issues: Aarhus Convention; UNESCO inscribed sites (Annex 3); implementation of the Barcelona Convention (Annex 4). These indicators are purely quantitative and static, but they are a first step towards taking into account the place of law within the MSSD. The accompanying mapping adds substantial value. In order to create an assessment tool to monitor the MSSD, it would be necessary to take into consideration real legal indicators of effectivity. These indicators would differ in part from tools for assessing the effectiveness of the Convention itself and its Protocols, by making a clear distinction between legal requirements under international and national law.

It should be noted that the text of the Barcelona Convention is particularly concerned with the role that the law must play in its implementation. According to Article 14.1, "Contracting Parties shall adopt legislation implementing the Convention and the Protocols". According to Article 26, the reports of the Contracting Parties shall cover "legal, administrative or other measures" taken for the implementation of the Convention, the Protocols and the recommendations adopted by the Meetings of the Parties, as well as "the

169 According to article 4.2 of the 1976 Convention for the Protection of the Marine Environment and the Coastal Region of the Mediterranean, amended in 1995, "the Contracting Parties shall take fully into account the recommendations of the Mediterranean Commission on Sustainable Development established within the framework of the Mediterranean Action Plan".

170 UNEP/DEPI/MED WG.441/Inf.3 and 441/6.

171 http://obs.planbleu.org/en.

effectiveness of the measures … and problems encountered in the implementation of the instruments" in question. This requires monitoring not only of the text of the implementing legislation, but also the legal, institutional, budgetary and material conditions of implementation. This will be the role of the Compliance Committee, established pursuant to Article 27 of the Convention on Compliance Control, by decision IG 17/2 adopted on 18 January 2008 at the 15th Conference of Parties in Almeria, Spain.

At the 21st Meeting of the Contracting Parties to the Barcelona Convention and its Protocols (Naples, 2–5 December 2019) consideration of legal indicators was, for the first time, officially called for within the framework of an international environmental convention. The report from the Chair of the Compliance Committee mentions them in three instances[172]:

- In paragraph 16: "In this context, the Compliance Committee also discussed the development of legal environmental indicators for measuring the effectiveness of the Barcelona Convention and its Protocols as an avenue that should be explored in future";
- In the program of work for 2020–2021, paragraph 6: "To develop specific legal indicators, both qualitative and quantitative, for effective implementation, and potential simplification of the reporting format";
- In the recommendations to promote compliance with the Convention and its Protocols and to improve their implementation, paragraph 20 reads as follows: "to develop indicators for evaluating the effectiveness of these strategies, plans and programmes" in relation to integrated coastal zone management.

In addition, in the Report on the State of the Environment and Sustainable Development, message 1 on enforcement recommends the following: "Develop and test a set of associated indicators to assess compliance".[173]

Lastly, the final report of the secretariat of the 21st Conference of the Parties states: "Meanwhile, enhanced evaluation of the effectiveness of the Convention and its protocols, which was crucial for the continued relevance of the system, called for the strengthening of legal and other indicators, assisted by partners such as the International Centre for Comparative Environmental Law".[174]

172 UNEP/MED IG 24/22, 21st Meeting of the Contracting Parties, Naples, 2–5 December 2019.

173 UNEP/MED/IG.24/22, p. 211.

174 UNEP/MED IG.24/22, para. 90, p. 17.

Yann Wehrling, French Ambassador for the Environment, also expressed this same concern in his speech: "If we want to maximize the impact of our commitments, let us give ourselves the means to evaluate the effective implementation of the Barcelona Convention. We have scientific and economic indicators, but we lack legal indicators. The International Centre for Comparative Environmental Law has carried out extensive work on this subject. The Centre is present and stands ready to work with us to develop these indicators together, to strengthen assessment of the implementation of our commitments under the Convention"[175]. A side event addressing this issue was held on 5 December 2019, under the auspices of the French Ministry of Ecological and Inclusive Transition and the International Centre for Comparative Environmental Law, an accredited partner of the Mediterranean Action Plan (MAP) under the Barcelona Convention.

8. UNEP Global Environment Outlook indicators, specifically in Africa

The UNEP Global Environment Outlook (GEO) program on the state of the global environment was launched in 1995. The first world report dates back to 1997. In its assessment of the world's environment, it relies on mainly scientific and economic statistical data and indicators. Legal data are rarely mentioned. However, there is an occasional reference to the need to monitor policy performance "with the aim of improving levels of implementation, enforcement and compliance"[176]. Legal data are sometimes provided, such as the chart displaying ratification of major multilateral environmental agreements, while underlining the need to ensure better treaty compliance and implementation[177].

The GEO 5 report, presented at the Rio+20 Conference in 2012, acknowledges the inadequacy of existing indicators (p. xx). The accompanying report, *Measuring Progress*[178], outlines the idea that the origin of the objectives pursued by environmental policies lies in international agreements, stressing that assessment does not take into account whether or not the objective is legally binding. This is the same approach that we have taken in this study. It justifies taking into consideration both hard and soft law in effectivity assessments of international

175 UNEP/MED/IG.24/22, p. 818.

176 *GEO 3*, 2002, p. xxix.

177 *GEO 4*, 2007, Figure 1.1.

178 UNEP, *Measuring Progress towards an Inclusive Green Economy, op. cit.*

environmental law. However, the lack of data to assess the implementation of environmental agreements was again highlighted in November 2012 by UNEP[179].

Interest in environmental law in Africa was expressed internationally within UNEP and the United Nations Economic Commission for Africa. For example, in 1981, the Commission organized a seminar for lawyers on the development of environmental law in Africa[180]. This highlighted both the need for a reinforced application of the law (para. 63) and the need for more effective monitoring (para. 66).

Africa Environment Outlook (AEO) reports are published as part of the African Ministerial Conference on the Environment (AMCEN), organized by UNEP every two years since 1985. The 1st report, published in 2002, is of particular interest. Chapter 5 deals with the contribution of international and national environmental law and suggests the limits of the law, but does not envisage a scientific assessment of its effectivity[181]. Subsequently, other African environmental reports have been released[182].

Following resolution 757 (XXVIII) of 4 May 1993 of the Conference of Ministers of the United Nations Economic Commission for Africa, the Conference of African Ministers Responsible for Sustainable Development and the Environment (CAMSDE) was established, and held its first meeting in Addis Ababa in March 1996. However, CAMSDE overlapped somewhat with AMCEN[183]. The latter continue to meet regularly. Its 16th session took place in Libreville, Gabon in June 2017 and its 17th session in Durban, South Africa in November 2019.

Specific GEOs for six regions were released in 2016[184]. The regional assessment for Africa[185] devotes part of Chapter 2 to "Determinants of policy effectiveness"

---

179 UNEP, *State of the environment and contribution of the United Nations Environment Programme to addressing substantive environmental challenges*, UNEP/GC.27/3, 29 November 2012, para. 53.

180 Economic and Social Council, Economic Commission for Africa, *Report of the Seminar for Lawyers on Development of Environmental Protection Legislation in the ECA Region*, E/CN.14/784, 21 October 1980.

181 UNEP, *Africa Environment Outlook. Past, present and future perspectives*, 2002; see chapter 5, "Policy intervention and the call for action".

182 *AEO 2*, 2006; *AEO 3*, 2013.

183 *Report of the First Session of the Conference of African Ministers Responsible for Sustainable Development and the Environment*, E/ECA/CAMSDE/16, 9 March 1996.

184 *Summary of the Sixth Global Environment Outlook Regional Assessments: Key Findings and Policy Messages*, UNEP/EA.2/INF/17, 22 May 2016.

185 *Global Environment Outlook: GEO-6, Regional Assessment for Africa*, 2016.

(pp. 94–102). One would have expected to find data on environmental law in Africa, which has often been a pioneer in this field (for example: inclusion of the human right to the environment in the African Charter on Human and Peoples' Rights of 1981; and introduction of the principle of non-regression in the legislation of the Ivory Coast in 2014). But it only briefly mentions the legal context (figure 2.5.4, p. 100), environmental impact assessment legislation and a few international conventions. The Africa regional report on the sustainable development goals refers to monitoring and evaluation and highlights the importance of the choice of indicators[186]. Legal indicators should also be introduced in assessments of institutional and strategic aspects of sustainable development[187]. It is therefore imperative that the next GEO 7 on Africa systematically integrates data regarding the contribution of international law and domestic legislation to the protection of the environment in Africa, through legal indicators.

9. The African Charter on Statistics

Within the framework of the African Union, a treaty establishing an African Charter on Statistics was signed in 2009 and entered into force in 2015. This treaty coordinates the law applicable to statistics in order to provide Africa with reliable measurement and evaluation tools. Article 1 refers to its application in the field of environment and governance. From 3 to 5 July 2017, in Libreville, Gabon, a workshop was organized by the United Nations Economic Commission for Africa, on the following theme: "Sound institutional environment, cooperation, dialog and partnerships for the production and utilization of SDG indicators". States Parties to the Charter and the African Union Commission responsible for implementing the Charter should be made aware of the urgent need to introduce legal indicators in the evaluation of progress in environmental protection.

10. ECLAC and ILAC Environmental Indicators in South America

The United Nations Economic Commission for Latin America and the Caribbean (ECLAC) has undertaken one of the first research projects on environmental indicators to incorporate legal data[188]. The results of this study in Brazil were disseminated in 2007: indicators for application and compliance with environmental

186 ECA, *Africa Regional Report on the SDGs*, Addis Ababa, 2015.

187 ECA, *Report on institutional and strategic frameworks for sustainable development in Africa*, Addis Ababa, 2012.

188 Study for the World Bank Institute and ECLAC, launched in 2003 for Brazil, Argentina and Mexico, on compliance with and implementation of environmental standards.

standards for air, water and vegetation in Brazil[189]. This report used the INECE-OECD network method adopted in Paris at a 2003 workshop (cited previously). It found that indicators for the implementation and enforcement of environmental law would surely serve as valuable tools for improving environmental management. There was unanimous agreement among respondents that a system of indicators would promote effectiveness in meeting environmental standards. As a result, at the initiative of the Brazilian NGO Law for a Green Planet, a working group was set up within the National Environment Council of Brazil to establish general guidelines for the development and implementation of indicators to measure application and compliance with environmental standards, including input indicators with reference to legal rules.

In 2009 ECLAC published a methodological guide for developing environmental indicators[190]. But it deals only with traditional statistical tools, ignoring the role of law in the environment. There is only a brief mention of the budgets and compliance with hazardous waste standards, with no details given as to how compliance should be measured.

In parallel, following the creation in 2002 of the Latin American and Caribbean Initiative for Sustainable Development (ILAC), which is part of UNEP, at the 13th meeting of the Forum of Ministers of the Environment in Panama in 2003 a working group on environmental indicators (*Grupo de trabajo en indicadores ambientales*, GTIA) was established by decision 6. Among the six themes selected, once again, environmental law does not appear as such. But there are some institutional aspects. The law occasionally appears within the other themes.

In the 2011 Regional Indicators Revision, the indicators on biological diversity include the number of protected areas, but not their status, and the existence of laws or decrees relating to access to genetic resources. Institutional indicators include reports on the state of the environment and the existence of a national council for sustainable development[191].

---

189 https://www.cepal.org/pt-br/publicaciones/3607-indicadores-aplicacao-cumprimentonorma-ambiental-ar-agua-vegetacao-brasil.

190 Rayén Quiroga Martínez, *Guía metodológica para desarrollar indicadores ambientales y de desarrollo sostenible en países de América Latina y el Caribe* (Santiago de Chile, CEPAL, 2009).

191 UNEP-ILAC, *Regional Indicators Revision 2011*, Latin American and Caribbean Initiative for Sustainable Development, www.geodatos.org.

The 2015 report from the ILAC working group on indicators encourages national assessments on the basis of a program of work[192]. The XX Meeting of the Forum of the Ministers of the Environment of Latin America and the Caribbean in Colombia in March 2016 recognized the progress made by the working group on environmental indicators in decision 2. It proposed the development of new indicators, particularly related to science and politics, but did not give mention to legal indicators. The XXI meeting of this Forum in Buenos Aires in October 2018 requested that the working group on environmental indicators continue to research indicators relevant to the region.

A 2016 report from Chile on sustainable development indicators related to the 2030 SDGs also fails to mention legal indicators[193]. However, it does mention indicators to be developed in relation to regulations and institutions (p. 170).

11. The INECE Environmental Compliance Indicators

The International Network for Environmental Compliance and Enforcement (INECE) brings together 4000 members, practitioners, governments and NGOs from over 150 countries. It was founded in 1989 by the environmental agencies of the United States and the Netherlands. It is supported in particular by UNEP, the World Bank, the European Commission and the OECD. The President and the Executive Director are heads of the Environmental Law Institute (ELI) in Washington, D.C. The objectives of INECE are to raise awareness of the importance of compliance and enforcement, to develop a network for cooperation on compliance, and to build capacity on compliance and enforcement through training seminars and research. These objectives fully correspond to our criteria for effectivity in environmental law. The advantage of INECE's approach is that it considers compliance with environmental law at all levels, from international to local.

Africa is one of the continents studied, especially English speaking Africa[194]. In fact, INECE is studying all the different ways of ensuring proper implementation

192 UNEP, Intersessional Meeting of the Forum of Ministers of Environment for Latin America and the Caribbean, *Working Group on Environmental Indicators of the Forum of Ministers of Environment of Latin America and the Caribbean*, UNEP/LAC-IC.1.2015/7, 17–19 November 2015.

193 Secretariat of the Environment and GreenLabUC, *Implementación de indicadores relacionados con los objetivos de desarollo sustentable y otras iniciativas in Chile*, Informe final, 15 December 2016.

194 See, however, Judge Nihunu Sama's report, *Criminal Law and Environment: Prosecutors, Inspectors and NGOs in Cameroon*, 9 April 2005; Mamann-Sani Issa, *Controlling Hazardous Waste in Cotonou (Benin) Port: What is Needed?*, 2 October 2011.

of environmental law, of which indicators are just one. Legal indicators should supplement those indicators recommended by INECE. Adopted on 15 April 2005 at the 7th INECE conference, the Marrakech Declaration is a strategic plan for 2012–2017. It recommended in paragraph 17 that indicators be developed to measure compliance with and enforcement of environmental standards, and directed INECE to continue to develop draft performance indicators. The final declaration at the 8th Conference, held in Cape Town on 11 April 2008, encouraged performance measurements, including effectiveness indicators for compliance and implementation of environmental law (para. f). There is a clear interest in a mixed approach to analyzing the conditions of implementation of the law through case studies, both quantitative and qualitative[195].

The methods used on the basis of terms of reference developed by the World Bank Institute were the subject of an OECD meeting in 2003[196]. Following work carried out by a working group on indicators, a guide was published in 2008[197]. However, unfortunately none of the numerous INECE studies directly addresses the issue of legal indicators[198].

Also of note was the 2006 establishment of a regional INECE network in the Maghreb, in Rabat, the Network for Environmental Compliance and Enforcement in the Maghreb (NECMA), with the aim of improving environmental law enforcement capacities. This network publishes a newsletter in French.

12. The Environmental Democracy Index

Since 1999, an international network called The Access Initiative (TAI) has brought together 250 NGOs from 60 countries, among which are 12 African States, including Benin, Cameroon and Madagascar. One of TAI's programs, the Open Government Partnership (OGP), looks at Tunisia in relation to action plans on natural resources. The objective of the TAI Network is to

195 JoyAnna S. Hopper, *A Mixed-Methods Approach to Analyzing Environmental Enforcement in the American States* (SAGE Research Methods Cases, 2019).

196 INECE-OECD, *Workshop on Environmental Compliance and Enforcement Indicators: Measuring What Matters* (Paris, 2004).

197 Performance measurement guidance for compliance and enforcement practitioners, 2nd ed., INECE, 2008.

198 Reports that address the issue: *Performance Measurement*, webinar, 5 February 2017; E. Messina, *Next Generation Compliance Measurement Technique*, February 2017; Shelley H. Mertzenbaum, *Environmental Compliance and Enforcement: Why, What and How?*, 19–29 March 2015.

develop environmental democracy by promoting Principle 10 of the 1992 Rio Declaration. The TAI Secretariat is operated by the World Resources Institute (WRI) in Washington, D.C. The aim is to establish and develop access to environmental law and justice through information and participation. TAI's programs include a reflection on regional standards for environmental democracy and the Environmental Democracy Index (EDI) launched in 2015 to assess law and practice in this area. It contains 75 legal indicators and 24 practical indicators across 70 countries[199]. They are based on international legal standards and the 2010 UNEP Bali Guidelines. These indicators have been validated by 140 jurists worldwide. The latest version of the EDI is from 2017. According to the EDI, legal indicators measure the strength of the law and practical indicators measure the conditions of its implementation. These data should help to mobilize environmental advocacy and help decision-makers prioritize reforms.

One example of a legal indicator for access to justice is: "To what extent does the law provide for broad access to justice in environmental matters?" One example of a practical indicator is: "Are measurements of air pollution in your capital city directly accessible online?" Each legal indicator is scored on a scale from 0 (lowest) to 3 (highest), according to the responses given. For the practical indicators, 3 answers are possible: yes, limited, or no.

It is important to note that the WRI and TAI refer to some of their indicators as "legal indicators". We can also find inspiration for our study in their experiences shared in a 2015 technical note[200].

13. The FAO Fisheries Indicators

In order to facilitate the implementation of the Code of Conduct for Responsible Fisheries, approved by FAO in resolution 4/95 of 31 October 1995, a study was carried out in 2001, entitled *Indicators for sustainable development of marine capture fisheries*. This publication is of interest to our study as it does not ignore the legal issues related to fishing. The objective is to create instruments to monitor the contribution of fisheries to sustainable development, integrating both ecological and institutional data. Thus, some of the proposed indicators reflect the administrative dimension, with legal factors such as compliance regime, property rights, transparency and participation, capacity to manage (see annex 4: governance/institutional criteria). The methodology of this report is relevant to our

199 *Environmental Democracy Index*, www.environmentaldemocracyindex.org.
200 Jesse Werker and Lalanath de Silva, *The Environmental Democracy Index*, Technical Note, World Resources Institute, 2015.

study in that it considers all three territorial levels: global, regional and national (see appendix A of annex 4: “Examples of governance criteria and indicators”).

14. The Land Indicators

The Global Land Indicators Initiative (GLII) has been in existence since 2012[201]. It brings together nearly 50 international and national, public and private institutions, with the Millennium Challenge Corporation, the World Bank and UN Habitat. The 2016 new Habitat III urban program further strengthened this initiative. The goal is to develop a methodology for comparable indicators as an aid to public decision-making. 15 comparable national indicators have been created, which have been linked to the 2030 SDG indicators relating to land since 2017. These are SDGs 1, 5, 11 and 15, as well as SDG 16, which is cross-cutting in nature. Land law and the environment are of course included. The following issues are therefore addressed: women's rights to manage and inherit land, land rights of indigenous peoples, access to land information, duration and cost of land transactions, urban and rural planning, efficiency of land administration services, and sustainable land use[202]. In 2017 the results of an experiment were published, which attempted to develop an indicator across 17 countries to achieve SDG 1.4.2. Once again this involved the examination of official statistical and legal data, interviews and expert evaluation, but no assessment of the actual legal effectiveness of the instruments in question[203].

In 2018 FAO released a publication that specifically referred to legal indicators on the issue of women's land rights[204]. Its aim is to contribute to the assessment process of indicator 5.a.2 of SDG 5. Although the law is at the heart of this initiative, the aim is to identify, with the help of a legal expert and through a questionnaire, the sources of the law and not the reality of the law's effectivity. As

---

201 *Global Land Indicators Initiative*, http://gltn.net/global-land-indicators-initiative-glii.

202 UN Habitat, *Proposed Global Land Indicators. Status Report on GLII Indicator Formulation, Disaggregation, Data Sources and Methodology*, GLII Working Paper No. 3, Nairobi, 2015; UN Habitat, *Sourcebook for Operationalisation of Global Land Indicators*, GLII Working Paper No. 4, Nairobi, 2016; Everlyne Nairesiae, *Reflections on GLII Achievements and Plans*, GLTN, GLII, 2018.

203 UN Habitat, *A Multi-Country Capacity Assessment of National Statistical Offices Preparedness to Report on SDG Indicator 1.4.2*, GLII, Working Paper No. 7, Nairobi, 2017.

204 FAO, *Realizing women's rights to land in the law. A guide for reporting on SDG indicator 5.a.2*, Rome, 2018.

there must be exact references to applicable law, this method covers national and international law and custom, but excludes case law.

15. Indicators of drought, desertification and pastoralism

The World Meteorological Organization and the Global Water Partnership published a technical manual on drought indicators and indexes in 2016[205]. Within the framework of the Convention to Combat Desertification, cooperation has begun between the Global Land Indicators Initiative (GLII) and the Committee on Science and Technology of the Convention. This also involves participation from the Rangelands Initiative[206], a network of institutions and NGOs. The aim is to develop global indicators on drought which have a much greater scientific content than previous versions, and which are framed as performance indicators and not as an assessment of the role of law in desertification. 102 States Parties to the Convention have released 408 drought indicators, 63 of which are socio-economic in nature[207]. A joint program of work was defined during COP14 in New Delhi (3–6 September 2019) under the Science-Policy Interface of the Committee on Science and Technology[208]. The aim is to harmonize global land indicators to better measure land tenure security and progress towards land degradation neutrality.

Pastoralism has also been the subject of assessment in the quest for better governance, in particular in a 2016 publication entitled *Improving Governance of Pastoral Lands*[209]. Section 3 sets out the policy and legal frameworks for pastoralism, and outlines legal indicators drawn from human rights law and environmental law, using sources from both national and international law.

---

205 WMO-GWP, *Handbook on Drought Indicators and Indices*, Integrated Drought Management Programme, Geneva, 2016.

206 http://rangelandsinitiative.org.

207 Convention to Combat Desertification, *Preliminary analysis – Strategic Objective 3: Mitigating, adapting to and managing the effects of drought to improve the resilience of vulnerable people and ecosystems. Note by the Secretariat*, E/C.16/2019/7, 24 January 2019.

208 Convention to Combat Desertification, *Work Programme of the Science-Policy Interface (2020–2021). Note by the secretariat*, ICCD/COP(14)/CST/6, 27 June 2019; *Practical recommendations arising from cooperation with other intergovernmental scientific groups and bodies. Report of the Executive Secretary*, ICCD/COP(14)CST/4, 5 July 2019.

209 FAO, *Improving Pastoral Land Governance*, Technical Guide for Land Tenure Governance 6, Rome, 2016.

C. Human rights indicators

It is rare for an international human rights convention to include the evaluation of data. One example is article 31 of the Convention on the Rights of Persons with Disabilities, which provides for statistics and data collection in order to assess how States are meeting their obligations and to identify obstacles. Human rights is likely the area of law that has been most studied in terms of the possibility of its measurement through indicators. Six more or less parallel projects were carried out by: the Office of the United Nations High Commissioner for Human Rights, the Inter-American Commission on Human Rights, the Core Humanitarian Standard, the European Union Fundamental Rights Agency, the Council of Europe and the Cato Institute in the United States.

1. The Office of the United Nations High Commissioner for Human Rights

The idea of developing indicators to measure the implementation and progressive realization of the International Covenant on Economic, Social and Cultural Rights originated in a 1990 report by Special Rapporteur Danilo Turk[210], and was taken up again in 1993[211] during a dedicated seminar[212]. It is interesting to note that during this seminar the idea emerged that certain principles are inviolable, such as the "right to a healthy environment" (para. 26). According to the conclusions of this seminar, the priority should be to better identify and clarify the content of different rights and obligations before moving on to developing possible indicators. According to one proposal, it would be useful to evaluate three different situations: the absence of laws or norms, the existence of laws that are ignored and the discriminatory or non-discriminatory application of texts (para. 30).

On 25 June 1993, the World Conference on Human Rights in Vienna approved a declaration and a program of action[213]. Paragraph 98 of this program

---

210 Economic and Social Council, Human Rights and Disability, Written Statement Submitted by Human Rights Advocates, a Non-Governmental Organization in Consultative Status, E/CN.4.Sub.2/1990/19.

211 According to Judith V. Welling, "International indicators and economic, social and cultural rights", *Human Rights Quarterly*, Vol. 30 (2008), p. 934.

212 World Conference on Human Rights, Preparatory Committee, 4th session, *Report of the Secretariat*, A/CONF.157/PC/73, 20 April 1993.

213 World Conference on Human Rights, *Vienna Declaration and Programme of Action*, A/CONF.157/23.

recommended the creation of indicators to measure progress in the realization of the rights set forth in the International Covenant on Economic, Social and Cultural Rights[214]. At that time the measurement of human rights was a topic that raised many methodological and theoretical questions. It wasn't until 2005 that an initiative was launched at the annual Inter-Committee Meeting of the human rights treaty bodies of the Office of the United Nations High Commissioner for Human Rights in Geneva. An expert meeting was organized in Finland, Turku, from 10 to 13 March 2005, on the topic of human rights indicators. This resulted in the *Report on indicators for monitoring compliance with international human rights instruments*, which was reviewed in June 2006[215]. This report was completed and validated at the meeting of chairpersons of the human rights treaty bodies and their Inter-Committee Meeting in June 2008[216]. After additional work, *Human Rights Indicators: A Guide to Measurement and Implementation* was published in 2012[217].

The aim is to develop quantitative indicators to better monitor States' implementation of international human rights conventions, particularly when submitting national reports. Special attention must also be given to the issue of data collection when there is a reference to statistics[218]. Four rights were tested in the beginning, not unrelated to the environment: the right to life, the right to adequate food, the right to health and the right to judicial review of detention. The goal was not to rank States along the lines of the benchmarking model used in the Human Development Index examined previously[219]. Instead the methodology consisted of a step-by-step approach at the conceptual level to:

---

214 Russell L. Barsh, "Measuring human rights: Problems of methodology and purpose", *Human Rights Quarterly*, Vol. 15 (1993), pp. 87–121.

215 International human rights instruments, *Report on indicators for monitoring compliance with international human rights instruments*, HRI/MC/2006/7, 11 May 2006.

216 International human rights instruments, *Report on indicators for monitoring compliance with international human rights instruments*, HRI/MC/2008/3, 16 May 2008.

217 Office of the High Commissioner for Human Rights, *Human Rights Indicators*, https://www.ohchr.org/EN/Issues/Indicators/Pages/HRIndicatorsIndex.aspx.

218 Office of the High Commissioner for Human Rights, *A human rights-based approach to data. Leaving No One Behind in the 2030 Agenda for Sustainable Development*, Geneva, 2018.

219 For country index methods, see Dipak K. Gupta and others, "Creating a composite index for assessing country performance in the field of human rights: Proposal for a new methodology", *Human Rights Quarterly*, Vol. 16 (1994), pp. 131–162.

- Determine the main characteristics of the right being studied, by examining its essence and normative content. It should be possible to select only 3 to 5 characteristics for each right examined;
- Formulate indicators corresponding to each of the characteristics selected, attempting to identify the Parties' intention in implementing the treaties.

There are three categories of indicators reflecting commitments and efforts to implement rights:

a) Structural indicators (or commitments): ratification of the treaty, adoption of national texts, nature of applicable national texts, basic institutional instruments, public policy documents and strategy, customary practices;
b) Method or process indicators (or efforts): support for public policy, efforts undertaken by duty bearers, measures taken by States, budgetary means, monitoring and controls, individual effects;
c) Outcome indicators: status of realization of the right (or overall impact).

The indicators are based on existing statistics, including those established by the courts, administrative documents, opinion and perception surveys, and expert advice.

The criteria for selecting indicators are that they are relevant, legitimate, reliable, simple, few in number, and are able to be broken down by sex, age or vulnerable group.

An important distinction must be made between sectoral indicators for each human right, and indicators that are common to all human rights. This distinction is important within environmental law.

Similarly, special attention should be paid to distinguishing between indicators that have universal relevance and those that are specific to one nation.

The 2012 guide to human rights indicators provides examples of indicators in 14 tables and 16 metadata sheets related to the selected indicators[220].

The Special Rapporteurs of the Human Rights Council have called for the development of sectoral indicators for every individual human right, in each of their respective fields. One example is Anand Grover, the Special Rapporteur on

220 Office of the High Commissioner for Human Rights, *Human Rights Indicator: A Guide to Measurement and Implementation* (Geneva, 2012). For an earlier country-specific experience, see Jeong-Woo Koo and others, "Measuring national human rights: A reflection on Korean experiences", *Human Rights Quarterly*, Vol. 34 (2012), pp. 986–1020.

the right of everyone to the enjoyment of the highest attainable standard of physical and mental health, in his 2012 report[221].

It is of particular interest for our study that the United Nations Special Rapporteur on the Right to the Environment (then independent expert) also reported on the growing importance of environmental indicators directly related to environmental law. In the 2015 good practice report, there are 5 mentions of indicators related to environmental law[222]: procedural rights, monitoring compliance with laws, citizen participation, the environment in the Constitution, and reporting on the state of the environment.

There have been some interesting experiments in parallel with the work of the Office of the High Commissioner for Human Rights, particularly with regard to the right to water, which comes under environmental rights. These could serve as inspiration for our study. A seminar was held under the auspices of the Böll Foundation in Berlin in October 2004, during which a very interesting report was presented by Virginia Roaf, Ashfaq Khalfoun and Malcolm Langford, entitled *Monitoring Implementation of the Right to Water: A Framework for Developing Indicators*. This report clearly sets out the challenges of reflecting legal obligations and appropriate methods in indicators. It proposes a matrix of all possible indicators on the right to water.

Among the very extensive work on indicators relating to compliance with international human rights law, one article by A. J. Rosga and M. L. Satterthwaite raises some important issues: the need for human rights compliance indicators that reflect both the progressive realization of the rights in question and allow for monitoring of respect for those rights; and the important role of convention monitoring bodies or compliance committees, which can utilize the indicators as tools. However, exclusive use of this type of tool can lead to technocratic rather than democratic governance[223].

The Office of the High Commissioner for Human Rights has also developed an important documentary source: the Universal Human Rights Index

---

221 Human Rights Council, 20th session, *Report of the Special Rapporteur on the right of everyone to the enjoyment of the highest attainable standard of physical and mental health, Anand Grover*, A/HRC/20/15, 10 April 2012, paras. 34 and 35.

222 Human Rights Council, 28th session, *Report of the Independent Expert on the issue of human rights obligations relating to the enjoyment of a safe, clean, healthy and sustainable environment, John H. Knox*, A/HRC/28/61, 3 February 2015, paras. 31, 34, 49, 77 and 81.

223 A. J. Rosga and M. L. Satterthwaite, "The trust in indicators: Measuring human rights", *Berkeley Journal of International Law*, Vol. 27–2 (2009), pp. 253–315.

(UHRI). This database contains 2218 country-specific recommendations from the treaty bodies, special procedures and the Universal Periodic Review. There are references to the right to water, the right to health as well as the Sustainable Development Goals[224].

2. The Inter-American Commission on Human Rights

Following the entry into force in 1999 of the Protocol of San Salvador on Economic, Social and Cultural Rights in the Americas, the General Assembly of the Organization of American States, in its resolution AG/RES.2074 (XXXV-O/05) to strengthen the periodic reports required of States under article 19 of the Protocol, decided to entrust the Inter-American Commission on Human Rights (IACHR) with the task of developing progress indicators to reduce the gap between reality and standards imposed[225]. To this end, the IACHR organized an expert meeting in October 2005 under the leadership of one of its members, Victor Abramovich. Consultants prepared a document for public consultation, which was approved by the IACHR in 2008: *Guidelines for preparation of progress indicators in the area of economic, social and cultural rights*[226]. The report follows the methodology favored by the Office of the High Commissioner for Human Rights, which distinguishes between structural, process and outcome indicators. These progress indicators were subsequently approved by the General Assembly of the Organization of American States in 2013[227]. In its advisory opinion on environmental and human rights, issued on 15 November 2017 at the request of Colombia, the Inter-American Court of Human Rights expressly refer to and make use of these progress indicators[228].

The above-mentioned 2008 report offers some interesting observations, suggesting three analytical categories which can be used to organize relevant information, taking legal data directly into account. These are: incorporation of the right, State capabilities and the financial context. Moreover, according to the principle of progressive realization, the report concludes that regressive

224 *Universal Human Rights Index*, https://uhri.ohchr.org/.

225 *Normas para la confección de los informes periódicos previstos en el Protocolo de San Salvador*, 6 June 2006.

226 Inter-American Commission on Human Rights, *Guidelines for preparation of progress indicators in the area of economic, social and cultural rights*, OEA/SER.L/V/II.132, 19 July 2008.

227 Organization of American States, *Progress indicators for measuring rights under the Protocol of San Salvador*, OEA/Ser.L/XXV.2.1, GT/PSS/doc9/13, 2013.

228 Advisory Opinion OC 23/17, 15 November 2017, para. 60 and notes 93–97.

measures should be banned, suggesting the need for indicators on this basis. This report is the first to make special mention of rights indicators, targeting strictly legal indicators, such as the constitutional recognition of a right; mechanisms of participation, transparency and accountability; institutions, programs and services devoted to the enforcement of rights; and the functioning of the justice system. It also refers to indicators to measure the capacity of individuals to demand that their rights are respected. The report is accompanied by model indicators for access to justice, access to information and participation, equality and non-discrimination, and the right to health. In each case, three distinct columns divide the structural, process and outcome indicators. These are then cross-referenced with the three analytical indicators.

3. The Core Humanitarian Standard indicators[229]

The Core Humanitarian Standard (CHS) indicators were developed by a network of international NGOs associated with the United Nations Office for the Coordination of Humanitarian Assistance (UNOCHA), the Sphere project and the CHS Alliance. Although the humanitarian standards are based on rules of international law (right to live in dignity, right to protection and security, right to health, etc.), the proposed indicators are not legal, but performance based, assessing progress towards compliance with the 2014 Core Humanitarian Standard on Quality and Accountability[230]. This standard sets out 9 voluntary commitments for institutions and individuals involved in humanitarian response, including natural disasters. To complement these 9 commitments and to make them operational, performance indicators were adopted and published in English in 2015[231]. There are 2 commitments that refer to rights: No. 4, “Communities and people affected by crisis know their rights and entitlements, have access to information and participate in decisions that affect them”; and No. 5, “Communities and people affected by crisis have access to safe and responsive mechanisms to handle complaints”[232].

229 *Core Humanitarian Standard on Quality and Accountability*, http://corehumanitarianstandard.org.

230 *Ibid.*

231 Core Humanitarian Standard, *Core Humanitarian Standard Guide and Indicators*, CHS Alliance, Sphere project and Groupe URD, 2015.

232 CAFOD, *Complaints Management Policy and Procedure for All International Programs*, 2010.

4. The European Union Fundamental Rights Agency

The European Union Fundamental Rights Agency (FRA) was established by European Council Regulation No. 168/2007. It is responsible for monitoring the Charter of Fundamental Rights of the European Union. Since 2012 it has been working on legal indicators for human rights.

The Agency believes that such indicators could help Member States and EU institutions to identify areas of improvement in respect for human rights, and draws inspiration from the methods put forward by the 2012 guide from the Office of the High Commissioner for Human Rights. In addition, a robust, rights-based framework of indicators has several positives, in particular increased accountability and transparency in actions taken by decision-makers. This can play a vital role in supporting democratic legitimacy.

The report entitled *Fundamental rights: challenges and achievements in 2014*, published by the Agency in 2015, is largely focused on indicators, in particular the section "Mainstreaming fundamental rights: turning words into action", and the paragraph "'What gets measured gets done': experience with fundamental rights indicators" (pp. 11–14)[233]. The FRA has worked on indicators for the rights of the child, family justice[234], political participation of persons with disabilities[235] and on Roma inclusion. In its 2017–2019 and then 2020–2022 work programs, the FRA planned to develop indicators to measure progress in human rights. Yet it seems this European Agency is not concerned with the right to the environment, even though Article 37 of the Charter of Fundamental Rights considers the environment as a human right[236].

5. The Council of Europe

Several indicators have been established in the areas of culture and human rights. Among these are human rights indicators for use by local populations[237]. In recommendation CM/Rec(2017)7 of 27 September 2017 (point h), the Committee

233 https://fra.europa.eu/sites/default/files/fra-annual-report-2014_en.pdf.

234 FRA, *Developing indicators for the protection, respect and promotion of the rights of the child in the European Union*, Vienna, 2010.

235 FRA, *The Right to Political Participation for Persons with Disabilities: Human Rights Indicators* (Vienna, 2014).

236 M. Prieur, "L'environnement dans la Charte des droits fondamentaux de l'Union européenne", in *Droit de l'environnement, droit durable* (Brussels, Bruylant, 2014), pp. 368–376.

237 Council of Europe, *Rule of Law Checklist*, CDL-AD (2016)007, 18 March 2016.

of Ministers recommended that States include "landscape" in sustainable development indicators, referring to the contribution of the European Landscape Convention to the exercise of human rights and democracy. This will require the establishment of legal indicators to assess the effectiveness of this Convention.

6. The Human Freedom Index

Since 2008, the Cato Institute and the Fraser Institute in the United States have developed a Human Freedom Index[238]. It consists of 76 performance indicators that determine the extent to which States respect this fundamental human right, on the basis of certain criteria. The 2019 study included 162 countries[239]. The following legal data is used: the rule of law with judicial proceedings (rights to life, fair trial, freedom from arbitrary interference with privacy), civil justice, criminal justice; the legal system with independence of the judiciary, impartiality of the courts, military interference in the rule of law, enforcement of contracts; and regulation of the markets, labor and business. There is no mention given to the environment. The indicators are based on data from existing texts and opinion surveys. The overall assessment, with a rating scale from 0 to 10, stems from the assumption that freedom is based 50 % on factors of individual freedom and 50 % on factors of economic freedom.

*

From this systematic review of 37 official, academic and NGO experiences with environmental assessment, we can draw the following conclusions:

- Environmental assessment is equivalent to the search for the Holy Grail: it is a never-ending and frustrating pursuit.
- Jurists who have studied the effectiveness of environmental law have never dared to seriously consider actually measuring the conditions of application of the law.
- Environmental texts refer to effectiveness, efficiency and efficacy often interchangeably. Confusion is often worsened by inconsistency in translations. In this publication we deliberately use the term "effectivity" to make a clear distinction in meaning and avoid confusion between other, similar terms.
- Aside from the environment, legal indicators have been used in studies and experiments within two other areas at the United Nations. These are human

---

238 *Human Freedom Index*, https://www.cato.org/human-freedom-index-new.

239 Cato Institute, *The Human Freedom Index 2019. A Global Measurement of Personal, Civil, and Economic Freedom* (Washington, D.C., 2019).

rights and the rule of law. The UN Statistics Division should take an interest in developing legal indicators in these areas that are already covered by the SDGs.

- While there is general agreement on the need for environmental indicators, legal indicators have only been regarded as necessary in exceptional circumstances, for instance at the 1993 Vienna Conference or in the 2012 guide for measuring human rights indicators.
- The term "legal indicator" could only be found on three occasions, in documents from the Inter-American Commission on Human Rights, the ILO and the Access Initiative.
- The most relevant work incorporates all three levels of environmental law in the assessment: international, regional and national.
- Where statistics are available on legal matters, they reflect the number of proceedings, the sanctions imposed or events relating to those proceedings, but never the processes and conditions of application of the rules.
- It is useful to distinguish between sector-specific and general indicators, as in the case of human rights. It would perhaps be advisable to adapt and adopt the distinction made in the area of human rights between structural, process and outcome indicators.
- Some institutions seem more open than others to integrate legal data directly into their environmental reviews. These include the IMPEL network, INECE, UNEP, OECD, the UN 2030 SDGs (see below) and the European Union.
- The Special Rapporteur J. Knox on the human right to the environment mentioned environmental indicators in his 2015 report.
- Africa could benefit from existing initiatives, such as the Ibrahim Index (mentioned previously) and UNEP's GEOs.
- Legal indicators should be treated separately at international and national levels by expanding the practices relating to the reporting system at the international reporting level.
- Legal indicators of effectivity can only be relevant if they supplement purely legal data with institutional, financial and social data.

III. Sustainable Development Goal indicators

On 25 September 2015, the United Nations adopted 17 Sustainable Development Goals through General Assembly resolution 70/1. States were invited to implement these goals, which are not legally binding, yet they constitute a political and moral commitment.

National implementation reviews are submitted by States voluntarily. Each year the conditions for implementation are analyzed for each SDG in turn. A handbook helps countries to complete their reports. It specifies that States must introduce "applicable legislation", thus clearly identifying the key role played by law in ensuring implementation of the SDGs[240]. These reports are examined by States each July at the High Level Political Forum on Sustainable Development.

In order to better identify sustainable development goals and to be able to measure progress in their implementation, the United Nations Statistical Commission developed a set of indicators, approved by the General Assembly in resolution 71/313 of 6 July 2017. 232 indicators were adopted to measure progress in implementing the 169 targets contained within the 17 SDGs. Of these 232 indicators, 93 address the environment and 2/3 address human rights. Each specialized international agency or organization is responsible for developing the methodology and collecting the data to enable States to apply the indicators. For instance, UNEP is responsible for 26 indicators.

Although not legally binding, the SDGs have become part of the landscape of environmental governance. They serve as a guide and reference point for political and legal action by States on environmental matters. The law's role within the SDGs should therefore be studied in order to verify whether official indicators successfully convey the effectivity of the law applicable to their implementation.

First, we will comment on the fact that the SDGs are moving increasingly away from the realm of soft law. This will be followed by an analysis of SDGs relating to the environment, complementary and alternative World Bank indicators, and finally academic and private indicators.

240 High-level Political Forum on Sustainable Development, *Handbook for the preparation of voluntary national reviews. The 2020 Edition* (New York, 2019), p. 24.

A. The gradual increase in indirect legal force of the SDGs

Legally non-binding, the SDGs were conceived from the outset as a common political and strategic plan or program for the entire planet. Like all plans and programs, the SDGs have a very general content that does not specify the conditions for their implementation. However, many of the targets are quantitative, which is quite remarkable and unheard of in a document of this nature. Each State is free to choose the technical, economic and/or legal application mechanisms it wishes to use. It should be noted that the law is mentioned in some SDGs and that several international documents suggest a certain legality, albeit subtle.

The SDGs do repeatedly refer to legal elements. In the 17 SDGs, the word "human rights" appears 11 times, the word "convention" 11 times, "international law" 8 times, "law" or "legislation" 5 times, "international agreements" 3 times and "rule of law" 3 times. Among the 169 targets, there are at least 15 direct references to the law[241]. Among the 232 indicators, the law, legislation, legal framework, application or implementation are referenced 35 times.

Therefore it is not surprising that a great deal of international soft law documents refer to the political, albeit voluntary, necessity to implement the 2030 Agenda. Upon adoption of the 2030 Agenda, Resolution 70/1 clearly stated that its implementation must be in accordance with international law and "consistent with the rights and obligations of States under international law" (para. 18). The Agenda setting out the SDGs was intended to be linked to human rights, through the Universal Declaration of Human Rights as well as other international human rights instruments (paras. 19 and 74.e). SDG implementation clearly implies the use of the law when referring to the "essential role of national parliaments through their enactment of legislation and adoption of budgets and their role in ensuring accountability for the effective implementation of our commitments" (para. 45).

In the run-up to the 3rd session of the United Nations Environment Assembly (UNEA 3), the Executive Director of UNEP stated that the aim is to "highlight how multilateral environmental agreements contribute to achieving the Goals"[242]. A special resolution was devoted to the SDGs at this 3rd Assembly

241 According to the UNEP publication *Environmental Rule of Law. First Global Report*, p. 226, there are in fact 76 such references.

242 *Progress in the implementation of resolution 2/5 on delivering on the 2030 Agenda for Sustainable Development. Report of the Executive Director*, UNEP/EA.3/5, 21 September 2017, para. 8.

which, like the UN General Assembly, brings together all of the UN Member States. According to Resolution 3/5, States commit to accelerating the effective implementation of the 2030 Agenda[243]. The final ministerial declaration, *Towards a Pollution-Free Planet*, is even more binding in nature: "we are determined to honor our undertakings … [through] the adoption of policies and approaches … including environmental agreements … [and] will strengthen and enforce … policies, laws and regulations"[244].

The 2019 political declaration of the High Level Political Forum on Sustainable Development, which is responsible for the annual SDG follow-up, was endorsed by the United Nations General Assembly in resolution 74/4 of 15 October 2019. It states: "We stand firm in our determination to implement the 2030 Agenda" (para. 2); ensuring "that ambitious and continuous action" is taken (para. 4); we commit "to action to remove all legal … barriers to achieve gender equality and the empowerment of … women" (para. 27-a); "to mainstream the 2030 Agenda into our national planning instruments … and financing frameworks" (para. 27-c); "to develop effective, accountable and transparent institutions" (para. 27-d); to strengthen "local action to accelerate implementation" (para. 27-e).[245]

The legality of the SDGs has also been touched upon in other international documents not related to the environment. Three examples can be given. Criminal justice is a very specific area which can support the legal effectivity of a measure by providing for criminal sanctions in the event of non-compliance. There is one United Nations General Assembly resolution that is entirely devoted to criminal justice within the SDGs, which clearly demonstrates that in order for the SDGs to be implemented, criminal sanctions must be created and applied. In terms of measures existing under national law, the UN relies on the Commission on Crime Prevention and Criminal Justice, one of the functional commissions of the United Nations Economic and Social Council. This Commission is requested to take an active role in the follow-up and implementation of the SDGs, in particular SDG 16[246]. In fact, the theme of the 14th United Nations Congress on

243 *Investing in innovative environmental solutions for accelerating the implementation of the Sustainable Development Goals*, UNEP/EA.3/Res.5, 5 December 2017, para. 1.

244 *Ministerial Declaration adopted by the United Nations Environment Assembly at its third session*, UNEP/EA.3/L.19, 5 December 2017, para. 8.

245 A/RES/74/4, 15 October 2019.

246 A/RES/73/183, 17 December 2018: Enhancing the role of the Commission on Crime Prevention and Criminal Justice in contributing to the implementation of the 2030 Agenda for Sustainable Development.

Crime Prevention and Criminal Justice was: "Advancing crime prevention, criminal justice and the rule of law: towards the achievement of the 2030 Agenda"[247].

Following the work of the Commission on Crime Prevention and Criminal Justice, the United Nations General Assembly adopted a resolution on the rule of law, crime prevention and criminal justice in the context of the SDGs[248]. It calls for the promotion of the rule of law when formulating legislation relating to the SDGs (para. 4), as well as the adoption of effective measures against crimes that have an impact on the environment, in pursuit of SDGs 13–16 (para. 11).

The United Nations General Assembly, in its resolution on "the rule of law at the national and international levels" of 20 December 2018, once again targeted the SDGs, reaffirming "its commitment to working tirelessly for the full implementation of the 2030 Agenda for Sustainable Development"[249].

In a broader sense, UNEP has highlighted the interrelationship between the law and the SDGs in the above mentioned 2019 publication, *Environmental Rule of Law*. In order to be effective, each of the 17 SDGs must rely on both existing law and very often the creation of new law to achieve the stated objectives. The law and the SDGs are mutually reinforcing[250].

B. The United Nations SDG indicators

1. Overview

Indicators related to the Sustainable Development Goals have been the subject of numerous studies and reports. The following are of particular note:

- Summaries of the voluntary national reviews, which States have been submitting annually since 2016, compiled by the United Nations Department of Economic and Social Affairs, specifying the indicators used[251];
- Monitoring of voluntary national reviews carried out by the IISD (International Institute for Sustainable Development), which published a summary of the voluntary reviews of 9 countries in June 2017, identifying those indicators chosen by each State[252];

247 Due to take place in Kyoto in April 2020 but postponed due to the Covid-19 pandemic.

248 A/RES/73/207, 20 December 2018, para. 7. The rule of law, crime prevention and criminal justice in the context of Sustainable Development Goals.

249 A/RES/73/207, 20 December 2018, para. 7.

250 See the illustration of this interrelationship in annex 3.

251 See references to these summaries in notes 38–41 above.

252 Livia Bizikova and Laszlo Pinter, *Indicator Preferences in National Reporting of Progress Toward the Sustainable Development Goals*, IISD, June 2017.

- Progress assessments of SDG implementation at the national level, based on the voluntary national reviews and conducted by the Canadian Council for International Co-operation in 2016, 2017 and 2018, the last of which recommended the development of national and sub-national indicators to complement the global indicators[253];
- Annual reports prepared by the UN Secretary-General on the SDGs from 2016 to 2019, the building blocks of the official global assessments, providing an overview of positive and negative developments in the implementation of each SDG, based on the indicators for which disaggregated data are available[254].

Following Decision 2015/2016 of the UN Economic and Social Council, an expert group was established to develop Sustainable Development Goal indicators, in response to the mandate given to the United Nations Statistical Commission by General Assembly resolution 70/1 of 25 September 2015 on the SDGs. This expert group is called the "Inter-agency and Expert Group on Sustainable Development Goals Indicators". The terms of reference of the Expert Group are contained in Annex I to the report of the 48th session of the Statistical Commission[255]. A report was submitted on 19 February 2016[256] including a final list of indicators for each of the SDGs in annex IV. This list was revised and supplemented by the Statistical Commission in March 2017[257], which included in annex 3 of the report the revised list of global SDG indicators. We will use this document in our proposals for legal indicators to complement existing scientific and economic indicators. The Committee of Experts on Public Administration of the Economic and Social Council has also made recommendations on measures

253 Canadian Council for International Co-operation, *Progressing national SDGs implementation: An independent assessment of the voluntary national review reports submitted to the United Nations High-Level Political Forum on Sustainable Development in 2018* (Ottawa, 2019).

254 Most recent report: ECOSOC, *Special Edition: Report of the Secretary-General on SDG progress 2019*, E/2019/68, 8 May 2019; see also: United Nations, *Sustainable Development Goals Report 2019* (New York, 2019).

255 E/CN.3/2017/2.

256 ECOSOC, *Report of the Inter-Agency and Expert Group on Sustainable Development Goal Indicators. Note by the Secretary-General*, E/CN.3/2016/2/Rev.1.

257 ECOSOC, *Report of the Inter-Agency and Expert Group on Sustainable Development Goal Indicators. Note by the Secretary-General*, E/CN.3/2017/2, 15 December 2016.

to be taken to ensure achievement of the Sustainable Development Goals. Based on this revised list of indicators, we will suggest adapted legal indicators for those SDGs that are more closely linked to the environment, namely SDGs 2, 3, 6, 7, 11, 12, 13, 14, 15, and 16.[258]

On 7 June 2017, the UN Economic and Social Council adopted a resolution on the work of the Statistical Commission pertaining to indicators related to the 2030 Sustainable Development Agenda[259]. This was subsequently endorsed by United Nations General Assembly resolution 71/313 of 6 July 2017, thus establishing a global framework of 232 SDG indicators. This framework is subject to ongoing change: it must be "refined annually and reviewed comprehensively by the Commission" in 2020[260]. Regular adjustments have therefore been made, based on recommendations from the SDG Expert Group. This group has proposed 36 significant changes, in the form of substitutions, additions, exclusions and revisions, approved by the Statistical Commission in 2018, 2019 and 2020[261]. Currently, the global framework is comprised of 231 unique indicators; while there appear to be 247, 12 indicators are in fact repeated under 2 or 3 different targets[262]. The SDG indicators are classified into 3 categories, or tiers: 1. Clear indicators, with internationally established methodology and used by 50 % of countries; 2. Clear indicators, with internationally established methodology, but not regularly used by countries; 3. No international established methodology yet available, but being developed or tested. A comprehensive review of the global indicator framework is expected to be carried out in 2020. While these adjustments have proved useful, the SDGs still lack truly legal indicators.

The Inter-Parliamentary Union published a practical document in 2016 to help national parliaments monitor progress of the SDGs. This document refers several times to the need for adequate indicators, without specifying the nature of these indicators, nor mentioning legal indicators[263].

---

258 ECOSOC, *Successfully achieving the Sustainable Development Goals: what is to be done? Note by the Secretariat*, E/C.16/2017/2, 30 January 2017.

259 ECOSOC, Resolution 2017/7 – Work of the Statistical Commission pertaining to the 2030 Agenda for Sustainable Development, E/RES/2017/7.

260 Resolution 71/313, para. 1.

261 The global indicator framework for the SDGs, as updated in 2020, is available at: https://unstats.un.org/sdgs/indicators/Global%20Indicator%20Framework%20after%202020%20review_Eng.pdf.

262 SDG indicators website: https://unstats.un.org/sdgs.

263 Inter-Parliamentary Union, *Parliaments and the Sustainable Development Goals – A self-assessment toolkit* (Geneva, 2016).

Various initiatives have also focused on SDGs with targets and/or indicators that concern the environment. They have led to assessments that are sometimes sectoral, focusing mainly on specific SDGs, and sometimes cross-cutting, horizontally exploring a given theme through a set of SDGs.

2. Sectoral assessments

Examples will be given of three sets of indicators. The first is related to health; second, water and sanitation; and third, justice and governance.

a) Health related indicators

The primary drive of SDG 3 is to enable all people to live in good health and to promote the well-being of all people at all ages. Yet this same concern for improving health and well-being is also reflected in various ways in almost 50 targets and across 14 SDGs. These include poverty eradication (SDG 1), food security (SDG 2), education (SDG 4), gender equality (SDG 5), water and sanitation (SDG 6), clean energy (SDG 7), decent work (SDG 8), reduction of inequality (SDG 10), cities (SDG 11), consumption and production (SDG 12), climate change (SDG 13), peace, justice and institutions (SDG 16), and partnerships (SDG 17). Progress is therefore needed on all these fronts to ensure health and well-being for all. For this reason, in 2019, 12 international agencies, including the World Bank, UN-Women, WFP, UNDP, UNFPA and UNICEF, led by WHO, developed a Global Action Plan[264] to strengthen global health collaboration by working together towards the harmonized implementation of all health-related targets, both those of SDG 3 and connected goals.

The links between the environment and health are clearly outlined in this plan. It recognizes the millions of deaths each year caused by various forms of pollution and serious diseases (malaria, yellow fever, cholera), which is exacerbated by climate change and natural disasters. Another study also highlighted the interrelationship between health and biodiversity, arguing that the right to health is "one of the most important indicators of sustainable development", and that "the conservation and sustainable use of biodiversity is imperative for the continued functioning of ecosystems at all scales, and for the delivery

264 *Stronger collaboration, better health: Global Action Plan for Healthy Lives and Well-being for All. Strengthening collaboration among multilateral organizations to accelerate country progress on the health-related sustainable development goals*, Geneva, WHO, 2019.

of ecosystem services that are essential for human health"[265]. The 2019 Global Action Plan advocates for legal determinants of health, by strengthening legal responses to environmental degradation to reduce health impacts, while emphasizing the utmost importance of the right to health for sustainable development and the centrality of rights-based approaches to health and well-being.

b) Water and sanitation related indicators

The aim of SDG 6, in addition to ensuring integrated water resources management, is to guarantee access to water and sanitation for all. In 2018, data revealed that billions of people still lacked access to safe water and sanitation, and that water pollution was worsening[266]. In the same year, SDG 6 was reviewed by the High Level Political Forum on Sustainable Development[267]. The targets and indicators related to SDG 6 have also been the subject of a detailed interpretation[268], specifically highlighting links with the constituent elements of the right to water and sanitation. This analysis can be illustrated, for example, through the prism of indicators 6.1.1 and 6.2.1.

The first indicator, which measures the proportion of the population using "safely managed" drinking water services to achieve "universal and equitable access" to safe drinking water (target 6.1), is consistent with the criteria of accessibility and affordability inherent in the right to water[269]. Access to water is understood according to its proximity to the place of residence (household connections) or the time it takes to collect water. Water should also be available in sufficient quantities at all times for personal and domestic use. Indicator 6.2.1 is used to measure the proportion of the population using "safely managed" sanitation services to achieve "access to adequate and equitable sanitation and

265 World Health Organization and Secretariat of the Convention on Biological Diversity, *Connecting Global Priorities: Biodiversity and Human Health. A State of Knowledge Review* (Geneva-Montreal, 2015).

266 UN-Water, *SDG Synthesis Report 2018 on Water and Sanitation*. New York, 2018.

267 *2018 HLPF Review of SDG implementation: SDG 6 – Ensure availability and sustainable management of water and sanitation for all*, https://sustainabledevelopment.un.org/content/documents/195716.29_Formatted_2018_background_notes_SDG_6.pdf.

268 Solidarity Water Programme, *Sustainable Development Goals for Water and Sanitation Services. Interpreting the targets and indicators* (Paris, 2018).

269 As recognized by the United Nations General Assembly in its resolution 64/292 of 28 July 2010 on the human right to water and sanitation, later reaffirmed in resolution 74/141 of 18 December 2019, as well as by the Human Rights Council in resolution 42/5 of 26 September 2019.

hygiene for all and end open defecation" (target 6.2). This is also in line with the definition of the right to sanitation. In particular, it implies that access to safe sanitation facilities, close to and not shared with other households, are essential requirements for the health, privacy, dignity and safety of users[270].

c) Justice and governance related indicators

SDG 16 is to promote peaceful and inclusive societies for sustainable development, provide access to justice for all and build effective, accountable and inclusive institutions at all levels. This goal is focused entirely on governance and its inclusion in the 2030 Agenda "was achieved through hard work and negotiation"[271]. Many countries were initially very resistant[272], but eventually gave their support, due in great part to the mobilization of African countries[273]. Its inclusion therefore marked "the culmination of a growth in importance of the theme of governance at the global level"[274]. It would appear that goal 16 is crucial for the achievement of many other SDGs.

Two targets under SDG 16 focus specifically on the demand for access to justice and information for the effective enjoyment of fundamental freedoms. The demand for justice is enshrined in target 16.3, which aims to promote the rule of law and ensure equal access to justice for all. However the two indicators that relate to this target only address criminal justice, focusing only on victims of violence (indicator 16.3.1) and the prison population (indicator 16.3.2)[275]. For this reason, in 2019 UNDP and OECD, with the support of the World Justice Project, submitted a proposal to the Expert Group on SDG Indicators for an indicator of access to civil justice[276]. Its creators suggested the addition of a third indicator, worded as follows: "Proportion of those who experienced a legal problem in the

---

270 See also indicators related to food and agriculture below.

271 Jean-Pierre Cling, Mireille Razafindrakoto and François Roubaud, "L'ODD 16 sur la gouvernance et sa mesure. L'Afrique en tête", *Afrique contemporaine*, No. 258, 2/ 2016, p. 73.

272 *Ibid.*, p. 75.

273 *Ibid.*, pp. 76 and 84.

274 *Ibid.*, p. 90.

275 This gap was pointed out by Sukti Dhital and Meg Satterthwaite, "New and inclusive measuring needed for SDG promise of access to justice for all", *Open Global Rights*, 5 February 2019.

276 UNDP/PCDE, "16.3.3. Indicator Proposal. Access to Civil Justice", 2019, https://worldjusticeproject.org/sites/default/files/documents/16.3.3%20Flyer_Access%20to%20Civil%20Justice_final_en.pdf.

last two years who could access appropriate information or expert help and were able to resolve the problem". Although this wording was not retained, it did contribute to the development of a new indicator, 16.3.3, which has been included in the revised global indicator framework: "Proportion of the population who have experienced a dispute in the past two years and who accessed a formal or informal dispute resolution mechanism, by type of mechanism"[277]. Worded in this way, this additional indicator can be applied to all types of disputes and resolution mechanisms, including those to do with the environment.

The information component is contained within target 16.10, which seeks to ensure public access to information and protect fundamental freedoms, in accordance with national legislation and international agreements. The main measurement criterion is the "number of countries that adopt and implement constitutional, statutory and/or policy guarantees for public access to information" (indicator 16.10.2)[278]. UNESCO is responsible for this indicator and ensures follow-up under the right to information. In 2019, in partnership with the Centre for Law and Democracy, UNESCO began a pilot project to collect data on legislation related to the right to information and to evaluate its implementation[279]. This assessment included 43 of the 51 States that have submitted voluntary national reviews under the 2030 Agenda[280]. Of the 43 countries studied, 26 had laws pertaining to the right to information. However, the practical effectivity of these measures remained relatively limited, mostly due to the absence of enforcement bodies in several countries[281].

With regard to Africa, the governance issues addressed in SDG 16 are also highlighted in Agenda 2063, a strategic framework for the long-term sustainable development of the continent, which was adopted by the Heads of State and Government of the African Union in January 2015. Its vision is based on

277 *Global indicator framework for the Sustainable Development Goals and targets of the 2030 Agenda for Sustainable Development*, A/RES/71/313, E/CN.3/2018/2, E/CN.3/2019/2, E/CN.3/2020/2 (2020), p. 18.

278 Committee of Experts on Public Administration, *Progress on institutional aspects of Sustainable Development Goal 16: access to information, transparency, participation and accountability. Note by the Secretariat*, E/C.16/2019/7, 24 January 2019.

279 Institute for Economics & Peace, *SDG16+ Progress Report 2019. A Comprehensive Global Audit of Progress on Available SDG16 Indicators*, March 2019.

280 Centre for Law and Democracy, "Pilot Data Collection on Sustainable Development Goal Indicator 16.10.2", 7 March 2019.

281 UNESCO, *Highlights from the 2019 UNESCO Monitoring and Reporting of SDG Indicator 16.10.2 – Access to Information* (Paris, 2019).

7 "Aspirations", broken down into 20 goals, with 66 indicators to measure their implementation. Aspiration 3 is an "Africa of good governance, democracy, respect for human rights, justice and the rule of law". It has two goals: (i) democratic values, practices, universal principles of human rights, justice and the rule of law entrenched (goal 11); (ii) capable institutions and transformative leadership in place (goal 12). These two goals are associated with 5 targets and 7 indicators, of which 3 relate to the effective implementation of the African Charter on Democracy, Elections and Governance (2007). Article 42 of the Charter calls for States Parties to implement "policies and strategies to protect the environment to achieve sustainable development for the benefit of the present and future generations". An initial assessment of the first 10-year implementation plan of Agenda 2063[282] shows modest progress of 27 % under aspiration 3[283].

3. Cross-cutting assessments

Here again three examples of horizontal analyzes will be given to illustrate the cross-cutting approach of SDG indicators related to food and agriculture, to culture and to human rights.

a) *Food and agriculture related indicators*

As a specialized agency for food and agriculture, including irrigation, fisheries and forestry, the FAO monitors SDGs within its areas of competence in order to assess progress on the indicators under its custodianship. In 2019, it published a first report analyzing global data and trends for 17 indicators associated with SDGs 2, 6, 14 and 15[284]. Some indicators have relied upon ad hoc studies[285].

---

282 African Union Commission, *Agenda 2063. The Africa We Want. A Shared Strategic Framework for Inclusive Growth and Sustainable Development. First ten-year implementation plan 2014–2023*, September 2015.

283 African Union, *First Continental Report on the Implementation of Agenda 2063*, February 2020.

284 FAO, *Tracking progress on food and agriculture related SDG indicators. A report on the indicators under FAO custodianship*, Rome, 2019.

285 FAO is actually responsible for monitoring 21 indicators, relating to six SDGs: 2, 5, 6, 12, 14 and 15. See: *FAO and the SDGs. Indicators: Measuring up to the 2030 Agenda for Sustainable Development*, Rome, 2017. Due to a lack of globally comparable data, four indicators could not be considered in the above-mentioned 2019 report. These are: agricultural sustainability (2.4.1), agricultural population with secure land rights (5.a.1), countries with a legal framework guaranteeing women's land rights (5.a.2) and

SDG 2 aims to eradicate hunger through the provision of safe, nutritious and sufficient food for all people, year-round (target 2.1), and is measured by the prevalence of undernourishment in the world (indicator 2.1.1). Undernourishment increased slightly in 2019, with more than 820 million people still suffering from hunger. This increase is due to a combination of factors, including environmental factors such as drought and extreme weather events. The eradication of hunger also requires the preservation of genetic diversity of seeds, crops, animals and related wild species (target 2.5), measured by the number of animal and plant genetic resources for food and agriculture secured in conservation facilities (indicator 2.5.1), as well as the proportion of local breeds, classified as being at risk, not at risk or at an unknown level of risk of extinction (indicator 2.5.2). For plant genetic resources, approximately 512,000 samples of 4,500 IUCN Red List species were conserved in 469 gene banks worldwide by the end of 2018. There has not been any significant progress in the conservation of animal genetic resources. Less than 1 % of the world's local livestock breeds has a sufficient stock of genetic material to ensure their recovery in the event of extinction. In addition, in the 70 countries that hold data on the issue, 60 % of local livestock breeds are endangered.

SDG 5 on gender equality was not included in the above-mentioned 2019 report due to a lack of meaningful data. However, a separate document on this indicator was published[286], and some findings have emerged from the analysis of available data for a limited number of countries, in relation to the two FAO indicators for target 5.a, to give women access to ownership or control over land[287]. Indicator 5.a.1 on women's access to ownership of agricultural land is broken down into two sub-indicators: (i) the proportion of total agricultural population with ownership or secure rights over agricultural land, by sex. Based on data from 10 countries,[288] the percentage secure land rights holders varies considerably, ranging from 4 % in Niger to 69 % in Ethiopia, through 19 % in Peru, 34 % in Cambodia and 49 % in Uganda. The percentage of women with these same rights is on average much lower, rarely reaching half that of men, with only one exception in Malawi: 47 % for women and 41 % for men; (ii)

---

food loss (12.3.1). Monitoring these indicators has nevertheless allowed for partial data to be collated regarding their implementation, which is reported separately.

286 FAO, *Realizing women's rights to land in the law. A guide for reporting on SDG indicator 5.a.2*, Rome, 2018.

287 http://www.fao.org/sustainable-development-goals/indicators/en.

288 Burkina Faso, Cambodia, Ethiopia, India, Malawi, Niger, Nigeria, Peru, Tanzania, Uganda.

the share of women among owners or rights bearers of agricultural land. Here again, the percentages reveal a significant disadvantage towards women, who represent only 10 % of holders of agricultural tenure in Niger, and 14 % in India, with exceptions of up to 51 % in Ethiopia and 58 % in Malawi[289]. For indicator 5.a.2, which measures the proportion of countries where the legal framework guarantees women's equal rights to land ownership and/or control, the analysis focused on the legal frameworks of 16 States[290]. The level of guarantees provided for women's equal access to land tenure was rated from 1 (lowest) to 6 (highest). The results were as follows: 2 countries at level 6 (Colombia, Paraguay); 4 countries at level 5 (Nicaragua, Portugal, Serbia, Sweden); 4 countries at level 4 (Italy, Slovakia, Switzerland, Uruguay); 2 countries at level 3 (Belarus, Uzbekistan); 1 country at level 2 (Suriname); and 3 countries at level 1 (Jordan, Pakistan, Qatar)[291].

With regard to SDG 6 on water management, the 2019 report looks at target 6.4 on increasing water-use efficiency across all sectors and ensuring sustainable withdrawals and supply of freshwater to address water scarcity. This is partially monitored by the FAO, with methodology developed for this purpose[292]. Two indicators relate to this target: (i) change in water use efficiency over time (indicator 6.4.1): particularly necessary are improvements in water productivity in irrigated agriculture, and loss reduction in municipal distribution networks and industrial and energy cooling processes; (ii) the level of water stress, indicated by freshwater withdrawal as a proportion of available resources (indicator 6.4.2). While water stress is considered to be low in 2/3 of countries, it is moderate in 20 % and high in 15 % of countries. Where water stress is high, countries should reduce freshwater withdrawal and increase the productivity and efficiency of its use.

With regard to SDG 14 on life below water, 4 targets that relate to the FAO are reflected in the 2019 report, 3 of which touch on the environment. The first aims to restore fish stocks to levels that can produce maximum sustainable yield as determined by their biological characteristics (target 14.4). This will be measured by the proportion of fish stocks within biologically sustainable levels (indicator 14.4.1). Here, the picture is one of a continuing decline in the percentage

289 http://www.fao.org/sustainable-development-goals/indicators/5a1/en.

290 Belarus, Colombia, Italy, Jordan, Nicaragua, Pakistan, Paraguay, Portugal, Qatar, Serbia, Slovakia, Suriname, Sweden, Switzerland, Uruguay, Uzbekistan.

291 http://www.fao.org/sustainable-development-goals/indicators/5a2/en.

292 FAO, *Incorporating environmental flows into "water stress" indicator 6.4.2 – Guidelines for a minimum standard method for global reporting*, Rome, 2019.

of the world's sustainably managed marine fish stocks, with one third being overexploited due to an increase in fishing overcapacity. The second target is to eliminate subsidies that contribute to illegal, unreported and unregulated fishing (target 14.6), measured by countries' progress in the implementation of international instruments to combat illegal fishing (indicator 14.6.1)[293]. Countries have made significant progress in this regard, but there is a need for increased effort for more widespread implementation. The third target is to provide access for small-scale artisanal fishers to marine resources and markets (target 14.b), which is measured by the progress made by countries "in adopting and implementing a legal / regulatory / policy / institutional framework which recognizes and protects access rights for small-scale fisheries" (indicator 14.b.1). The majority of States have effectively put in place such legal and policy tools for artisanal fisheries, in addition to establishing mechanisms to involve small-scale fishers in decision-making processes[294].

SDG 15, life on land, aims to manage forests sustainably, combat desertification, halt and reverse land degradation and halt biodiversity loss. The four targets of relevance to the FAO are reflected in the 2019 report. First, target 15.1 to ensure the conservation, restoration and sustainable use of ecosystems, is measured by the forest area as a proportion of the total land area (indicator 15.1.1). Forests continued to decline between 2000 and 2015, with total forest area falling from 31.1 % to 30.7 % of the world's land area. The largest declines occurred in tropical zones. Target 15.2, to promote the sustainable management of all types of forests, halt deforestation, restore degraded forests and significantly increase afforestation and reforestation globally, is measured by progress towards sustainable forest management (indicator 15.2.1). Recent data reveals progress in the sustainable management of the world's forests. Despite the reduction in forest area, the rate of forest loss decreased by about 25 % between 2010 and 2015 compared to the period 2000–2005. In addition, the proportion of protected forest areas and forests under management plans either remained stable or increased in every region of the world.

---

293 These instruments are: United Nations Convention on the Law of the Sea, 1982; FAO Agreement to Promote Compliance with International Conservation and Management Measures by Fishing Vessels on the High Seas, 1993; United Nations Fish Stock Agreement, 1995; FAO Agreement on Port State Measures to Prevent, Deter and Eliminate Illegal, Unreported and Unregulated Fishing, 2009.

294 On these indicators, see also: FAO, *The State of World Fisheries and Aquaculture 2018 – Meeting the sustainable development goals*, Rome, 2018.

Target 15.4 aims to ensure the conservation of mountain ecosystems, as measured by the Mountain Green Cover Index (indicator 15.4.2). According to the first data collected in 2017, 76 % of the world's mountain environments were covered by vegetation (forests, grasslands or shrub land, arable land). While forests always decline at altitude, this varies depending on the location and can result from climatic factors, overgrazing, land clearing, urbanization, logging and fires. Finally, target 15.6 encourages the fair and equitable sharing of the benefits arising from the utilization of genetic resources. This is quantified by the number of countries that have adopted "legislative, administrative and policy frameworks to ensure fair and equitable sharing of benefits" (indicator 15.6.1)[295]. Since 2012, one third of the States Parties to the International Treaty on Plant Genetic Resources for Food and Agriculture have provided information on legal measures taken under the Treaty in their national reports. In addition, the Treaty has led to the establishment of standard genetic material transfer agreements to determine the conditions of use and benefit-sharing. By 2019, there were more than 75,000 such agreements.

b) *Culture related indicators*

SDG 4 aims to ensure "equitable, inclusive and quality education" for all, as well as "opportunities for lifelong learning". On the basis of this goal, which promotes the right to education and broadens cultural perspectives, in 2019 UNESCO adopted a framework of thematic indicators for culture, called the "Culture|2030 Indicators". They aim to measure the contribution of culture to the achievement of the SDGs at national and local levels, complementing the indicators for the 2030 Agenda[296]. Their conceptual framework is made up of four cross-cutting themes: environment and resilience; prosperity and livelihoods; knowledge and skills; and inclusion and participation. Each dimension brings together several goals and targets in order to capture the multiple ways in which culture contributes

---

295 Note that the FAO, while not fully responsible for this indicator, contributes to its monitoring jointly with UNEP and the Secretariat of the Convention on Biological Diversity.

296 UNESCO, *Culture Indicators 2030*, Paris, 2019. An earlier UNESCO publication assessed the multidimensional role of culture in development, in terms of values and norms guiding human action and promoting an inclusive vision of the interactions between culture and development: *Culture for Development Indicators. Methodology Manual*, Paris, 2014.

to sustainable development[297]. "Environment and resilience" emphasizes the role of natural and cultural heritage, both tangible and intangible, in relation to the "planet" component of the SDGs. The indicators assess in particular countries' commitment to safeguarding natural and cultural heritage with regard to the relevant UNESCO conventions and from the perspective of the SDG targets to which they relate.

There are six treaties that draw attention to this issue: the Convention for the Protection of Cultural Property in the Event of Armed Conflict (1954); the Convention on the Means of Prohibiting and Preventing the Illicit Import, Export and Transfer of Ownership of Cultural Property (1970); the Convention concerning the Protection of the World Cultural and Natural Heritage (1972); the Convention on the Protection of the Underwater Cultural Heritage (2001); the Convention for the Safeguarding of the Intangible Cultural Heritage (2003); and the Convention on the Protection and Promotion of the Diversity of Cultural Expressions (2005). Each of these conventions correlates with the implementation of various targets under several SDGs. In total, they contribute to progress within 26 wide ranging targets, spread across no less than 12 SDGs. They address, for example, the protection of the world's cultural and natural heritage (target 11.4), the preservation of marine and coastal areas (target 14.5), and terrestrial and freshwater ecosystems (target 15.1), the improvement of capacity on climate change adaptation (target 13.3), the promotion of sustainable tourism that promotes local culture (target 8.9) and monitoring its impacts for sustainability (target 12.b), enhancing policy coherence for sustainable development (target 17.14), returning stolen assets and combating organized crime (target 16.4) or strengthening institutions responsible for preventing and combating crime (target 16.a). This form of horizontal evaluation is highly instructive and can be useful in terms of methodology in trying to capture the contribution of other environmental conventions to the achievement of the SDGs in relevant areas, such as biodiversity or climate change, using indicators selected on a thematic basis.

297 For a similar approach, see: Katia Vladimirova and David Le Blanc, *How well are the links between education and other sustainable development goals covered in UN flagship reports? A contribution to the study of the science-policy interface on education in the UN system Department of Economic & Social Affairs*, DESA Working Paper No. 146 (New York, October 2015).

c) *Human rights related indicators*

Aspiring to "a world in which human rights are universally respected", the 2030 Agenda reaffirms the importance of "international human rights instruments". Thus it explicitly states that the SDGs seek to "realize the human rights of all" and that follow-up and review processes must be "people-centered" and "respect human rights" so that "no one is left behind"[298]. Approximately 92 % of the SDG targets reflect international rules on human and labor rights. With this in mind, the Danish Institute for Human Rights developed a digital guide to human rights within the framework of the SDGs[299]. It illustrates the human rights foundation of the 17 goals by making concrete links between the 169 targets and 81 international legal instruments dealing with human rights in general (17 universal and 15 regional), labor standards (38 instruments) and the environment (11 instruments)[300]. Therefore the guide helps to understand the interdependencies between the SDGs and these three categories of law.

It is linked to the SDG-Human Rights Data Explorer, a database created in collaboration with the Office of the United Nations High Commissioner for Human Rights, which facilitates searches by goal, target, instrument, instrument article, group of instruments, country or group of countries, as well as combinations of these entries. Let us take the example of a search on Benin, for target 12.4 which is to achieve environmentally sound management of chemicals and wastes in order to minimize their adverse impacts on health and the environment, a component of SDG 12 on sustainable consumption and production. The results of this search would refer to all the relevant provisions of the six international instruments that Benin is bound by in this area: the International Covenant on Economic, Social and Cultural Rights (art. 12); the United Nations Declaration on the Rights of Indigenous Peoples (art. 29); the African Charter on Human and Peoples' Rights (art. 16); the Protocol to the African Charter on Human and Peoples' Rights on the Rights of Women in Africa (art. 18); the entire Convention on the Control of Transboundary Movements of Hazardous Wastes and their Disposal; and the United Nations Convention on the Law of the Sea (arts. 207–210 and 216)[301].

---

298 Transforming our world: the 2030 Agenda for Sustainable Development, UNGA Resolution 70/1, 25 September 2015.

299 https://sdg.humanrights.dk/en/node/10.

300 https://sdg.humanrights.dk/en/instruments/overview/list.

301 https://sdg.humanrights.dk/en/targets2?combine_1=xxx&goal=81&target=12.4&instrument=All&title_1=&field_country_tid=27&field_instrument_group_tid=All&combine=.

In addition, the database allows users to explore approximately 150,000 recommendations issued to States by the 67 international human rights bodies and mechanisms (UN Charter bodies, Universal Periodic Review, Special Procedures, Treaty Bodies, etc.). Almost 60 % of these recommendations are closely, yet not explicitly linked to the SDG targets. With this search engine, they can be easily identified and used directly for national implementation of the SDGs, based on the related indicators. Recommended reforms can therefore be implemented on the basis of the indivisibility and interdependence of human rights, following the global vision of the SDGs and related instruments that are offered by the guide.

Of the 556 recommendations concerning Benin, 345 (62 %) are linked to specific targets, distributed among 13 SDGs, including 179 for SDG 16 alone. For example, in relation to target 16.a (national human rights institutions), the Committee on Economic, Social and Cultural Rights recommended that Benin ensure that the rights contained in the International Covenant on Economic, Social and Cultural Rights be directly applicable in domestic courts and that legal and judicial training take into account the justiciability of these rights. In another example, referring to target 6.1 (universal and equitable access to safe drinking water), the Universal Periodic Review recommended that Benin should improve both hygiene conditions in schools by providing access to drinking water, as well as conditions of detention in prisons through provision of water and sanitation[302].

C. The World Bank SDG indicators

The World Bank has extensive experience with indicators. They are regularly updated and are now in line with the Sustainable Development Goals. Three sets of documents provide a numerical overview of every country, including those in Africa. They refer to data far removed from environmental law, but nevertheless provide useful information. Among the tools leading to these indicators are the following:

- The World Development Indicators, international data related to 217 economies and comprising 1600 indicators, of which more than 140 are related to the environment since 2015[303]. These address clean water and sanitation; clean

302 https://sdgdata.humanrights.dk/en/taxonomy/term/800.

303 World Bank, *World Development Indicators 2015*, Washington, D.C., 2015; *World Development Indicators 2016*, Washington, D.C., 2016; *World Development Indicators*

energy; sustainable cities; responsible consumption, including waste; climate action; oceans; life on earth, in particular forests and biodiversity; and peace, justice and institutions;

- The World Development Reports, which occasionally contain chapters that address environmental themes, such as a section on green growth in the 2017 edition[304], and an examination of the environmental dimension of global value chains in the 2020 edition[305];
- The Atlas of Sustainable Development Goals, a visual guide published in 2017 and 2018[306] which provides updated information on the progress made by countries on the 17 SDGs, in particular those related to the climate, oceans, environment and institutions.

D. SDG indicators of academic and private origin

Two organizations have developed indicators for the 17 SDGs, complementing the official UN indicators. They are Bertelsmann Stiftung, a German foundation, and the Sustainable Development Solutions Network (SDSN) at Columbia University in New York[307]. Together they have developed a methodology for ranking States according to the implementation of the SDGs at the national and local levels. This ranking is based on a scale from 0 (worst) to 100 (best). 144 indicators are applied in 162 States to enable decision-makers to identify priorities for action to achieve the SDGs. Under the direction of Jeffrey Sachs, Professor of economics at Columbia University, the 2019 report[308], as in previous editions[309], ranked countries as can be seen in this example of 4 African States:

2017, Washington, D.C., 2017. Since 2018, these indicators have been available in digital form at: http://datatopics.worldbank.org/world-development-indicators.

304 World Bank, *World Development Report. Governance and the Law*, Washington, D.C., 2017.

305 World Bank, *World Development Report 2020. Trading for Development in the Age of Global Value Chains*, Washington, D.C., 2020.

306 World Bank, *Atlas of Sustainable Development Goals 2018. World Development Indicators*, Washington, D.C., 2018; World Bank, *Atlas of Sustainable Development Goals 2017. World Development Indicators*, Washington, D.C., 2017.

307 *Sustainable Development Solutions Network*, www.unsdsn.org.

308 Bertelsmann Stiftung and SDSN, *Sustainable Development Report 2019. Transformations to achieve the Sustainable Development Goals*, June 2019.

309 Bertelsmann Stiftung and SDSN, *SDG Index and Dashboards Report 2017. Global Responsibilities, International Spillover in Achieving the Goals*, July 2017; *SDG Index and Dashboards Report 2018. Global Responsibilities, Implementing the Goals*, July 2018.

- Tunisia, 63rd in the world ranking with a score of 70.0;
- Cameroon, 127th in the world ranking with a score of 56.0;
- Benin, 151st in the world ranking with a score of 50.9;
- Madagascar, 158th in the world ranking with a score of 46.7.

At the top of the list of 162 nations is Denmark, with 85.2, and at the bottom is the Central African Republic, with 39.1.

Previous to this, in 2015, the SDSN produced a report commissioned by the United Nations Secretary-General proposing a set of SDG indicators[310]. This report set out 100 indicators for monitoring SDGs. It is interesting to note that the authors seem to have been aware of the difficulties of using of legal data. While noting that countries may introduce "nationally appropriate indicators on policies and law", it argues that this "would be difficult to harmonize at the global level" (p. 19). On the contrary, our view is that, at least within the realm of environmental law, harmonization is facilitated by its universal nature. The same document cites an example from the Mongolia national report on the implementation of the Millennium Development Goals, which assesses the compliance of Mongolian law with international human rights law (p. 11). We have seen that human rights, like environmental law, facilitate comparisons between States because of the large number of international conventions that are binding on them.

In its 2015 proposals, the SDSN makes several references to legal indicators, but does not propose a method for assessing the effectivity of the law. Examples include indicator 57 for SDG 8, "Ratification and implementation of fundamental ILO labour standards and compliance in law and practice"; and indicator 93 for SDG 16, "Existence and implementation of a national law and/or constitutional guarantee on the right to information". Even though in a 2014 report assessing gaps in the coverage of indicators the SDSN made no mention of the law[311], they may be open to widening the scope of the indicators to include legal aspects. This is suggested in the 2019 report, which emphasized that, in addition to the commitments of the executive branch, the legislative power also has significant leverage on policy direction and laws for SDG implementation. However, it is also argued that the lack of comparable data on the frequency and content

310 SDSN, *Indicators and a Monitoring Framework for the Sustainable Development Goals: Launching a Data Revolution for the SDGs*, 12 June 2015.

311 SDSN, *Assessing Gaps in Indicators Availability and Coverage*, July 2014.

of debates on SDGs in parliaments makes it difficult to accurately assess their contribution[312].

Since 2018, the SDSN has devoted a specific report to Africa. While its first edition[313] included only 11 African nations in a preliminary analysis of the implementation of the SDGs, the 2019 report covered all 54, using 97 indicators to rank countries on the same scale as that used in the global index (from 0 to 100). The highest ranking country was Mauritius, with a score of 66.19, and the lowest was South Sudan, with 29.19. The 4 African States mentioned earlier are ranked as follows:

- Tunisia, 2nd with a score of 66.12;
- Cameroon, 28th with a score of 51.57;
- Benin, 29th with a score of 51.52;
- Madagascar, 44th with a score of 45.57.

The same report assesses both the progress made by African countries towards the achievement of the SDGs and the strategies put in place to achieve them, particularly at the institutional level. One of the inputs is to do with "legislative actions", monitoring whether or not a special task force had been created within parliament to discuss the implementation of the SDGs. In 2019, only 7 countries had a task force in their parliament (Algeria, Comoros, Mali, Nigeria, Sierra Leone, Uganda and Zimbabwe), while 21 countries had established an inter-ministerial committee or task force to coordinate the implementation of the SDGs in relevant ministries or other bodies.

Finally, there is another academic initiative being led by Oxford University: *Our World in Data*[314]. It consists of a platform for collecting data on the major problems and changes shaping the world, grouped around 16 major themes. These include the environment, health, demographics, food, energy, peace, society, culture, values, education, knowledge, rights, living conditions, political system, etc. The 17 SDGs are monitored interactively through a dedicated tool: the SDG Tracker[315]. This provides the most up-to-date data available according to the UN global indicator framework for SDGs.

312 Bertelsmann Stiftung and SDSN, *Sustainable Development Report 2019. Transformations to achieve the Sustainable Development Goals*, June 2019, p. 9.

313 Bertelsmann Stiftung and SDSN, *Africa SDG Index and Dashboards Report 2018*, July 2018.

314 https://ourworldindata.org.

315 https://sdg-tracker.org.

IV. Why create legal indicators for the environment?

Through the creation of legal indicators for the environment, better monitoring of public policies and governance in this area will be possible. Legal indicators first identify ineffective processes within environmental law. They can then be used in a combination of different ways, as they have multiple functions.

A. Respond to ineffective processes in environmental law

Environmental law is widely criticized for being ineffective. This is due to both its rapid development and growth, internationally and nationally, as well as the fact that its demands often lead to infringements upon rights assumed to be acquired. Is it useful? Why hasn't the environment been better protected since its creation? These are valid questions that call into question the many inspection reports and state of the environment reviews that, throughout the year, desperately seek to illustrate existing environmental progress. As a political consequence, at international meetings and conferences in recent years, governments have repeatedly called for more effective implementation of both international conventions and national laws. This demand for effectiveness is always quite general and abstract, lacking any tangible suggestions on how to combat ineffectiveness. However, in order to know how the law can be better applied, it is necessary to know why it is poorly applied, or not applied at all. Aside from a few academic studies that have dared to tackle this apparently taboo subject, there is still no scientific method to detect the precise causes of non-effectivity[316]. This is why the creation of legal indicators should make it possible to provide guidelines and recommendations for improving the effectivity of environmental law. Society demands accountability. But it is necessary to have the right tools. It is no longer enough to simply study the wording of legislation, ignoring all the difficulties associated with its application.

316 J. Bétaille, "L'effectivité en droit de l'environnement", in S. Brimo and Ch. Pauti (dir.), *L'effectivité des droits. Regards en droit administratif* (Paris, Mare et Martin, 2019).

B. Inform the public about the social value of environmental law

Legal indicators should first of all be able to provide information to the public to create awareness of the social benefit of the law and its role in environmental protection. Given that the environment is part of our common heritage, both the general public and professional interest groups must be able to assess whether environmental law is serving a purpose and is working correctly. This information will first of all serve to raise awareness of environmental law, which is still largely ignored by citizens even in countries where there exists an environmental code. An environmental code is intended to collate scattered pieces of legislation into an easily accessible format. However these efforts have mostly been directed at legal professionals. As texts can also now be accessed via the internet and legal databases, the public will begin to question their relevance, their clarity and their complexity. Therefore legal indicators will enable the public to gain a concrete understanding of the difficulties encountered in the application of the law and to better appreciate the progress achieved. Moreover, a greater understanding of the usefulness of the law in solving environmental problems enables stakeholders, both public and private, to better accept rules as legitimate, thus making compliance more likely. It is a known fact that effectivity in law only exists if there is conscious support from all actors concerned.

C. Inform decision-makers

Legal indicators also have a political and operational function. Public policy assessment mechanisms used by governments and parliaments will be given a scientific basis, providing numerical data on the practical application of the law. Thus, proposed reforms will no longer be carried out blindly, but rather they will be fully informed. The use of legal indicators will make it possible to highlight the real obstacles hampering or preventing the effective application of the legal rule. Hence, the findings revealed by legal indicators will be used as a basis for impact assessments for draft bills and regulatory acts. Public decision-making will be evidence-based, thus giving justification to proposed solutions. Policy-makers will have at their disposal a new and innovative tool to assist with much needed future reforms.

D. Scientifically measure progress and regressions in environmental law

Finally, legal indicators also have a scientific function. They will make it possible to scientifically measure effectivity, via a methodology that calls attention to both advances and regressions in the law. They will also be an invaluable tool for supplementing the data used in both national and international scientific reports on the state of the environment. These reports have so far paid no attention to the place and role of law in pollution levels and the state of biodiversity. The absence of references to environmental law in reports on the state of the environment shows a lack of respect for the rule of law. Environmental law now forms part the rule of law[317]. Democratic regimes are generally no longer able to ignore the contribution of environmental law to public policy. Environmental reports will be able use legal indicators to inform governments and the public about what role the law actually plays in determining the state of the environment.

Legal indicators are hugely useful for the effective implementation of international environmental conventions at both national and international levels. At the formal level, they can be used to better reflect actual levels of compliance with general obligations by the contracting parties. In addition, they will help States to better fulfill their specific obligation to submit periodic reports. Finally, they will enable the contracting parties, during their meetings, to better assess compliance with the commitments they have entered into, and to wisely guide their decisions and recommendations. They will also enable parties to be fully informed when accepting the conclusions put forward to them by compliance committees, which are a common feature of most multilateral environmental conventions.

At the substantive level, legal indicators will make it possible to regularly document the strengths and weaknesses in the implementation of international conventions, providing specific insights into the obstacles, gaps, progress and regressions in their application. They will provide a scientifically sound tool to measure the degree of effectiveness of the legal measures taken by States Parties to incorporate the international convention into their national law. Finally, they will be a valuable tool for compliance committees, enabling them to better understand the legal challenges involved in implementing the conventions and

---

317 UNEP, *Environmental Rule of Law. First Global Report, op. cit.*

to formulate detailed recommendations on how to overcome these challenges. Indeed, the diagnosis provided by legal indicators will make it immediately possible to identify what needs to be done by States, specifically targeting current flaws in implementation, such as problems with procedure, human or financial resources, institutional organization or unsuitability of the very content of the rule.

V. How to create legal indicators based on criteria of effectivity in environmental law

The creation of legal indicators is a complex multidisciplinary task that requires a strong team of jurists specializing in environmental law, as well as experts in other disciplines such as mathematics, sociology, ecology and political science. Before presenting our method, we will describe three similar experiments in international and comparative law. Although they did not lead to a real measure of the effectivity of applicable law, they are nevertheless helpful to consider. Following this, we will present our preliminary choice of the area of environmental law to be assessed, and then the theoretical framework for the distribution of the legal indicators into broad categories, referred to as families. Finally, we will describe the different stages involved in formulating the legal indicators. We will also give examples of model questionnaires, designed for both international and national law and focusing either on general or special legal indicators.

A. Similar experiments

It is interesting to examine three other projects that also aim to identify legal criteria for the application of environmental law. While these examples do seek to go beyond simply analyzing the content of rules of international and national law, they do not include question weightings nor measure the results, which is ultimately the only way to achieve reliable results that reflect a reality that is difficult to grasp.

1. Criteria for Assessing the Effectiveness of International Environmental Law, by Peter H. Sand

The collective publication prefaced by Peter Sand in July 1992[318], shortly after the adoption of the Rio Declaration, is a veritable textbook of international environmental law. It explains the legal conditions for the implementation of chapter 39 of Agenda 21, relating to international legal instruments and mechanisms. It is based on the proposals of the Preparatory Committee for the Rio Conference,

318 Peter H. Sand (ed.), *The effectiveness of International Environmental Agreements: A Survey of Existing Legal Instruments* (Cambridge, Grotius, 1992).

which set out "criteria for evaluating the effectiveness of existing agreements"[319]. The effectiveness assessment covered 124 international agreements. However, effectiveness is limited to the field of international law, without addressing the application of treaties in national law, which is something we consider to be essential. It is nevertheless an interesting document that can serve today as a basis for the development of legal indicators of effectivity for international environmental law. Effectiveness is divided into 6 criteria, each subdivided into indicators and sub-indicators. In total there are 32 indicators.

At its second session in March-April 1991, Working Group III was established by the Preparatory Committee for the United Nations Conference on Environment and Development. This open-ended group was established to deal with legal, institutional and all related matters. It was specifically entrusted with the task, among others, to "prepare an annotated list of existing international agreements and international legal instruments in the environmental field, describing their purpose and scope, evaluating their effectiveness and examining possible area for further development of international environmental law, in the light of the need to integrate environment and development, especially taking into account particularly the special needs and concerns of developing countries" (Decision 2/3, A/46/48, Part I, Annex I).

At its third session, in August-September 1991, the Preparatory Committee formulated a set of proposed "criteria for evaluating the effectiveness of existing agreements and instruments", to serve as a basis for compiling the necessary background information for an agreed list of such agreements and instruments, in cooperation with the international secretariats concerned, as applicable (Decision 3/25, A/46/48, Vol. II). The criteria, which thus provided the framework for the survey, read as follows:

Criteria for assessing the effectiveness of existing agreements and instruments

(Some of the criteria below may not apply to all agreements or instruments being assessed).

A. Objectives and achievement

1. What are the basic objectives formulated in the international agreements and instruments evaluated, and how do these objectives relate to the effective integration of environment and development?

---

319 Decision 3/25, A/46/48, Vol. II.

2. In the case of regional agreements and instruments, what is their actual and potential bearing on global environmental protection and sustainable development?
3. Do these agreements or instruments take into account the special circumstances of developing countries?
4. To what extent have the basic objectives (environmental/ developmental) formulated in international agreements and instruments been met, and how is goal achievement measured?

B. Participation

5. Is membership limited or open-ended?
6. Are reservations possible, and to what extent have they been used?
7. What is the current geographical distribution of membership in existing environmental agreements and instruments, especially as regards developing countries?
8. What is the record of actual participation by developing countries in the negotiation and drafting of these agreements and instruments, and in program activities and meetings organized under these agreements and instruments?
9. Which incentives (e.g., financial, trade technology benefits) are available to encourage participation and facilitate implementation by developing countries?
10. Which measures have been taken to promote and support the effective participation of developing countries in the negotiation and operation of international agreements or instruments, including technical and financial assistance and other available mechanisms for this purpose?
11. Which factors influenced the participation, especially of developing countries, in the agreement or instrument? For example:
    a. Financial resources required and available for participation in the agreement or instrument;
    b. Technical assistance required and available for participation in the agreement or instrument;
    c. Scientific assistance required and available for participation in the agreement or instrument;
    d. Information on the (operation of the) agreement or instrument to governments, parliaments, press, non-governmental organizations, industries and the general public;
    e. Role of parliaments, press, non-governmental organizations, industries and public opinion in general;
    f. Availability of reservations.

C. Implementation

12. To what extent has the implementation of agreements or instruments been constrained or accelerated by provisions regarding their entry into force?
13. What are the commitments imposed on parties by these agreements and instruments, and how is compliance by parties with their commitments monitored and measured?
14. How do parties report on their performance in implementing agreements and instruments, and to what extent have they complied with reporting duties?
15. Which are the specific requirements (if any) of data supply and data disclosure, and to what extent have they been met by the parties?
16. Which possibilities exist to promote compliance and to follow up on non-compliance, and to what extent have they been used?
17. What mechanisms are available to deal with disputes over implementation and to what extent have they been used?
18. Which factors influenced the implementation? For example:
    a. Financial resources required and available for implementation of the agreement or instrument;
    b. Technical assistance required and available for implementation of the agreement or instrument;
    c. Scientific assistance required and available for implementation of the agreement or instrument;
    d. Information on the (operation of the) agreement or instrument to governments, parliaments, press, non-governmental organizations, industries and the general public;
    e. Role of parliaments, press, non-governmental organizations, industries and public opinion in general;
    f. International supervisory or implementing bodies;
    g. Obligations to report on compliance and/or to supply and disclose data;
    h. Non-compliance procedures and procedures for settlement of disputes (including fact-finding procedures).

D. Information

19. In which form and in which languages are the texts of existing agreements and instruments published and disseminated?
20. How is current information on the operation and implementation of international agreements and instruments made available to governments, to the industries concerned and to the general public?

21. What additional materials are available to provide guidance for the implementation of international agreements and instruments at the national level?
22. To what extent is the above information used in international and national training and education programs?

E. **Operation, review and adjustment**

23. Which are the institutional arrangements for international administration of existing agreements and instruments?
24. What are the annual (1990) costs of international administration (secretariat, meetings, programs) of agreements and instruments, and how are they financed?
25. Which are the main benefits and the main cost elements of national participation in existing agreements and instruments, and which possibilities exist to reduce participation costs for developing countries?
26. Which mechanisms are available to ensure that scientific knowledge and advice is taken into account in policy-making decisions under these agreements and instruments?
27. How do these arrangements and mechanisms ensure the effective participation of (a) national authorities, especially from developing countries; and (b) non-governmental participants, including the industries concerned and the scientific community?
28. Which mechanisms are available to ensure periodic review and adjustment of international agreements and instruments in order to meet new requirements and to what extent have they been used?

F. **Codification programming**

29. Which new drafts or draft revisions of existing agreements and instruments in the environmental field are currently under preparation or negotiation?
30. To what extent and through which mechanisms is drafting coordinated with related work regarding other agreements and instruments?
31. Which are the remaining gaps that need to be covered by legal provisions?
32. To what extent are mechanisms other than formal agreements or instruments contributing to the development of international law in the field of the environment?[320]

Some indicators require a yes/no answer. Most however are either multiple choice or require a more detailed, qualitative response, which makes measurement very difficult.

---

320 Source: Peter H. Sand (ed.), *The Effectiveness of International Environmental Agreements: A Survey of Existing Legal Instruments*, *op. cit.*, pp. 4–7.

Peter Sand returned to the theme of effectiveness in a more recent publication in which he reviewed the international literature on the subject[321]. In this study, he mentioned the existence of databases with indicators to measure and compare States' performance in implementing an environmental treaty[322].

The R. B. Mitchell database is a remarkable tool that catalogs every international environmental treaty (1280 multilateral treaties, 2100 bilateral treaties), thus making them accessible. However, it only provides static data and scientific performance indicators (150), but not legal indicators of the effective application of international law into national law.

2. Gerd Winter's indicators for the Aichi Targets

An interesting experiment was carried out by Professor G. Winter of the University of Hamburg on the Aichi Targets, as a non-binding program of action for implementing the Convention on Biological Diversity. Unlike the previous example, it addresses soft law, and therefore may serve as inspiration for the creation of indicators for the SDGs. In a report for IUCN of 12 December 2014, he examines how legal indicators could be used to assess the effectiveness of the Aichi Targets, in the context of maritime fishing[323]. He rightly points out that the legal factor is not the only factor to be taken into account, and that alongside the law "in the books" there is the law "in real society", which determines how the law is applied. To evaluate the success or failure of a policy, he proposes a list of 12 questions, which are equal to indicators, but they are not quantified nor classified. Only the 12th question relates to law enforcement measures. Actually, the aim is to evaluate the effectiveness of a policy by taking into account legal factors, and not the effectivity of the law as a process, in the sense we mean it.

321 Peter H. Sand, "The Effectiveness of Multilateral Environmental Agreements: Theory and Practice", in Melissa Lewis, Tuula Honkonen and Seita Romppanen (eds.), *International Environmental Law-making and Diplomacy Review 2016* (Joensuu, University of Eastern Finland Law School, UNEP Course Series 16, 2017), pp. 1–25.

322 H. Breitmeir, O. R. Young and M. Zurn, *Analyzing International Environmental Regimes: From Study to Database* (Cambridge, MIT Press, 2006); R. B. Mitchell, *International Environmental Agreements: Database, Performance Indicator Data*, http://iea.uoregon.edu; see also the set of environmental law instruments in the ECOLEX database, http://www/ecolex.org.

323 G. Winter, *Assessing law as a factor towards the Aichi Biodiversity Targets* (2014) https://www.iucn.org/sites/dev/files/assessing_law_as_a_factor_toward_the_aichi_biodiversity_targets_0.pdf.

3. The evaluation of law for sustainability: Case study

A case study was carried out for IUCN, using partly legal indicators, to assess how States apply certain general principles of environmental law[324]. The report focused on the application of the precautionary and participation principles in protected areas, including marine protected areas, and for endangered species. The authors identified four levels, or criteria of indicators:

- Instrumental criteria relating to the existence of the above-mentioned principles and to their sources, both legal and non-legal, such as industry codes or market standards;
- Institutional criteria relating to the establishment of institutions or implementation arrangements, with accompanying programs and budget, to apply the principles;
- Behavioral criteria: the attitude of people and organizations towards these principles and the way in which this is reflected in their behavior. For this reason, practical implementation action is also sought;
- Outcome criteria: the measurement of ecological and social outcomes that demonstrate achievement of the principles' aims.

This project is clearly ambitious, integrating not only law per se, but also social, psychological and scientific data. The authors of the report admit to having encountered many obstacles in their search for reliable data, particularly with regard to the outcome criteria.

The methodology combined the use of existing data, working group meetings with stakeholders, interviews and involvement of multidisciplinary expert groups.

B. Initial selection of the area of law to be evaluated

The first step in the creation of legal indicators is to determine the area of environmental law that will be evaluated. This is referred to as the area of measurement. However, as this is not something necessarily easy to identify, and given that the evaluation of effectivity concerns the environment, first we will attempt to identify the question, based on four different inputs:

---

324 Paul Martin, Ben Boer and Lydia Slobodian (eds.), *Framework for Assessing and Improving Law for Sustainability. A Legal Component of a Natural Resource Governance Framework*, Environmental Policy and Law Paper No. 87 (Gland, IUCN, 2016).

a) Is this a study of the effective application of the law within a particular environmental topic? In international law? In regional law? In domestic law, including national application of international law? The area of law may be chosen from among 35 specific environmental topics covered by the law:
   - Hunting;
   - Fishing;
   - Pastoralism;
   - Water;
   - Air;
   - Soils;
   - Forests;
   - Noise;
   - Landscapes;
   - Waste;
   - Chemicals;
   - Endocrine disruptors;
   - Industrial pollution;
   - Genetically modified organisms;
   - Pesticides;
   - Glyphosate;
   - Bees;
   - Plastic;
   - Coastal areas;
   - Marine environment;
   - Mountains;
   - Natural disasters and hazards;
   - Energy;
   - Wildlife;
   - Flora;
   - Protected natural areas;
   - Islands;
   - Wetlands;
   - Cultural and historical heritage;
   - Town planning;
   - Agriculture;
   - Billboards and advertising;
   - Mines and quarries;
   - Light emissions;
   - Shale gas.

b) Or is this an attempt to evaluate the effective application of the law in relation to a general principle, for example:
   - Information;
   - Participation;
   - Access to justice;
   - Prevention;
   - Precaution;
   - Polluter pays;
   - Compensation for ecological damage;
   - Non-regression;
   - Integration;
   - Education;
   - Planetary limits.
c) Or is this an evaluation of the effective application of the law in relation to a cross-cutting environmental or legal theme or a general issue, for example:
   Environmental impact assessment;
   - Sustainable development;
   - The environment in the constitution;
   - Human right to the environment;
   - Common heritage;
   - Rule of law;
   - Criminal sanctions;
   - Administrative sanctions;
   - Easements;
   - Taxation;
   - Governance;
   - Biodiversity;
   - Rights of nature;
   - Ecological solidarity;
   - Climate change;
   - Environmental justice;
   - Access to justice;
   - Emergency measures;
   - Renewable energies;
   - Nuclear power plants;
   - Agri-food industry;
   - Ecological transition;
   - Circular economy;
   - Environmental plans and programs;

- Sustainable Development Goals;
- Non-governmental organizations (NGOs).

(d) Or is this an attempt to evaluate the effective application of the law within an institution, for example:
- Ministry of the Environment;
- Advisory bodies;
- Environmental agencies;
- Local and regional authorities;
- Independent administrative authorities;
- Environmental Ombudsman;
- Airports;
- Inventories;
- Courts;
- Constitutional judge;
- UN;
- FAO, UNEP, etc.
- Secretariat of an international convention.

In view of the complexity and large number of environmental areas subject to regulation, and to assist in the choice of the area of law to be assessed, an inventory will first be carried out of all environmental topics that are covered by legal texts, for example as they may be found in environmental codes. This will be followed by a survey among experts in order to select the theme or themes considered to be a priority. The existence of an environmental code, however, is not necessarily a guarantee that all environmental issues have been included. In France for instance, forests, which are a crucial component of biodiversity and in the fight against climate change, are not contained within the environmental code but in the forest code.

In assessing the effectivity of international law, irrespective of its application in national law, the same four inputs can be used as a basis:

a) By environmental sector, as above, by researching the body of applicable rules in international law, both binding and soft law. In this scenario, the assessment of effectivity of international environmental treaties, both universal and regional, will be decisive. It will lead to the development of an appropriate methodology, as envisaged by the Barcelona Convention for the Protection of the Marine Environment and the Coastal Region of the Mediterranean and its Protocols (see above).
First of all, the internal functioning of the Convention can be assessed within its General Secretariat and its interactions with the Contracting Parties. This

is an institutional assessment, regarding governance. An international convention can also be assessed in terms of monitoring its effective implementation vis-à-vis international law. The challenge will be to create indicators capable of reporting on the actual functioning of the reporting duties, and also on the functioning and impact of the compliance committees established under the Conference of the Parties. The indicators will be mainly formal and will need to be combined with national indicators, as they alone are capable of assessing the application of the Convention at national level, which is required by international law.

b) By general principles of international law recognized by international jurisprudence, international custom and doctrine. All reports from the various international institutions, expert committees and doctrine should be used as sources, and surveys of resource persons should be carried out by means of questionnaires or interviews.
c) By cross-cutting environmental theme or general issue. The same sources will be used as above in b).
d) By the functions and activities of an international organization or the secretariat of an international convention. This search for legal indicators will amount to a kind of external audit to assess the governance and functioning of the institution. The questionnaires will be drawn up on the basis of activity reports, databases, internal interviews and surveys of the institution's partners, namely member States and accredited NGOs.

In order to prioritize the area of law to be assessed, a survey should first be carried out, either with elected officials, the government or the public, or simply a panel of experts. Each State, depending on its culture, geography, resources and development model, generally has its own priorities and varying degrees of ecological awareness. This results in the existence of current or old laws that are inappropriate, or environmental sectors that are not yet covered by the law.

Using the 35 environmental topics listed above, it may be interesting to propose a list of environmental areas, to be ranked in order of importance, as indicators of a State's ecological awareness. A similar question could be posed to a panel made up of elected representatives, civil servants, NGOs, ordinary citizens, legal experts and ecological experts.

By considering the existence of these texts and not their content, and assuming that they are legally applicable, it is possible in each country to rank, in the above list, the areas covered by a legal rule in order of importance and according to their legal usefulness for a better environment (1 to 35, 1 being the most important; for texts considered to be of equal importance, the same figure may be used). This will result in a country-specific ranking that will make it possible to determine priorities, with a view to either adopting or reinforcing texts.

C. Families of effectivity criteria in environmental law

Having specified the environmental or legal field in which to create legal indicators, the next thing to identify are the broad categories or families of indicators considered to be relevant criteria, in that they contribute to effectivity in applying the legal rule. These are all general criteria of effectivity. By convention, we have divided the different components of the implementation of environmental law into six criteria of effectivity. This division is not specific to environmental law, but could apply to any assessment of the stages of application of a particular field of law. It is on the basis of these six families of indicators that the various questionnaires can be constructed and then measured numerically.

These six families of criteria make it possible to take into account elements of the legal process, from the text or area of law being evaluated to its possible application in court. These are all necessary steps to ensure that the rule, having been written and effectively applied, can lead to beneficial effects for the environment. As explained earlier (I.B), the goal of this study is not to directly assess these beneficial effects, which would rely more on performance or output indicators, but rather to assess whether the law has been correctly applied in the first place.

Of these six families of criteria, five are purely legal and one lies outside the law:

1. Existential criteria and legal sources;
2. Applicability criteria and legality;
3. Substantive criteria;
4. Organic or institutional criteria;
5. Enforcement criteria;
6. Non-legal criteria which nevertheless affect the application of the law.

Before examining the content of each of these criteria, it is useful to examine another doctrinal set of criteria for effectivity. In his law thesis, Julien Bétaille[325] listed what he considered to be the necessary conditions for assessing the effectivity of national legal norms. He offers a detailed breakdown that reflects the complexity involved in conducting a legal analysis of the effectivity of a norm. He identifies eleven criteria:

325 J. Bétaille, *Les conditions juridiques de l'effectivité de la norme en droit public interne…*, *op. cit.*

1. Indicators related to the internal coherence among legal orders;
2. Indicators related to the coherence of the national legal order;
3. Indicators related to the sanction of the national norm;
4. Indicators related to the judicial review of the legality of the norm;
5. Indicators related to the liability of public authorities for breaching environmental law norms;
6. Indicators related to the knowledge of the norm;
7. Indicators related to the quality of the norm;
8. Indicators related to the legitimacy of the norm;
9. Indicators of implementation of the norm;
10. Indicators of reception of the norm by its addressees;
11. Indicators of reception of the norm by the judge.

Julien Bétaille collaborated with this publication to detail the precise content of each of these eleven criteria. This resulted in 127 indicators:

Legal Conditions for Effectivity in Environmental Law[326]

1. ***Indicators related to the internal coherence among legal orders***
   1.1. **Formal Indicators**
      - Ratification
      - Publication
      - Incorporation into an ad hoc law
      - Diffuse incorporation
      - No incorporation

   1.2. **Institutional Indicators**
      - Institutions
      - Monitoring of implementation
      - Affected staff and budget

   1.3. **Substantive Indicators**
      - Primacy of the international legal order
      - Content of the reception of each article in a treaty

   1.4. **Indicators of judicial review of compliance with international law**
      - Review of conventionality of the constitution
      - Review of conventionality of the law
      - Review of conventionality of the regulation
      - Justiciability of external norms
      - Criteria of direct effect assessed by the national judge

326 List based on the thesis by Julien Bétaille, *ibid.*

2. ***Indicators related to the coherence of the national legal order***
   2.1. **Existence of constitutional norms** that lay down general norms (rights, obligations or principles)
   2.2. **Number of normative levels** within the broad categories of norms (law, regulation, etc.):
      - Programming law (*loi de programmation*)
      - Number of regulatory acts governing the same issue, e.g. number of environmental planning levels
   2.3. **Relationship between environmental and other norms** (urban development law, economic law, health law, etc.).
   2.4. **Extent of the required relationship between national norms**: conformity, compatibility, inclusion

3. ***Indicators related to the sanction of the national norm***
   3.1. **Formal Indicators**
      - Existence of criminal sanctions
      - Existence of environmental damage as a specific offense
      - Existence of administrative sanctions
      - Requirement of formal administrative notice
   3.2. **Institutional Indicators**
      - Competent bodies to detect violations of the norm
      - Investigative powers of these bodies
      - Public bodies responsible for initiating sanction procedures
      - Affected staff and budget
      - Discretionary power of the sanctioning authority
      - Independence and impartiality of the sanctioning authority
   3.3. **Substantive Indicators**
      - Legal qualification of the criminal sanction: crime, misdemeanor, contravention
      - Nature of the administrative sanction: provisional suspension, closure, exclusion from public procurement contracts, etc.
      - Proportionality between the severity of the sanction and the seriousness of the offense
   3.4. **Indicators of judicial review of sanctions**
      - Private individuals and NGOs able to initiate criminal sanctions
      - Private individuals and NGOs able to initiate administrative sanctions
      - Right of defense
      - Possibility to challenge the weakness of a sanction

4. ***Indicators related to the judicial review of the legality of the national environmental norm***
   4.1. **Formal Indicators**
      - Right of appeal against a law:
        ✓ By a natural person
        ✓ By a public legal person
        ✓ By a legal person
        ✓ By an NGO
      - Right of appeal against an administrative act:
        ✓ By a natural person
        ✓ By a public legal person
        ✓ By a legal person
        ✓ By an NGO
   4.2. **Institutional Indicators**
      - Against the law:
        ✓ Existence of a constitutional judge
        ✓ Independence of the constitutional judge
        ✓ Number of assistants per judge
      - Against an administrative act:
        ✓ Independence of the judge
        ✓ Number of competent jurisdictions per inhabitant
        ✓ Number of judges per inhabitant
   4.3. **Substantive Indicators**
      - Against the law:
        ✓ Review of human rights violations
        ✓ Review of environmental law violations
        ✓ Effects of annulment
      - Against an administrative act:
        ✓ Sanctions for procedural violations
        ✓ Substantial Formalities Theory
        ✓ Effects of annulment

5. ***Indicators related to the liability of public authorities for breaching environmental law***
   5.1. **Sanction for breaching international law before the national judge**
      - Admissibility
      - Grounds: fault/liability under treaties
   5.2. **Sanction for breaching a national norm**
      - Admissibility
      - Grounds: simple negligence/gross negligence/risk/legal liability

- Damage: material/moral
- Compensation: by equivalent/in kind

5.3. Sanction for non-compliance: public authority inaction and failure

- Admissibility
- Failure:
  - ✓ In the exercise of regulatory powers
  - ✓ In the exercise of administrative police powers
  - ✓ In the exercise of sanctioning power
- Grounds: simple negligence/gross negligence
- Compensation

5.4. Sanction for environmental damage or liability for pure ecological damage

- Admissibility: natural person/legal person and NGO
- Grounds for compensation: negligence/no negligence
- Damage: material/moral
- Compensation: by equivalent/in kind

6. *Indicators related to the knowledge of the norm*

- Publication of the norm
- Access to the norm via the internet
- Existence of a codification
- Completeness of the codification
- Dissemination of comments and explanations of the norm

7. *Indicators related to the quality of the norm*

7.1. Indicators related to the formal quality of the norm

- Clarity and precision
- Accessibility and intelligibility
- Stability (legal certainty)

7.2. Indicators related to the substantive quality of the norm

- Mandatory prior legal expertise
- Level of ambition of the norm
- Binding nature of the norm
- Permissive nature of the norm

8. *Indicators related to the legitimacy of the norm*

8.1. Indicators related to the evaluation of the norm a priori

- Requirement for an impact assessment of the laws
- Requirement for an impact assessment of administrative acts

8.2. Indicators related to the democratic legitimacy of the norm

- Public information on the draft law
  - Public information on the draft administrative act
  - Public's right to comment on the draft law
  - Public's right to comment on the draft administrative act
  - Report on public comments referring to the law
  - Report on public comments referring to the administrative act
  - Consideration of public opinion in the legal text
  - Consideration of public opinion in the administrative act
  - Rationale for the decision in the light of the various comments from the public
  - Admissibility of an appeal against the adopted text for breaching the participation procedure

8.3. Indicators related to the evaluation of the norm a posteriori

- Assessment of the application of the norm arranged by parliament
- Assessment arranged by the executive
- Assessment by an independent authority

9. *Indicators of implementation of the norm*

9.1. Formal adoption of application norms

- For the constitution
- For the laws
- For the regulations

9.2. Adoption of enforcement instruments

- Policing measures
- Easements
- Contracts
- Taxation
- Exchange of rights

9.3. Confidence factors of the norm addressees

- Motivation behind norms
- Exemptions
- Regularizations
- Administrative tolerances

10. *Indicators of reception of the norm by its addressees*

10.1. Indicators of access to justice

- Constitutional and conventional protection of the right to access to justice
- Admissibility of natural persons and NGOs

- The cost of legal action
- Legal costs and fines for abuse of process

11. ***Indicators of reception of the norm by the judge***
    11.1. Number of environmental disputes
    - Constitutional
    - Criminal
    - Administrative
    - Civil and commercial

    11.2. The judge's interpretation of the rule
    - Existence of interpretation *contra legem*
    - Interpretation more or less favorable to environmental protection

    11.3. The judge's powers
    - Summary proceedings and suspension of environmental damage
    - The judge's expertise
    - The judge's power of injunction
    - The judge's power of reversal

    11.4. Enforcement of judicial decisions

This list includes indicators that concern the very existence of the norm, as well as formal, substantive, institutional and enforcement indicators. In particular there are many procedural indicators and indicators related to judicial review.

The ideal scenario would be to utilize this detailed range of eleven effectivity criteria. However this would clearly involve a considerable effort to formulate questions corresponding to each criterion and sub-criterion. Some call for yes or no responses that are easy to measure, but others are open-ended and qualitative and should be appropriately worded in order to be measurable.

But the main problem is that, firstly, eleven criteria are too many, and secondly, they focus on strictly legal elements alone. The indicators correspond well to each stage of application of the law, but so much detail is given that respondents may become confused or discouraged, which would certainly distort the reliability of the results. Moreover, by failing to take into account what we have referred to here as non-legal effectivity criteria, they remain outside the realms of social reality, which is also important to the application of the law. The law is only abstract in the way it is worded. It is actually a part of society. Assessing the effectivity of the law without taking into account social, cultural or economic factors is misleading. For even by limiting our study to the effectivity process, without addressing the impact on the environment, non-legal factors are a reality and can obstruct or distort the legal conditions for the application of the law.

This is why we have chosen to abandon this range of indicators, and focus on just six families of indicators, taken from the main categories outlined in this list of eleven. By limiting our study in this way, it will be more effective. The list could also be used to draft some of the questions to appear within the six selected categories.

The six families of effectivity criteria are explained below with the use of hypothetical model questions.

1. Existential criteria and/or legal sources from the area of law in question

To be effective, a rule must first of all exist. This is obvious. When assessing a legal text, its existence will be observed by identifying its legal sources: what is the legal basis of the text (international convention, international resolution or recommendation, constitution, law, decree, circular, private convention or agreement, ISO standard, plan, program, jurisprudence, etc.)? Is it a unilateral or contractual act? A planning instrument?

When evaluating a problem or an issue, the existence and visibility of their triggering factor, a legal act or a political or programming instrument, will be sought. Is there a specific direct or indirect law that forms the basis of this problem or issue? What are its sources of both hard and soft law? Is this norm or area of action subject to legal implementation? In what form (political declaration, voluntary commitment or international recommendation)? In summary, what is the formal and/or informal root of the issue being assessed?

2. Applicability criteria

To be effective, a norm must be legally applicable with varying degrees of force. This determines its enforceability, that is, that it can be invoked by both public authorities and private individuals. Applicability is observed primarily through procedure, according to the way in which the norm is made public (display, publication, notification). Its applicability may also be determined by the enactment of implementing legislation. The following questions will be asked: if the norm in question is based on a law, is there implementing legislation? At what level: national, local? Are there any time limits? Are there any procedural prerequisites to its application? Is a publication necessary?

To be applicable, a norm must also be legally valid. Legality must therefore be assessed. Is there a review of legality or constitutionality? When? A priori or a posteriori? When there is a conflict between an environmental norm and other norms, is there a report assessing compliance, compatibility or inclusion? How is this carried out? Is there primacy of the international legal order? Does the international norm have a direct effect on national law in order to be valid?

3. Substantive criteria

To be effective, a norm must be either specific or general in its content. Does it consist of general principles or detailed rules? How is the content of the norm articulated? What does it include? What does it forbid? What does it allow? Is this a progressive or a regressive norm?

Since the document is divided into several articles, questions can be posed under each article or only select articles of importance.

4. Organic or institutional criteria

To be effective, a norm must be implemented by appropriate institutions with sufficient staff and budgetary resources. Do these institutions exist? At what territorial level? How are they organized? What are their human, technical, scientific and financial resources?

5. Enforcement criteria

To be effective, a norm must actually be enforced. Its enforcement must be subject to three types of review: administrative, judicial and by the public.

Do administrative review bodies with inspectors exist? How many are there? Do they have general or special administrative police powers? Are there criminal sanctions? Administrative sanctions? Are they used? How? Is it possible to appeal against sanctions?

Are legal remedies available to NGOs? Are the judge's decisions enforced? What are the forms of public scrutiny? Is there a review of conventionality of the constitution, the laws and regulations?

6. Criteria reinforcing and conditioning effectivity

Lastly, to be effective, a norm must correspond to economic, social and cultural requirements and data. The aim here is to consider and assess the influence that non-legal factors can have on the application of the law.

Is there awareness of the norm or issue in question? Is it understandable and clear? Is it too technical? Is it overridden by corruption? Is it ignored by companies and NGOs? Is it economically viable? Is it compatible with customs and local culture? Does it meet the expectations of the population? Their beliefs? Does it clash with common behaviors?

In summary, the questions within this 6th criterion of effectivity depend on the political, socio-economic, cultural, international, national and local context. The aim is to identify non-legal obstacles to the effective application of the law.

D. Stages leading to the formulation of legal indicators in questionnaires

Designing and using legal indicators involves a rigorous 12-stage development process.

1. Establishment of a committee of experts

This committee should be made up of a maximum of 10 to15 members, possessing legal and scientific expertise, two thirds of whom should be jurists with knowledge of or experience in environmental law. The jurists will be law professors, magistrates, lawyers, jurists in an environmental administration and jurists from environmental NGOs. Non-jurists will be statisticians and mathematicians familiar with the field of indicators, sociologists, political scientists and historians. There will be an odd number of members in the event that decisions require a vote due to a lack of consensus. This committee may be assisted by a group of 3 to 5 researchers in environmental law working on document or data research, for example PHD candidates in environmental law.

In view of the work to be carried out by this committee and the innovative nature of the exercise, training and explanatory sessions will need to be organized during the first committee meetings in order to avoid uncertainties along the way that might call into question its purpose, target or programming.

2. Determining the area to be evaluated, or the area of measurement

The committee will determine the area(s) to be evaluated for effectivity. Given the wide range of topics covered by the environment, it is clear that it will not be possible to measure compliance with all environmental law. The complexity of application of the law depends on the area in question, on how scientific it is in nature and how complex the legal text itself is. It will therefore be necessary to choose the area of law to be assessed according to certain criteria: timeliness of the issue, and political or social demand. Priority will be given to areas where it is known that there are implementation problems.

Once the area of law has been chosen, the territorial scope of the assessment, whether international, national, regional or local, will have to be determined. This may be dependent upon the area of law chosen.

We anticipate that the committee of experts may go on to rank the various environmental areas in order of importance or urgency in order to determine those that are a priority.

3. Inventory of sources of applicable law

All sources of law that may apply to the chosen area of evaluation should be clearly identified. This will include international, regional and national law, in particular those acts that apply international law. Consideration should also be given to national and international political and declaratory acts, even if they are not legally binding.

When drafting the questions in the questionnaire, it will not be necessary to repeat each of these sources. The committee of experts will need to select the key sources. This selection from the inventory will then be used to formulate certain questions.

The committee of experts may be asked to rank the sources of applicable law from 1 to x, depending on their estimate of the importance of each in terms of its contribution to the effectivity of the area to be assessed. This will be used for guidance in drafting the questions.

4. Creating the questionnaire through question identification and formulation

After explaining the content of the six families of criteria in detail to the committee of experts, they then go on to identify the relevant questions and sub-questions for each criterion that will be put to actors involved in the application of the law. It is essential to always keep in mind the ultimate goal: to measure the effectivity of the implementation of the law. The way in which the questions are worded should allow for the responses to be measured mathematically. Specific guidance on this is provided in Part VI of this publication.

For each criterion, one single-choice, closed-ended question will be formulated to allow measurement of effectivity. Where appropriate, a criterion may require the question to be divided into sub-questions to measure an alternative or combination of ways in which the law can be effectively applied.

It is essential that the committee of experts adopt a common position by consensus for each question and sub-question, which can take time. Otherwise there will be a vote.

5. Determining the grading scale for answers to questions

Each of the questions and sub-questions requires a single response that cannot be justified. It demonstrates the respondent's knowledge of the problem, their perception or ignorance. The possible answers are ordered according to a range of values assigned to each. The highest value is given to the answer that reflects the greatest effectivity. The answers are: yes, often, sometimes, rarely, no, and don't know. The committee of experts chooses which to include and agrees on the value to be given to each answer, thus resulting in the grading scale of the response options.

6. Orderly formatting of questions and sub-questions

All questions and sub-questions in each of the six families of criteria should be reviewed at this point in order to ensure they can be easily understood and always with a view to maximum effectivity. This may lead to a change in the initial order of questions.

Also at this stage, the possible answers for each question and sub-question will be reviewed.

7. Weighting of questions and sub-questions

This involves assessing the weight or importance of the question and sub-question in relation to other questions in the same family of criteria. This assessment, which may be on a scale from 10 to 1 (from most to least important), is decided by the committee of experts with a view to future measurement of effectivity. The committee will assess the relative importance of each question as a factor of effectivity in the application of the law.

Although this is clearly a subjective assessment, it is adopted by consensus after debate or, if necessary, by voting. This provides a quantitative scale of effectivity, based on a peer review of the importance of the particular stage of implementation in question. Within the same family of criteria, questions and sub-questions may have the same weighting.

The questionnaire respondents are not informed of this weighting as this could influence their responses.

Weighting should be the result of an evaluation by legal experts of what is more or less necessary in order for the law to be effectively applied.

8. Weighting of families of criteria

In the same way, the committee of experts shall go on to set the weighting of the six families of criteria. This will involve applying a ratio, expressed as a percentage, by considering the relative importance of each. The highest ratio denotes the family of criteria considered most important for ensuring effectivity in the area in question. The lowest ratio denotes the family of criteria considered to be of least importance. The sum of these values across the six families of criteria will be equal to 100 %. Of course, the six families of criteria could be considered to be of equal importance in ensuring effectivity in law. In this case each family would be awarded the same ratio of 1/6.

Once again, the respondents will not be informed of this weighting. It is simply a reflection of the opinion of legal experts, drawn from their experience.

9. Validation of questionnaires

After a final critical review, the committee of experts will validate the questionnaire(s). They will also include an explanatory note for respondents, which will briefly introduce the relevance of legal indicators, explain the key elements of the methodology used and the rationale for the questionnaire.

10. Composition of the panel of respondents

The panel of respondents should be representative of all categories of actors involved in the effective implementation of the norm or problem that has been selected. The composition of this group will vary according to the field of environmental law chosen.

The same method will be used as the World Justice Project and the Rule of Law Index, which relies on individuals that are especially qualified to assess compliance with the law (qualified respondents questionnaire).

A typical panel will be comprised of 15 to 17 carefully selected legal actors involved with the application of the law. Composition will depend upon the area of law being assessed.

It will need to include: (i) an official from the environmental authority concerned with the enforcement of the law in question; (ii) an environmental inspector (thus at least 2 representatives of the authority responsible for enforcing the norm); (iii) 1 or 2 representatives of the norm addressees, who, depending on the field in question, will be farmers, industrialists, craftsmen or traders; (iv) 2 or 3 representatives from interest groups (chamber of industry, chamber of commerce, federation of hunters or fishers, forest owners, etc.); (v) 2 representatives from environmental NGOs (1 national, 1 local or regional); (vi) 4 representatives from legal professions (a lawyer, a criminal magistrate, a civil magistrate, an administrative magistrate); (vii) a representative of an environmental consultancy firm; (viii) a professor of environmental law (not a member of the committee of experts); (ix) 2 elected officials (1 national and 1 local or regional).

The panel of respondents would ideally be managed by professional polling institutes, replicating the composition presented above on a large scale.

Depending on the area of law in question, the survey may be carried out at an international, national, regional or local level.

11. Planning and execution of the survey

If possible, the survey will be carried out by means of direct interviews to better mobilize and guide the respondents, provided that legal investigators are trained beforehand.

Otherwise, the survey will be conducted by e-mail, which carries the risk of a low response rate, unless respondents have been given prior explanatory information on the purpose of the survey and on the process of assessing the effectivity of law by means of legal indicators.

12. Questionnaire processing and interpretation of results

The answers are processed mathematically according to the description in Part VI of this publication.

The results of the measure of the effectivity will be examined by the committee of experts, which will then formulate a diagnosis, highlight the progress observed and make recommendations to the public authorities and interested parties with a view to making the necessary improvements and reforms.

E. Examples of model questionnaires

Here we will present examples of model questionnaires containing legal indicators. However we did not go on to measure their respective weighting as this would have required further work and the help of mathematicians. Part VI provides explanatory and methodological avenues on the method of measurement and its graphical representation.

Research conducted in 2017 for the IFDD included an experiment to develop questionnaires evaluating the effectivity of environmental law in Africa. A total of 17 questionnaires containing indicators were tested in 4 French-speaking African countries: Benin, Cameroon, Madagascar and Tunisia. 8 referred to international law and 9 to national law. In the absence of a committee, individual experts participated in the experiment, all specialists in environmental law in their own countries[327]. It received validation at a seminar in Yaoundé (Cameroon) from 5 to 9 February 2018.

327 Benin: Pulchérie Donoumassou Simeon; Cameroon: Parfait Oumba; Madagascar: Saholy Rabelisoarajo; Tunisia: Leila Chikhaoui. All are representatives of their country at the International Centre for Comparative Environmental Law.

Legal indicators can be used to assess and measure either general environmental law issues or specific issues.

1. General legal indicators

General legal indicators address international treaty law, international law connected to the 2030 SDGs, and domestic law.

a) Within international environmental treaty law

The aim here is to assess the legal factors that contribute to the effective implementation of the legal requirements imposed by international conventions. For completeness, other factors relating to the effectivity of general principles of international law should be developed in parallel, such as international custom, soft law instruments, international jurisprudence and findings from compliance committees under international conventions. We have observed that work on effectiveness in environmental law has tended to focus more on international law than national law. This is why our proposals also include mention of the indicators put forward by P. Sand (above).

The indicators are formulated in a simplified manner, in questionnaires organized according to six families of criteria. These are designed to be answered by jurists familiar with the vocabulary used in international law (lawyers, judges, administrators, law professors, NGO lawyers). This first list of indicators aims to assess the formal mechanisms and procedures that allow for the treaty in question to be considered as effectively implemented and not just existing on paper. Yes or no responses allow for simple and fast processing. The substance of the law is not addressed here.

For each question and sub-question, the possible responses will be: yes, no, sometimes, and don't know.

i) At the institutional level

– Secretariat:	Existence
– Conference of the Parties:	Existence
	Power to adopt recommendations
	Power to impose sanctions
– Focal point:	Existence

ii) *Monitoring the implementation of the treaty*

– Periodic reports:	Mandatory
	Made public by the secretariat
	Transmitted to the Parties
	Made public by the State concerned
	Evaluated by the secretariat
	Evaluated by a committee of experts
– Compliance committee:	Existence
	State representative members
	Independent members
	Referral to the committee by States
	Referral to the committee by the secretariat
	Referral to the committee by NGOs
	Referral to the committee by private persons
	Follow-up of the committee's decisions by the committee
	Follow-up of the committee's decisions by the COP
	Planned technical assistance for implementation.

iii) *Settlement of disputes*

- Arbitration
- Recourse to the International Court of Justice.

The criteria proposed by Peter Sand in 1992[328] are much more ambitious as they deal with both the form and the substance of the treaties in question.

b) *With reference to the Sustainable Development Goals (2030 SDGs)*

Given the political, strategic and financial importance of the SDGs adopted by the United Nations in September 2015[329], and the fact that their implementation is monitored internationally, regionally and nationally, there is no doubt that the

328 P. Sand, *The Effectiveness of International Environmental Agreements…*, *op. cit.*

329 Resolution 70/1 of the General Assembly of the United Nations, 25 September 2015 (A/RES/70/1).

tools for their implementation are to be found in the law, in particular environmental law. However, the targets of the 17 SDGs only give minimum reference to the law. Only human rights and the rule of law are mentioned as fundamental requirements, but environmental law is given very little attention. The United Nations does monitor the SDGs with indicators specially developed for this purpose. The "global indicators" for the SDGs is a list which has been regularly updated and revised since the global indicator framework was approved by the United Nations Economic and Social Council on 7 June 2017.

The question of whether the indicators should be global or national was a matter of great debate in relation to the MDGs, and subsequently for the SDGs, with statisticians rightly arguing that globally agreed indicators must be used by all States in order to obtain comparable data. Some countries that lack the (often considerable) human and financial resources to comply with the global indicator framework, adopted by the UN General Assembly in 2017, are requesting to be able to use "alternative" indicators that they themselves determine and that cost much less. These countries appear to have won their case at the 51st session of the Statistical Commission in March 2020, which seems to have opened the door to these "alternative" national indicators. This was criticized by Mr Gennari, Chief Statistician of FAO, as it may represent a regression in terms of the level of requirement for implementation of the SDGs[330]. The FAO had previously been criticized for agreeing, under pressure from some States, to relax certain criteria for assessing the area and density of the world's forests on the basis of "alternative" national or regional indicators.

These "alternative" national indicators can include any type of indicator, and could therefore be legal indicators at the national level. When the Statistical Commission referred to "complementary" indicators in 2020, it took terminology used by the UN General Assembly in resolutions related to the SDGs. The Statistical Commission "reiterated that the application of the global indicator framework is a voluntary and country-led process and that alternative or complementary indicators for national and subnational levels of monitoring will be developed at the national level on the basis of national priorities, realities, capacities and circumstances"[331]. These complementary indicators are new indicators, negotiated and agreed upon by the Statistical Commission, which could also be

330 P. Gennari and D. Kalamvrezos Navarro, *A bold call for action needed on measuring SDG indicators* (IISD, 28 April 2020).

331 Decision 51/101, para. e, adopted by the Statistical Commission at its 51st session, 3–6 March 2020, E/CN.3/2020/37.

of a legal nature. They could function as replacements, revisions, additions or withdrawals.

Our research on legal indicators for the environment should complement this list of indicators by strengthening the role of environmental law as an operational tool for sustainable development.

Among the 17 SDGs, some are more linked to the environment and require the use of legal instruments for implementation. These are SDGs 2, 3, 6, 7, 11, 12, 13, 14, 15 and 16.

In the pilot test carried out in 2017 and published by IFDD in 2018, four national experts were asked to propose specific legal indicators for those targets that obviously require legal instruments for implementation. Their proposals for Benin, Cameroon, Madagascar and Tunisia can be found in annexes 5 to 8 of the above mentioned 2018 publication[332].

On the occasion of a seminar held in 2020 as part of the Normandy Chair for Peace in Caen, a questionnaire was developed by an international group of researchers, brought together by videoconference due to the pandemic. It focused on SDG 14 on Oceans, "Conserve and sustainably use the oceans, seas and marine resources for sustainable development".

Indeed, it is interesting to note that the law has considerable presence within SDG 14. All of its targets imply the use of legal enforcement measures:

- 14.1: "prevent and reduce";
- 14.2: "take action";
- 14.4: "regulate";
- 14.5: "national and international law";
- 14.6: "prohibit … eliminate";
- 14.b: "guarantee";
- 14.c: "international law … legal framework".

Some of the proposed indicators refer to the use of the law to some extent:

- 14.2.1: "exclusive economic zones";
- 14.5.1: "marine protected areas";
- 14.6.1: "international instruments";
- 14.a.1: "total budget";

332 *Les indicateurs juridiques, outils d'évaluation de l'effectivité du droit de l'environnement, op. cit.*, pp. 115–159.

- 14.b.1: "legal framework … right of access";
- 14.c.1: "ratification … legal framework … institutional … international law … law of the sea".

c) *Within national environmental law*

In view of the large number of international environmental treaties, it is important to first address the question of effectivity of international law within national law. This concerns ratification, incorporation, implementation, NGO and public involvement, and international custom. We have included non-legal indicators that reflect obstacles to treaty implementation in States.

We will then propose two potentially complementary approaches, the conditions of which will be validated by peers, taking into account the modalities of indicator measurement that will be established later.

i) *Assessment of the effectivity of international law within national law*

The possible responses will be: yes, no, sometimes, under certain conditions, don't know.

1. *Ratification:*
   - Does ratification always require legislation?
   - Is the ratification procedure usually long or short?
   - Must ratification be preceded by a review of the constitutionality of the treaty?
   - Must the treaty be published in the official gazette prior to application?
2. *Incorporation into national law:*
   - Does the constitution provide for the primacy of international law over national law?
   - Is this primacy recognized by judges?
   - Does this primacy mean that treaties are self executing, thus always regarded as having direct effect?
   - Does this primacy depend on the precise content of the treaty articles in question?
   - Does ratification imply, legally or de facto, the prior adoption of domestic legislation to incorporate the requirements of the treaty?
   - Does the application of a treaty always require an act of incorporation into national law?
   - Are the act or texts of incorporation preceded by references mentioning the incorporated treaty?

3. *National treaty implementation:*
   - Is the proper implementation of treaties under national law an indicator of democracy building?
   - Is implementation entrusted to:
     ✓ the Ministry of Foreign Affairs?
     ✓ the Ministry of the Environment?
     ✓ both?
   - Are the technical norms imposed by the treaty adopted?
   - Is there a special monitoring service for each treaty?
   - Is there a mechanism for evaluating implementation of the treaty?
   - Is there a structure for coordinating implementation of the treaties?
   - Are there any problems concerning interpretation of the treaty?
   - Have the national focal points required by each treaty been designated?
   - Is there coordination between the focal points?
   - Are there any mechanisms to follow up on the resolutions and decisions from the conferences of the parties?
   - Is there any control of compliance of the laws with the treaties?
   - Is there any control of compliance of the administrative acts with the treaties?
   - Are national judges trained in treaty application?
   - Are national lawyers trained in treaty application?
   - Can courts be accessed by all to challenge decisions that do not respect a treaty?
4. *NGO and public involvement:*
   - Are NGOs and the public provided with information on the existence and implementation of the treaties?
   - Do NGOs have difficulties in being admitted by the conferences of the parties?
   - Are NGOs invited to be part of the official delegation of the conferences of parties?
5. *Applicability of custom in international law:*
   - Is international custom recognized in domestic law?
6. *Other conditions of effectivity:*
   - What obstacles prevent national application of environmental treaties? (rank from 1 to 9, 1 being a minimal obstacle and 9 being a major obstacle):
     ✓ Clarity and understanding of the treaty texts or their dissemination;
     ✓ Information on the existence of the treaty;
     ✓ Access to the treaty text;

- ✓ Technical capacity;
- ✓ Lack of knowledge of English;
- ✓ Conflicting local custom or belief;
- ✓ Pressure from interest groups to prevent the application of the treaty;
- ✓ Awareness of universal concepts relating to the global environment;
- ✓ Lack of interest from NGOs.

ii) General assessment of the effectivity of national environmental law

Presented below is a proposed list of indicators requiring a simple yes or no answer, which will later be measured and placed in a ranking. Non-legal indicators have been included to assess the causes of a lack of effectivity in the law. This set of indicators will provide an overview of effectivity in environmental law in a particular country, with a view to identifying priorities for action through legal instruments. Three inputs were selected: institutions, legal instruments and justice.

1. *Institutions:*
   - Is there a ministry of the environment?
   - Does it oversee forests?
   - Does it oversee water?
   - Does it oversee desertification?
   - Does it oversee the urban environment?
   - Are there jurists within the ministry of the environment? How many?
   - Is there a national environmental commission or council?
   - Does this body oversee sustainable development?
   - Is there a coordination structure between ministries on environmental matters?
   - Are there specialized agencies for different areas of the environment?
   - Is there legal provision for the supervision of these agencies?
   - Are there any local representatives of the ministry of the environment?
   - Are there any jurists among these local representations?
2. *Legal instruments:*
   - Are plans relating to environmental issues outlined in legal texts?
     - ✓ If so, are these plans legally binding?
   - Is there an environmental code?
   - If not, is there a general environmental law instead?

- Does this code or general law also deal with forests?
- Does this code or general law also deal with mines?
- Is land tenure an obstacle to environmental measures?
- Does custom play a role in environmental matters?
  - ✓ In a sense of environmental protection?

3. *Justice:*
   - Do special environmental courts exist?
   - Is access to justice for all enshrined in the constitution?
   - Is it acknowledged for NGOs?
   - Are there any judicial decisions on the environment?
   - Are there many?
   - Why not? (rank the choices from 1 to 8, with 1 being the least important and 8 being the most important):
     - ✓ Ignorance of the legal texts;
     - ✓ Ignorance of rights;
     - ✓ Requirement of prior administrative appeal;
     - ✓ Transaction;
     - ✓ Cost of justice;
     - ✓ Fear of appearing in court;
     - ✓ Lack of confidence in the justice system;
     - ✓ Reliance on customary justice;
   - Does free legal aid exist?
   - Are judicial decisions on the environment enforced?
4. *Non-legal factors limiting the effective application of the norm* (rank in order of importance, from most to least):
   - Corruption;
   - Political clientelism;
   - Poverty;
   - Political instability;
   - Administrative instability;
   - Weight of beliefs;
   - Legislative wording and poor drafting;
   - Technicality of the rule;
   - Absence of NGOs.

2. Special Legal Indicators

The development of legal indicators for all of environmental law would only be possible through an in-depth collective effort. Therefore we have randomly selected a limited number of areas of effective application of environmental law.

Six international conventions (2 universal and 4 regional) have been assessed in terms of the effectivity of their application in national law

In national law, mainly general principles have been selected, such as having less technical content than special laws, as well as two specific areas: protected areas and environmental impact assessments.

a) National application of certain international environmental conventions

The model of indicators is the same for all conventions in that the legal questions of effectivity are the same, with just a few exceptions. We propose the following elements as legal indicators: the legal existence of the convention in national law; the applicability of the convention; the organic content of application; the evaluation of substantive application; the institutional and legal conditions of application; and finally non-legal indicators relating to obstacles encountered.

This model of indicators first addresses the national application of two universal conventions: the Convention on Wetlands of International Importance especially as Waterfowl Habitat (Ramsar Convention) and the Convention concerning the Protection of World Cultural and Natural Heritage (UNESCO Convention).

This is followed by an assessment of the effectivity in national law of four regional conventions: the African Convention on the Conservation of Nature and Natural Resources (Algiers and Maputo Conventions), the Convention for the Protection of the Marine Environment and the Coastal Region of the Mediterranean (Barcelona Convention), the Convention for Cooperation in the Protection, Management and Development of the Marine and Coastal Environment of the Atlantic Coast of the West, Central and Southern Africa Region (Abidjan Convention) and the Convention for the Protection, Management and Development of the Marine and Coastal Environment of the Eastern African Region (Nairobi Convention). The Regional Convention for the Conservation of the Red Sea and Gulf of Aden Environment (Jeddah Convention) could be added if there were interest from countries in the Horn of Africa, such as Djibouti and Comoros.

In addition to formal and institutional aspects, specific questions have been included for each article of each convention dealing with the substance of the law (substantive content).

i) The legal existence of the convention
   - Has it been:
     ✓ signed by the State?
     ✓ ratified by the State?
     ✓ published by the State?
   - Is publication a condition of application?
   - Other suggested indicators?

ii) Is this law applicable?
   - Is the convention incorporated into national law:
     ✓ In a single specific text?
     ✓ In several texts?
     ✓ In no text?
   - Does this convention have a direct effect in national law even if it has not been incorporated?
   - Other suggested indicators?

iii) Organic content
   - Planned and established institutions;
   - Planned procedures;
   - Other suggested indicators?

iv) Substantive content:
   - For each substantive article:
     ✓ has a legal measure been taken?
     ✓ been partially taken?
     ✓ did it already exist?
     ✓ not been taken?
     ✓ Other suggested indicators?

v) Is this law applied?
   - Institutions responsible for monitoring: general; specific; non-existent?
   - Number of officials affected?
   - Sanctions: envisaged; not envisaged?
   - Appeal available in case of non-application: envisaged; not envisaged?
   - Number of judicial decisions concerning the application of the convention?
   - Budget allocated?
   - Other suggested indicators?

vi) Other factors limiting application (number in order from 1 to 5, 1 least, 5 most):
  - Corruption;
  - Poverty;
  - Political instability;
  - Local custom;
  - Legislative wording, poor drafting;
  - Other suggested indicators?

It should be made clear that in terms of the substantive content in point iv), each question addresses only the formal application of the treaty article under consideration. To evaluate the scientific adequacy of the content of the treaty article with the national implementation measure would require sharing of expertise between scientists and jurists. This is normally carried out by the secretariat of the conventions and their compliance committees, where they exist.

We have selected the articles under each convention for which implementation indicators are envisaged:

- Ramsar Convention: Articles 1 to 5;
- UNESCO Convention: Articles 1 to 6;
- Algiers Convention: Articles 2 to 15; Maputo Convention: Articles 2 to 21;
- Barcelona Convention: Articles 1 to 15;
- Abidjan Convention: Articles 1 to 11 and 13;
- Nairobi Convention: Articles 1 to 10 and 13.

b) Evaluation of the effectivity of national law

We have retained five areas of assessment relating to general principles of law and case law: the environment in the constitution; the right to information; the right to public participation; access to justice in environmental matters; and the principle of non-regression.

In addition, there are two sectoral areas of assessment: natural protected areas and impact assessments of projects and activities that are detrimental to the environment.

In each case, the indicators seek to answer the following six questions, which correspond to the six families of criteria detailed above:

- Does the law in question exist; what are its sources?
- Is this law applicable?
- What is its substantive content?
- What is its organic content and institutional framework?

- Is this law subject to effective monitoring of its application by the administration, the judge or the general public?
- What non-legal factors may explain its non-application or poor application?

i) The environment in the constitution

1. *Existence and sources of law:*
   - Does the word "environment" appear in the constitution:
     ✓ in the preamble?
     ✓ in the body of the constitution?
2. *Is this law applicable?*
   - Is it included in the legally applicable provisions?
   - Does application depend upon a future law?
   - Does application depend upon a future organic law?
   - Have these laws been enacted?
3. *Organic content:*
   - Institutions: does the constitution create an institution, a council or committee for the environment?
   - Procedures: does the application of the constitution require the establishment of specific procedures?
   - Does the constitution give the parliament competence in:
     ✓ the environment?
     ✓ the fundamental principles alone?
   - Does the constitution allow for a referendum on the environment?
     ✓ Directly?
     ✓ By interpretation?
   - Does the constitution give citizens the right to petition or objection?
   - Is this law limited to environmental matters?
4. *Substantive content:*
   - Does the constitution refer to the following principles:
     ✓ Prevention?
     ✓ Precaution?
     ✓ Polluter pays?
     ✓ Remedying environmental damage?
     ✓ Non-regression (question asked again in the questionnaire on principles contained in laws)?
     ✓ Information?
     ✓ Participation?
     ✓ Access to justice?
     ✓ Duty to protect the environment?

- Does the substance of the law address:
  - ✓ The right to the environment?
  - ✓ The rights of future generations?
  - ✓ Sustainable development?
  - ✓ Education and training?
  - ✓ Research?
  - ✓ Biodiversity?
  - ✓ Climate change?
  - ✓ Disasters?
  - ✓ Waste on national territory?
  - ✓ A ban on the import of radioactive waste?
  - ✓ A ban on the import of hazardous waste?

5. *Is the constitution applied in environmental matters:*
   - by the constitutional judge?
   - by the civil judge?
   - by the criminal judge?
   - by the administrative judge?
   - by customary authorities?
6. *Non-legal factors limiting effective application:*

   Rank in order of importance from 1 to 8, 1 being the factor with the least impact:

   - Corruption;
   - Poverty;
   - Political instability;
   - Legislative wording and poor drafting;
   - Others.

ii) The right to information

1. *Does the right to environmental information appear:*
   - in a law?
   - in a decree?
2. *Is this right legally applicable:*
   - by a reference to the right to information in general?
   - by a special implementing text?
   - through custom?
3. *Organic context of the exercise of this right and procedures:*
   - Is there a specialized national institution for monitoring?

- Is there an information officer in each department of environmental administration?
- Is there a time limit within which the administration must respond?
- Does the information have to be requested first from a specialized body?

4. *Substantive content:*
   - Is confidential information listed?
   - Does a refusal to provide information have to be justified?
   - Is information on hazardous activities disclosed?
   - Is the pollution level of companies disclosed?
   - Are the reports of the administration's inspectors disclosed?
   - Are the preparatory documents disclosed?
   - Are unfinished documents disclosed?
   - Are contingency plans at hazardous sites disclosed?
5. *Is this law effectively applied?*
   - Are there any statistics on the number of requests and responses?
   - Are these statistics recurring?
   - Is it possible to appeal to a court of law against refusal?
   - Is appeal available to NGOs?

     Is deferment or urgency procedure admissible?
   - Is there any case law referring to compliance with this law?
     ✓ Is there a significant amount?
   - Is it necessary to first resort to an ad hoc body?
   - Is the illegal refusal to disclose information subject to a sanction?
   - Is the illegal refusal to disclose information sanctioned?
6. *Non-legal factors limiting application of the right to information:*

   Rank in order of importance from 1 to 5, 1 being the factor with the least impact:

   - Corruption;
   - Ignorance on the part of citizens;
   - Unwillingness on the part of the administration;
   - Legislative wording and vagueness of texts;
   - Absence of NGOs;
   - Others to be specified.

iii) The right to public participation

1. *Does the right to public participation in environmental matters appear:*
   - within the constitution?
   - in a law?

- in a decree?
- only in case law?
- only in administrative practice?

2. *Is this right legally applicable:*
   - through reference to the right to participation in general?
   - through a special environmental text?
3. *Organic context of the exercise of this right, procedures and substantive content:*
   - Is there an environmental service responsible for participation?
   - Is the participation procedure open to legal persons?
   - Does participation allow NGOs to participate in advisory bodies?
   - Are experts and qualified individuals invited to sit on advisory bodies?
   - Are environmental jurists invited to participate in advisory bodies?
     ✓ Often or rarely?
   - Can participation in decision-making take place via the internet?
   - Can participation in decision-making take place only via the internet?
   - Is there a special procedure (such as a public inquiry) prior to individual approvals?
     ✓ If yes, what is the duration of participation: <10 days or >10 days?
   - Is there a procedure for participation in the development of environmental regulations?
     ✓ If yes, does participation concern all environmental texts?
     ✓ What is the duration of participation in this case?
   - Is there a procedure for participation in the development of plans and programs?
   - Is there a procedure for participation in the development of laws?
   - Is there a procedure for participation prior to the ratification of treaties?
   - Is there an independent guarantor during and after the participation process?
   - Does the public authority have to account for what takes place during the participation process?
   - Does the public authority have to justify its decisions in taking into account participation?
   - Is a referendum on environment matters provided for in the texts:
     ✓ at the national level?
     ✓ at the local level?
   - Has it ever been used?
   - Was the result in favor of the environment?

4. *Is this right effectively applied?*
   - Is it possible to appeal against an act adopted as a result of public participation on the grounds of a breach of the participation procedure?
   - Is the appeal admissible from any person?
   - Is the appeal only admissible when the applicant has participated?
   - Is there any case law on participation?
     ✓ Is there a significant amount?
   - Is it necessary to first appeal to the administration?
5. *Non-legal factors limiting application of the right to participation:*

   Rank in order of importance from 1 to 8, 1 being the factor with the least impact:
   - Corruption;
   - Illiteracy;
   - Ignorance on the part of the public of the right to participation;
   - Public fear of participation;
   - Legislative wording and vagueness of texts related to participation;
   - NGOs that lack scientific expertise given the technical nature of the texts;
   - NGOs that lack jurists;
   - Reluctant administration;
   - Others?

iv) The principle of access to justice in environmental matters

1. *Is the principle of access to justice:*
   - enshrined in general terms:
     ✓ within the constitution?
     ✓ in a law?
     ✓ by case law?
   - specifically enshrined for the environment:
     ✓ within the constitution?
     ✓ in an environmental law?
     ✓ by case law?
2. *Is this law legally applicable?*
   - Is an implementing text required?
   - Does this text exist?
3. *Organic and institutional content:*
   - Is there an administrative judge for appeals against the administration and the State?

- Is a preliminary appeal to an administrative authority necessary before appearing before the judge?
- Is there a special prosecutor's office for environmental criminal proceedings?

4. *Substantive content:*
   - Is the public informed about their right to appeal?
   - Are environmental NGOs admissible:
     ✓ before the administrative judge?
     ✓ before the civil judge?
     ✓ before the criminal judge?
   - Do claimants have to justify sufficient standing to act?
   - Do claimants have to assert an infringement of a right?
   - Is it possible to appeal against an omission or abstention of the administrative authority?
   - Can the judge issue injunctions?
   - Is justice swift?
   - Are the costs of justice high?
   - Are court decisions published:
     ✓ in hard copy?
     ✓ electronically?
5. *Is this right effectively applied?*
   - Are there statistics for judicial decisions on the environment:
     ✓ before the administrative judge?
     ✓ before the civil judge?
     ✓ before the criminal judge?
6. *Non-legal factors limiting application of the right of access to justice:*

   Rank in order of importance from 1 to 8, 1 being the factor with the least impact:

   - Corruption of judges;
   - Number of judges;
   - Absence of NGOs;
   - Complexity of the procedure;
   - Cost of lawyers;
   - Ignorance on the part of the claimants;
   - Fear of going to court;
   - Others?

v) The principle of non-regression of the environment

1. *Is the principle of non-regression enshrined:*
   - in the constitution?
   - in a law?
   - only in case law?
2. *Is this principle legally applicable?*
   - Is implementing legislation required?
   - Is the principle considered only a political and not a legal objective?
   - Is opposition to the principle based on the idea of parliamentary sovereignty?
   - Is opposition to the principle based on the power to repeal any rule?
3. *Organic context:*
   - Are there any reports or studies on this issue?
   - Have there been any political statements in support of this principle?
4. *Substantive content:*
   - Does it concern the entire environment?
   - Does it concern only nature?
   - Does it concern only pollution control?
   - Does it concern urban space?
5. *Is this principle effectively applied?*
   - Are there any specific examples?
   - Is there any case law?
   - Does this case law support the principle?
   - Does this case law oppose the principle?
6. *Non-legal factors limiting application of the principle of non-regression:*

   Rank in order of importance from 1 to 7, 1 being the factor with the least impact:

   - Ignorance of the principle;
   - Official opposition to the principle;
   - Doctrinal opposition to the principle;
   - Opposition to the principle in economic circles;
   - Misunderstanding of the scope of the principle;
   - Fear of blocking progress;
   - Desire to remain flexible and adapt freely to new situations.

vi) Protected natural areas

1. *Sources of law on protected natural areas:*
   - The constitution?
   - A specific law?
   - An environmental law?
2. *Is this law legally applicable?*
   - Is implementing legislation necessary?
     - ✓ if so, has it been created?
   - Is a specific text required for each protected area?
   - Are there any obstacles related to land tenure?
   - Are there any obstacles related to the application of local custom?
3. *Organic content:*
   - Is there any control over protected areas at national level:
     - ✓ by the ministry of the environment?
     - ✓ by a specialized national body?
   - Are there several categories of protected areas:
     - ✓ How many?
     - ✓ Are they modeled after the IUCN categories?
   - Are they created by central government?
   - Are they created by a local authority representing the State?
   - Are they created by an elected local authority?
   - Does their creation provide for public participation (by survey or other means)?
   - Does the elimination of protected areas respect the principle of congruent forms?
   - Does the elimination of a protected area require a higher act in hierarchy to that required for its creation?
   - Is the elimination of protected areas prohibited?
   - Does the procedure for elimination of a protected area provide for public participation?
   - Are protected areas managed locally?
   - Is there a director?
   - Is there a board of directors?
   - Is there a scientific council?
4. *Substantive content:*
   - Are the regulations applicable in the protected area uniform for each of the categories?
   - Do applicable regulations vary from one protected area to another?

- Are bans on the exercise of certain rights possible?
- Are certain activities subject to authorization?
- Can obligations be imposed?
- Is hunting allowed in the protected area?
- Is fishing allowed in the protected area?
- Is deforestation permitted?
- Is scientific research possible?
- Is mining and quarrying permitted in the protected area?
- Can activities outside the protected area but adjacent to it be controlled?
- Is a management plan mandatory?
- Does this plan need to be reviewed periodically?
- Is it binding on local activities and plans?

5. *Application controls:*
   - Are there local control officers?
   - Do they have the power to issue fines?
   - Are any criminal sanctions provided for in the texts?
   - Are they applied?
   - Are there any administrative sanctions?
   - Are they applied?
   - Is there litigation over protected areas?
6. *Non-legal factors preventing effectivity in law for protected areas:*

   Rank in order of importance from 1 to 7, 1 being the factor with the least impact:

   - Corruption;
   - Lack of interest from citizens;
   - Legislative wording and vagueness of texts;
   - Lack of interest from NGOs;
   - Inadequate management and monitoring personnel;
   - Poaching;
   - Illegal hunting and trafficking of species.

vii) Impact assessment of projects and activities that cause harm to the environment

1. *Sources of law for impact assessments:*
   - The constitution?
   - A general environmental law?
   - A specific law on impact assessments?
   - Other?

2. *Is this law applicable?*
   - Does implementing legislation exist?
   - Are there any explanatory leaflets?
   - Is the project required to have a significant effect on the environment?
   - Is there a financial threshold for work that is always exempt from impact assessment?
3. *Organic content of the law:*
   - Is there a special department in the ministry?
   - Is there a central technical advisory body?
   - Is there an independent body for evaluating impact assessments?
   - Can the petitioner request a preliminary scoping to aid in planning?
   - Are the projects subject to impact assessment included in an agreed list of projects?
   - Are proposed works or activities not on this list exempt from impact assessment?
   - Or are impact assessments required for such works or activities on a case by case basis?
   - Is the impact assessment carried out under the responsibility of the petitioner?
   - Can the petitioner entrust the assessment to a consultancy firm?
   - Must consultancy firms be officially approved?
   - Must the consultancy firm include a jurist?
   - Is there usually a jurist on the team?
   - Is the public informed in advance of specific projects that are subject to an impact assessment?
   - Is there a national database or a website listing all current projects?
   - Is there a national database or a website allowing access to impact assessments carried out in the past?
   - Can the public intervene while the impact assessment is being carried out?
   - Does the public have to give an opinion or be consulted at the end of the impact assessment?
4. *Substantive content of law on impact assessments:*
   - Is the content accurately described by the texts?
   - Do the health effects of the project need to be presented?
   - Is a study required of the effects on the landscape?
   - Should there be a non-technical summary?
   - Should there be a presentation of the methods used and the difficulties encountered?
   - Must there be a mention of the applicable environmental legal texts?

- Is there a requirement to mention affected protected areas?
- Is there a requirement to assess the effects of the project on climate change?
- Is there a requirement to assess the effects of the project on biodiversity?
- Is there a requirement to assess cross-border environmental effects?
- Is there a requirement to present alternatives?
- Should the zero alternative be studied (i.e. abandonment of the project)?
- Can the petitioner propose compensation measures?
- Must the petitioner demonstrate that they cannot take measures to eliminate or reduce the environmental effects?

5. *Control of effective application:*
   - Is a specialist scientific review of impact assessments carried out by an independent body?
   - Is there an administrative review?
   - Is an official evaluation notice of the impact assessment required prior to the decision to authorize the project?
     ✓ if so, is the notice made public?
   - Is it possible to appeal against the impact assessment before the administration?
   - Is it possible to appeal directly before the judge?
   - Is a prior administrative appeal required?
   - Can appeals only be made against the authorization given to the project: yes or no?
   - Does the judge examine the content of the impact assessment?
   - Does the judge only consider the form of the impact assessment?
   - If an impact assessment was required but not carried out, does this result in automatic suspension of the project?
   - Is the lack of an impact assessment subject to a criminal penalty?
   - Is the author accountable for errors in the impact assessment?
   - Is there a criminal penalty for knowingly providing inaccurate information in the impact assessment?
   - Is there a significant number of impact assessment disputes in courts?
   - Does the judge carry out a thorough evaluation?
   - Are there any projects that the petitioner has given up on because of an impact assessment deemed insufficient by the administration?
6. *What are the non-legal factors that limit or prevent the effectivity of law on impact assessments?*

   Rank in order of importance from 1 to 8, 1 being the factor with the least impact:

   - Corruption;
   - Ignorance or disinterest on the part of citizens;

- Inadequate scientific review by the public authorities;
- Absence of an independent expert body;
- Legislative wording and vagueness of texts;
- Lack of competent consultancy firms;
- Unwillingness on the part of the petitioners;
- Lack of pressure from donors and lenders for serious studies;
- Others?

This list of indicators can be complemented by those proposed by C. Wood[333] :

1. Is the EIA system based on clear and specific legal provision?
2. Must the relevant environmental impacts of all significant actions be assessed?
3. Must evidence of the consideration, by the proponent, of the environmental impacts of reasonable alternative actions be demonstrated in the EIA process?
4. Must screening of actions for environmental significance take place?
5. Must scoping of the environmental impacts of actions take place and specific guidelines be produced?
6. Must EIA reports meet prescribed content requirements and do checks to prevent the release of inadequate EIA reports exist?
7. Must EIA reports be publicly reviewed and the proponent respond to the points raised?
8. Must the findings of the EIA report and the review be a central determinant of the decision on the action?
9. Must monitoring of action impacts be considered at the various stages of the EIA process?
10. Must the mitigation of action impacts be considered at the various stages of the EIA process?
11. Must consultation and participation take place prior to, and following EIA report publication?
12. Must the EIA system be monitored and, if necessary, be amended to incorporate feedback from experience?

333 C. Wood, *Environmental Impact Assessment: A Comparative Review* (London, Prentice Hall, 1995), p. 12, quoted by C. McGrath, *Does Environmental Law Work?, op. cit.*, p. 142.

13. Are the financial costs and time requirements of the EIA system acceptable to those involved and are they believed to be outweighed by discernible environmental benefits?
14. Does the EIA system apply to significant programs, plans and policies, as well as to projects?

Concluding remarks on examples of model questionnaires:
In the scientific evaluation of the contribution of environmental law to the progress or decline of biodiversity and pollution, legal indicators will add real value to the numerous national and international state of the environment reports.

These reports will then be able to better serve policy-makers in guiding decision-making, whilst also giving visibility to the law. This can only serve to enhance its effectivity. The first time a government made regular reporting on the state of the environment obligatory, it demanded that it address issues relating to the state of the environment and enable proposals for legislation to remedy any identified weaknesses[334].

In order to report on the effectivity of environmental law, it is essential that the indicators chosen are simple and clear, yet retaining key elements of legal terminology. Previously we examined the relevance of human rights indicators, focusing on repression and sanctions and divided into three categories (structural indicators, process indicators and outcome indicators). This breakdown should be analyzed and debated in order to assess whether it corresponds to the needs and content of environmental law, except for the result indicators, which are of scientific and economic nature.

The six families of criteria presented above will enable a scientifically valid assessment of effectivity, based on a formal assessment of both the legal text and the practical application or material assessment of the implementation process. The outcome evaluation, that is, review of the causal link between the legal text and the level of pollution observed, is deliberately left aside. This would require a different, complementary and multidisciplinary study, to be undertaken at a later stage.

To employ the terminology used by R. Bartlett, our focus is only on process and institutional indicators[335].

---

334 United States, *National Environmental Policy Act* (NEPA), 1969.

335 R. Bartlett, "Evaluating Environmental Policy Success and Failure", in N. Vig and M. Kraft (eds.), *Environmental Policy in the 1990s: Towards a New Agenda*, No. 24 (Washington, D.C., CQ Press, 1994), p. 170.

VI. How to measure and represent legal indicators?

Legal indicators respond to a real demand from the international community to find a way of demonstrating that each State is setting up legal mechanisms that strengthen environmental protection. The question therefore arises of how to measure and represent these legal indicators to improve the application of the law.

Indicators are tools for evaluation and decision-making. **Legal indicators** primarily serve to evaluate the **processes involved with the application of the law**, thus making it possible to measure **effectivity**. In addition, they offer a way to improve the application of the law, making it more effective.

Measuring effectivity requires four different competencies: legal, sociological, mathematical and statistical:

1. **Legal**, since the criteria to be measured should respond to a factual state within the processes of application of the law;
2. **Sociological**, since these criteria will have to fully reflect the roles of all those involved in the application of the law;
3. **Mathematical**, since these same criteria will need to be aggregated in order to generate the legal indicators of effectivity;
4. **Statistical**, since these same criteria will be monitored over time to measure progress towards sustainable development.

Measuring the effectivity of the law is therefore quite a complex undertaking, requiring input from individuals with a multidisciplinary skillset brought together in a committee.

A. The object of measurement

A legal measurement of environmental protection goes beyond a mere evaluation of the effects of the law, or its effectiveness. Instead it calls for an assessment of the impact resulting from the stages of implementation of the law, thereby its level of effectivity.

Effectivity describes that which is effective, that which produces an effect and exists in reality. The effectivity of the **law** is therefore determined according to **criteria that describe the processes of its application**. Previously we outlined six families of criteria that allow for a scientific assessment of the effectivity of the law: existence and sources, applicability, content or substance, organization or institution, enforcement, and non-legal factors.

1. Method of measurement to determine effectivity of the law

To measure legal indicators, it is useful to translate the concept of effectivity of the law into a mathematical model.

It is not as an attempt to redefine the concept of effectivity in law, but to apply a means of measurement.[336]

Here we discuss the **measurement of effectivity**.

a) Premise

To measure the implementation of the law is to measure its outcomes. The law has an effect on the environment. We measure its effectiveness.

To measure the stages of implementation of the law, the effectivity of the processes necessary for its application must be evaluated. This measurement of effectivity makes it possible to determine whether or not the law is being effectively applied.

b) Principles

Measuring effectiveness makes it possible to:

1. Evaluate the effects of the law in relation to environmental protection goals;
2. Identify its level of effectiveness in relation to set objectives (effectiveness of the outcome, or performance), by measuring compliance.

This "state effectiveness" does not take into account measurement of the necessary legal stages that determine the effective application of the law.

The **measurement of effectivity** looks at the processes involved in the implementation of the law, not the result of its application.

This is an important distinction. It enables the following:

1. To focus not only on the expected impact of the law;
2. To assess the effects of implementing the law in relation to legal criteria;
3. To determine the effectivity of defined legal conditions and implementing processes (effectivity of processes), in relation to purely legal criteria ("action effectiveness").

336 J. Bétaille, *L'effectivité en droit de l'environnement…*, *op. cit.*

This “action effectiveness” takes into account legal criteria as expected conditions of the stages of implementation of the law.

Measurements of effectivity help towards meeting the requirements of compliance with environmental protection legislation. In addition, they support the rhetoric of governance by guaranteeing that all of the conditions for application of the law have been evaluated and measured.

2. Data to be measured

Effectivity is measured on the basis of legal criteria. These criteria make it possible to produce data corresponding to each level of application of the law.

A **criterion** is a tool used to carry out an evaluation. A **legal criterion** is a factual element relating to the application of a legal rule or principle.

a) Application of legal criteria

The legal criteria are applied on the basis of data compiled from a questionnaire on a specific legal subject.

These data describe to what extent the law has been applied, for each criterion, on the basis of a graded response and supported by factual elements.

This leads to a set of qualitative data, to be converted into quantitative data.

b) From subjective data to objective measurement

“It is in its subjectivity, the way in which it is experienced, that an event acquires its real significance”[337].

The data collected is subjective. It is the expression of an opinion, albeit supported by factual elements. The repetition of different opinions on the same legal criterion over time provides objectivity to the measurement.

Specifically, the measurement method allows for the following under each criterion:

1. To convert an individual perception based on facts into a set of perceptions;
2. To adjust the subjectivity of the measurement based on the average perceptions and the extent to which they are held;
3. To gain objectivity of the measurement by repeating it over time based on the same legal criterion.

---

337 Jean-Pierre Martel, *Les œuvres complètes de Marguerite T. De Bané* (Montreal, Cercle du Livre de France, 1973).

B. The method of measurement

Since 2017, inventory and comparison studies have been carried out to identify scientific methods for the development of legal indicators.

We have established that legal indicators do not yet exist, therefore there is no frame of reference in this area. For this reason we have developed an innovative ad hoc method for the creation of legal indicators to describe the effectivity of environmental law.

1. Choice of method

Measurements of effectivity are rarely used within the application of law. They are also rarely used outside disciplines such as mathematics, information mechanisms for complex systems, and philosophy.

a) Inspiration

It was therefore important to search for areas of activity where this concept is applied. It was found within industry, in particular the aerospace industry, where process control is the only way of guaranteeing product compliance.

It is not easy to identify analogies. Neither the aerospace industry nor the law can guarantee the outcome of its product a priori. It is only known afterwards if a rocket has reached its target or if a law has produced the desired effect.

In the aerospace industry, efforts to ensure the proper functioning of the product focus on process control, from design to implementation. Efforts to ensure the proper application of the law must focus on the stages of implementation of the law.

In industry, different methods of process control are used. The most widespread and proven method is Statistical Process Control, or SPC. This will serve as inspiration in our study for the development of a methodology to measure the effectivity of the law with legal indicators.[338]

---

338 Maurice Pillet, *Appliquer la maîtrise statistique des processus MSP/SPC*, 6th ed. (Paris, Eyrolles, 2005); François Bergeret and Sabine Mercier, *Maîtrise statistique des procédés. Principes et cas industriels* (Paris, Dunod, L'Usine Nouvelle, 2011); Emmanuel Duclos, *La maîtrise statistique des procédés MSP/SPC* (Doussard, Emmanuel Duclos Conseil, 2008).

b) Adaptation

Just as industry calls for a control of variability in goods manufacture and services provided, the law should be measured according to variations in the effectivity of its rules. The following basic concepts have been adapted from SPC:

1. Monitoring of variability and management of key points in the processes involved in the implementation of the law;
2. Evaluation of effectivity by **process capacities**;
3. **Capacity of stages of implementation of the law**. This can be understood as the ability of a rule or principle to achieve a required level of enforcement. It allows for measurement of the capacity to reproduce levels of effectivity within the accepted range laid out by the rule, based on the following legal criteria: existential, applicability, substantive, organic, enforcement and non-legal.

c) Principles

Legal indicators are the product of collective multidisciplinary reflection. This reflection is necessary in order to rationalize the subjectivity of each actor's perception of the application of the law, to create a collective objectivity surrounding this application. It allows for measurement of achieved legal progress.

In order to rule out subjectivity in the effectivity measurement, and therefore ensure confidence in the results, this method applies strict rules for implementation and control. This will help to frame subjectivity through repetition.

> If the procedure is carried out in isolation, it is impossible to guarantee framing of subjectivity in the measurement of effectivity and objectivity in the measurement of progress.

The measurements are based on a frame of reference. Only the measurements produced by this frame of reference can be compared. This guarantees repeatability of the survey processes and the objective comparison of the results of each survey to measure legal progress towards sustainable development.

None of the processes leading to the application of the law are capable of always producing exactly the same result. There will always be some dispersion. This variability is unavoidable and is part of the very nature of all processes of application of the law.

Through analysis of these processes, 5 basic components can be identified that contribute to this dispersion, namely: MATERIAL, METHOD, MANNER, MEANS, ENVIRONMENT.

This 5-component concept can be adapted from industry to outline the 6C principles. These are 6 fundamental legal criteria for measuring the effectivity of the law that explain this dispersion, and therefore non-effectivity of the law:

1. **Existential criteria:** environment in the area of application of the law;
2. **Applicability criteria:** material in the area of application of the law;
3. **Substantive criteria:** method in the area of application of the law;
4. **Organic criteria:** manner in the area of application of the law;
5. **Enforcement criteria:** means in the area of application of the law;
6. **Non-legal criteria:** external environment in the area of application of the law.

This provides greater precision and methodological tools that will help to control and improve the effectivity of the law. These criteria are **mathematical targets** of effectivity control[339].

2. Area of measurement for the application of law

The area of measurement involves all dimensions of the law relevant to the mathematical expression of the target. In the context of effectivity, these dimensions are the various ways in which the law is applied. They are interdependent.

The area of measurement encompasses all dimensions, not only where they relate to each other, but also integrating non-legal parameters that enhance effectivity.

a) Object

The way a target is expressed is key to establishing the area of measurement. The clearer the target description, the more precise the area of measurement.

For example, the study of a protected area is a very broad field of environmental protection, therefore certain aspects should be specified and broken down into several targets to fully cover the area of measurement. These are: its category (nature reserve, national park, natural monument, species management area, etc.); geographical area (location, environment, etc.); and conservation objectives (fauna, flora, ecosystem, etc.).

This lays the foundations of the mathematical model of the method by reflecting the constraints of the area of measurement:

339 Expressing targets mathematically discards the analytical approach in favor of focusing on one aspect of the stages of implementation of the law. The target uses mathematical models that help to improve effectivity management.

1. When there are several targets for the same area of measurement, it is easier to carry out inventories and then group them into specific areas of application of environmental law to be measured, for each target in turn;
2. Each country is bound by its national law and by the translation of international law into national law. The areas of application of the law are therefore different in each country and cannot be compared with each other; even if the targets are similar, the areas of application will differ.

b) *Mathematical predominance of the areas of application of law*

The application of a legal norm has an impact on the effectivity of one or more targets within the area of measurement, depending on:

1. The level of interdependence with the application of other legal norms;
2. The influence of its implementation on the application of other legal norms.

The respective importance of the targets varies from one legal norm to the other. It is therefore necessary to reflect them in the calculation of effectivity, by modeling the predominance of the areas of application of the law between them within a particular area of measurement.

This predominance is established by a hierarchy:

1. By convention without a ranking;
2. By convention of criticality that measures the level of impact – critical, major or minor – of that area on the effectivity of the area of measurement. The higher the criticality, the more important the area of application of the law.

c) *Weighting of areas of application of the law*

Ratios are the most appropriate form of weighting to represent the relative importance of each area of application of the law. The more important the area of application of the law, the higher its ratio.

The sum of the ratios of all areas of application of the law in one area of measurement is equal to 100 %.

This ratio is used to aggregate measurements of effectivity of:

1. Each target;
2. Each area of measurement;
3. All environmental law.

3. The legal topics within the area of measurement

In order to be measured, the target must undergo a functional breakdown into legal and non-legal criteria according to the 6 criteria (6C) that form a legal topic.

a) Breakdown of the area of measurement into legal topics

An area of measurement is either:

1. Basic: involving a single target, therefore a single legal topic;
2. Complex: involving several targets, and therefore as many legal topics.

b) From specific to comprehensive measurement

An area of measurement that responds to only one target will produce a specific measurement. If a broader measurement is desired, it is necessary to indicate other targets, resulting in as many specific measurements.

The more targets there are for the same area of measurement, the more they will allow for an overall measurement of the effectivity of the areas of application of the law.

This modeling of the global measurement makes the following possible:

1. To observe the variability in effectivity within the area of measurement;
2. To distinguish the strengths and areas for improvement in the stages of implementation of the law within the area of measurement.

c) Mathematical predominance of legal topics

When the area of measurement is limited to one target, there is no predominance since there is only one legal topic.

When this area includes several targets, the legal topics will have a predominance only if there is a priority of implementation among the targets in relation to a legal measure expressing:

1. A timescale;
2. A priority;
3. A decision.

4. The measurement of criteria by legal topic

The legal criteria forming the legal topic are subject to a set of measurements:

1. Measurement specific to each criterion;
2. Aggregated measurement of each criterion within one family of criteria;

3. Aggregated measurement of all criteria within one family of criteria;
4. Aggregated measurement of all families of criteria.

To be representative of effectivity, the criterion determines a key point to consistently measure one stage of an implementation process. This does not take into account the evolution of the content of the rule, nor the expected result.

These measurements are obtained through surveys using a questionnaire for each legal topic.

a) *Questionnaire, question wording and choice of answers*

The validity of a questionnaire is based on the presence of the six families of effectivity criteria: the existence of the law and its sources, its applicability, substance, institutions, enforcement, and the non-legal criteria reinforcing its effectivity. At least one question per family of criteria is required.

A question corresponds to a criterion by:

1. Identifying an element that contributes to the stages of implementation of the law;
2. Being formulated with a view to strengthening effectivity;
3. Breaking it down into sub-questions if the response calls for a combination of conditions to be met;
4. Respecting a single-choice interrogative form;
5. Having a common range of possible responses throughout the questionnaire.

Examples:

i) Choice of an element that contributes to the stages of implementation of the law
   Imagine that one of the expected results of one stage in the process of application of the law is to measure the effectivity of the procedure for issuing a report on the rate of particle emission in the air. In this case, effectivity is judged by the systematization and reproducibility of the procedure through key points such as:
   1. Calibration of control devices;
   2. Staff authorization to draw up a report;
   3. Listing of the conditions of measurement;
   4. Publicity of observed levels of pollution, etc.;
   and not the result of the measurement.

ii) Formulation with a view to strengthening effectivity
The focus of the question should contribute to measuring the effectivity of the law and not its non-effectivity:
1. Rather than the following question: "Does the lack of interest among forest holders have an impact on the protection of a specific protected animal?": the greater the lack of interest, the greater the non-effectivity;
2. We ask: "Does interest among forest holders have an impact on the protection of protected animals?": the greater the interest, the greater the effectivity.

iii) Breakdown into sub-questions
A legal criterion may satisfy one of several conditions. This could represent:
1. An alternative;
2. A combination;
3. Or both.

It will be possible to divide the question into sub-questions to satisfy the measurement. For example, to determine the legal status of a protected area, the question will be made up of sub-questions. Instead of asking: "Do you know whether the status of the protected area is regional, national and/or European?", this question is divided into three sub-questions: "Does the protected area have:
1. Regional
2. National
3. Or European status?".

iv) Respect of the single-choice interrogative form
All questions have the same format:
1. Interrogative;
2. Offering a single choice from a set of possible answers.

The question is then divided into sub-questions to satisfy the measurement.

Two opposing questions may have the same investigative purpose, but will result in opposing measurements:
1. Rather than the following question: "Are control measures not taken?"; this negative question form measures non-effectivity;
2. We ask: "Are control measures taken?"; this question form measures effectivity.

In order to determine a measurement, question responses cannot be open ended. It is therefore necessary to outline possible responses that will be the same throughout the whole questionnaire.

The question: "Are control measures taken?" can be answered with:

1. Yes;
2. In part;
3. No;
4. Don't know.

v) Range of possible responses

The range of possible responses corresponds to the mapping of all possible answers to all questions. It is a mathematical necessity in order to ensure:

1. Standardization of measurements in the questionnaire;
2. Aggregation of comparable data.

The response "don't know" is systematically applicable to all questions. Other choices are possible depending on the question.

b) Gradation of responses

Gradation is a mathematical necessity in order to transform qualitative data into quantitative data to be aggregated, thus producing the different legal indicators.

The range of possible answers throughout the questionnaire is graded. These gradings express the decreasing level of effectivity of each response.

This ordering of choices constitutes a **gradation** that is common to all the questions.

Examples:

1. The range of options lists the responses in the questionnaire.
2. The ordering of most effective to least effective responses is done by convention. The range of options translates into a **grading scale**.
3. This gradation is translated into a **logarithmic value scale** by convention, assigning the highest value to the highest grading, and the lowest value to the lowest grading. The logarithmic value scale allows for differences in the level of effectivity to be highlighted in the aggregations, making it easier to identify strengths and areas in need of improvement.

Range of options					
Yes	*No*	*Sometimes*	*Rarely*	*Often*	*Don't Know*
Translation					
Grading scale					
Yes	*Often*	*Sometimes*	*Rarely*	*Don't Know*	*No*
Translation					
Scale of values					
Yes	**Often**	**Sometimes**	**Rarely**	**Don't Know**	**No**
8	**5**	**3**	**2**	**1**	**0,001***

* The use of the value 0 is prohibited to avoid operating impossibilities. A decimal value to the 1000th is chosen.

c) Logical order of questioning

The sequence of questions follows a logical order that helps respondents to better understand the questionnaire.

Two logical orders must be followed:

1. The first is the ordering of families of criteria:
   - Existential criteria;
   - Applicability criteria;
   - Substantive criteria;
   - Organic criteria;
   - Enforcement criteria;
   - Non-legal criteria.
2. The second is the sequence of questions by family of criteria respecting causal links.

d) Weighting of questions

Weighting is carried out by the legal committee or expert group that drafts the questions, none of whom will be asked to complete the questionnaire. The weighting must never be communicated to interviewers nor respondents, so as to avoid influencing responses.

Weighting of the questions and sub-questions makes it possible to assess their order of importance within a family of criteria, that is, their importance as a factor of effectivity. It is a subjective assessment, the result of consensus among the group of experts. It makes it possible to obtain a purely quantitative scale, determined by coefficients within a range established by convention.

A question that is very important for one family of criteria may have a different coefficient to another question that is very important for another family.

Within the same family of criteria, questions and sub-questions may have the same coefficient.

If the family of criteria consists of questions and sub-questions, the coefficients are assigned in two stages:

1. According to the relative importance of the questions;
2. According to the relative importance of the sub-questions within each family of sub-questions.

Example:

Weighting convention applied to questions and sub-questions

Ranked in order of importance by assigning a coefficient of between 1 and 10, from least to most important.

The use of the value 0 is prohibited to avoid operating impossibilities.

Criteria family question		*Coefficient*
Question 1		7
Sub-question set 2	*Sub-question 2.1*	4
	Sub-question 2.2	2
	Sub-question 2.3	7
Question 3		10
Sub-question set 4	*Sub-question 4.1*	5
	Sub-question 4.2	3
Question 5		6
Question 6		7

e) Mathematical predominance of families of criteria

A family of criteria impacts the effectivity of its legal topic, according to:

1. The level of interdependence with other families of criteria;
2. The influence of its own effectivity on that of others.

The respective importance of each family of criteria varies. It is therefore necessary to represent them in the calculation of effectivity by modeling the predominance of families in relation to each other within the legal topic.

This predominance of families of criteria is expressed by a ratio representing their level of influence on the effectivity of the legal topic.

This predominance is established by a hierarchy linked to a weighting, either:

1. By convention without a ranking nor weighting;
2. By convention of criticality that measures the level of impact – critical, major or minor – of each family of criteria on effectivity within the area of measurement. The higher the criticality, the more important that family of criteria.

Where the six families of criteria are of equal importance, their respective weight is 1/6, or 16.66 %.

> The use of the ratio 0 is prohibited to avoid operational impossibilities; by convention, a minimum applicable ratio is determined.

Example:

Predominance of the six families of criteria						
Existential	*Applicability*	*Substantive*	*Organic*	*Enforcement*	*Non-legal*	*Total*
5 %	***20 %***	***15 %***	***30 %***	***20 %***	***10 %***	***100 %***

5. The panel of respondents

The make up of the panel depends on the legal topic addressed by each questionnaire. This may mean choosing different actors involved in various areas of application of the law.

At the start of the project, the legal committee presents the profiles of the panel. Then, depending on the work sequences, the profiles are fine tuned according to:

1. Their involvement in the stages of implementation of the law;
2. Their capacity to answer all of the questions.

The panel follows the rules of representative sampling.

The empirical method of quota sampling is the preferred and most representative approach, when the typology of legal actors is known and can be associated with all or part of the legal criteria.

If it is not possible to know the typology of legal actors involved, the random sampling method is applied. This second approach should be avoided where possible, as it is more complex and difficult to implement.

a) Statistical definition of the target panel

i) By quota sampling

The principle of this empirical method is to identify the distribution of legal actors within the target population of the panel. The same distribution must then be maintained in the sample.

If the group of legal professionals is made up of 15 % magistrates, 25 % lawyers, 27 % managers, 8 % controllers, 5 % professionals, 16 % users, 2 % representatives of associations and 1 % elected officials, and if 100 legal actors are to be interviewed, then the sample should include 15 magistrates, 25 lawyers, 27 managers, 8 controllers, 5 professionals, 16 users, 2 representatives of associations and 1 elected official.

The quota method is based on the assumption that by framing the sample structure on the basis of these criteria, which are known to the population, the results obtained will be transferable to all legal actors.

ii) By random sampling

The method of random sampling assumes the preexistence of a sampling frame corresponding to the population of legal professionals that meet the survey criteria.

Four approaches are possible:

1. Simple random sampling, using actors selected from a sampling frame on a random basis, ensuring that all profiles of legal professionals have the same chance of being part of the sample;
2. Systematic sampling, using an existing or constructed sampling frame listing all profiles of legal professionals to select a random starting point for the first profile in the sample. The other profiles are then selected at fixed intervals throughout the list. The interval is calculated based on the sample size and the size of the population in the sampling frame. This calculation takes into consideration the desired level of confidence and the margin of error;
3. Cluster sampling, which divides the sampling frame into subgroups with strong similarities. This allows either a random selection of a few sub-groups from which all legal actors are interviewed, or choosing more clusters at random and creating samples in each cluster;

4. Stratified sampling, by subdividing the legal actors in the sampling frame into subgroups according to one or more factors to extract a simple random sample for each subgroup.

b) Representativeness of the sample

The sample size depends on:

1. The size of the parent population of legal actors related to the questionnaire;
2. The level of confidence in the outcome;
3. The margin of error in responses;
4. The number of invitations to participate in the survey.

Example:

Example of parent population size	*Sample size*			*Sample size*		
	Confidence level 95 %	*Margin of error 5 %*	*Number of invitations*	*Confidence level 99 %*	*Margin of error 1 %*	*Number of invitations*
20	**20**		*100*	**20**		*100*
50	**45**		*225*	**50**		*250*
100	**80**		*400*	**100**		*500*
500	**218**		*1090*	**486**		*2430*
5000	**357**		*1785*	**3843**		*19215*
20000	**377**		*1885*	**9068**		*45340*

c) Conditions for launching the survey

Questionnaire and survey respondents have, depending on the country, differing rights regarding their personal data. If there is not complete anonymity in the responses, the companies or organizations carrying out these surveys take on new responsibilities.

According to this methodology, the questionnaire is conducted on the basis of anonymity.

There should be no identifiable elements in the survey, such as the actor's profile, their affiliation nor anything that would reveal an individual's identity in the questionnaire.

No personal data should be processed or recorded.

However, for the purposes of the survey, different means of communication may require the use of personal data, such as contact lists, to:

1. Distribute the questionnaire by e-mail or post;
2. Disseminate a weblink to conduct the questionnaire online;
3. The way in which questionnaires are returned may allow for the identification of respondents, such as e-mail addresses.

It is therefore advisable to take some precautions, depending on the legislation of the country where the survey is carried out:

1. Gain consent of the data subject when collecting personal data for contact lists;
2. Explain the reason for processing personal data, the data recipients, the retention period;
3. Guarantee access to personal data at any time, to have data corrected or deleted (right to be forgotten), to request data portability, to contest processing operations or to request their limitation;
4. Guarantee confidentiality and security of data and establish a procedure in the event of a breach or loss of data.

In some countries other legal obligations may need to be taken into account, depending on the nature of the survey. These include:

1. Authorization request;
2. Disclosure of subcontracting (IT, research firm, etc.);
3. Basic disclosure;
4. Establishment of an ethics committee;
5. Disclosure of data files;
6. Authorization and/or obligation to publish outcomes; etc.

We recommend the support of specialized companies or the presence of a specialist in the survey team, given the complexity that this can add to the launch of a study.

6. The questionnaire instructions

The questionnaire instructions must meet requirements for:

1. Framing subjectivity;
2. Data collation (factual substantiation);

3. Autonomous completion of the questionnaire by the respondent is therefore not advised. Supervision is recommended to ensure that the responses given are factual.

a) Supervision of the questionnaire

Supervision of the questionnaire is entrusted to a professional with significant skills and experience in the relevant area(s) of law in order to monitor the respondent's answers in the questionnaire.

This supervisor shall receive skills training in connection with the norm and data collation according to the chosen criteria of effectivity of the law.

The supervisor will therefore be able to monitor data collation while respecting the respondent's independence in giving their answers.

b) Data collation

Collation involves checking for documents and other forms of justification that can verify a given response. It consists of fact checking to support the responses, using hard copy and electronic documents and checklists. Where there is no factual evidence, the respondent is requested to give a rationale for their response.

7. Data processing

Data processing is a mathematical necessity to enable the creation of indicators, by carrying out the following steps:

1. Scoring of responses;
2. Data checks;
3. Validation of the survey.

a) Scoring of collected data

The scoring is the input element for all aggregations. It defines the first measurement of effectivity.

The scoring of a question is calculated by the product of the value of the response in the grading scale and the weighting specific to that question.

The scoring of a sub-question is more complex, depending on the conditions to be met in each case.

Examples:

i) Take the scale of values

Scale of values					
Yes	*Often*	*Sometimes*	*Rarely*	*Don't Know*	*No*
8	*5*	*3*	*2*	*1*	*0,001**

ii) Question scoring

Apply to the questionnaire

Question from family of criteria	*Response*	*Coefficient*	*Scoring*
Question 1	***Sometimes*** / ***3***	***7***	***21***
Question 2	***Yes*** / ***8***	***10***	***80***
Question 3	***Don't Know*** / ***1***	***6***	***6***
Question 4	***No*** / ***0,001***	***7***	***0,007***

iii) Sub-question scoring

The scoring of a sub-question depends on the following:

1. Selection from among the sub questions: the highest product will be kept from among the sub-questions to establish the scoring;
2. Combination of all sub-questions: the sum of the products of the sub-questions;
3. Combination and selection from among the questions: the sum of the product(s) of the combined sub-questions and of the highest product(s) from among those selections.

Question from family of criteria		*Response*	*Condition*	*Coefficient*	*Scoring*
Sub-question set 1	*Sub-question 1.1*	***No***	***OR***	**4**	~~***0,002***~~
		0,001			
	Sub-question 1.2	***Yes***		**2**	***16***
		0,001			
	Sub-question 1.3	***Yes***	***AND***	***7***	***56***
		8			
Sub-question set 2	*Sub-question 2.1*	***Don't Know***	***AND***	**5**	**5**
		1			
	Sub-question 2.2	***Often***	***AND***	**3**	***15***
		5			

b) Control of collected data

Collection control involves the use of control charts to process a sample statistically, identifying the distribution of responses to the same questions in order to detect their variability and potential spread (using the normal distribution): either the curves (of each control chart) differ and remain centered (evidence of dispersion in the processes of implementation of the law); or the curves are off-center, which brings into question the sincerity of the response and therefore suggests tampering[340].

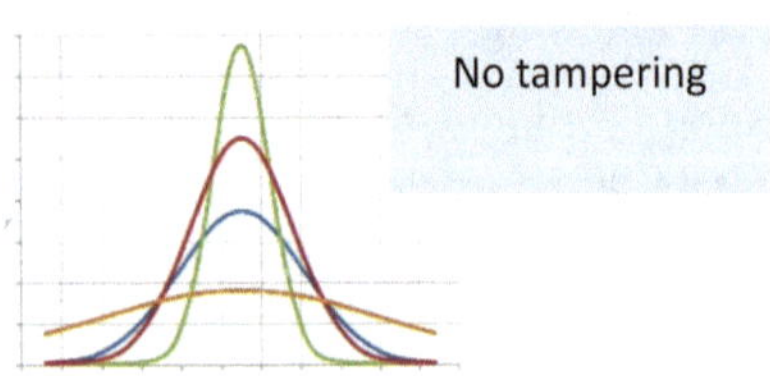

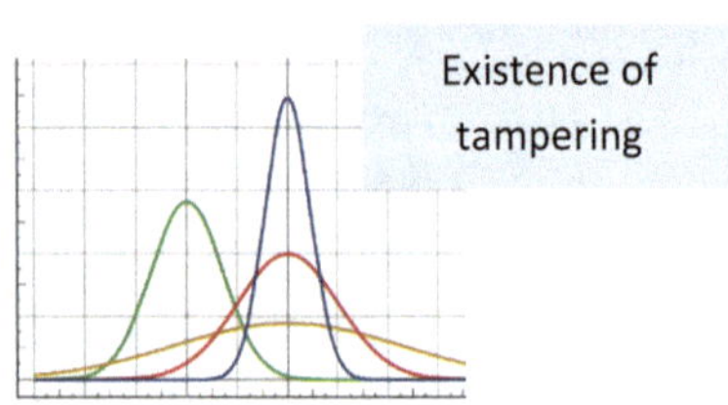

340 Tampering: action of rigging the answers, not respecting the requirements of data collection. See: Rémy Caveng, "La production des enquêtes quantitatives", *Revue d'anthropologie des connaissances*, vol. 6, n° 1 (2012), pp. 65–88, https://www.cairn.info/revue-anthropologie-des-connaissances-2012-1-page-65.htm.

c) Validation of the collation

This validation consists of reviewing the effectivity results, before publication, in order to remove any doubts about their "sincerity", in particular when the survey process controls highlight tampering, a lack of reliability in responses or non-compliance on the part of the panel of respondents (sampling plan). It is then decided whether to:

1. Discard those results that suggest tampering and proceed with the creation of indicators;
2. Repeat all or part of the survey;
3. Not publish the results of the survey.

C. The resulting indicators

Legal indicators are the result of aggregations. Before aggregation, effectivity must be declared to be "under control". In the same process of implementation of the law, no two situations are ever exactly the same. This is due to two causes of dispersion:

1. Dispersion due to common causes;
2. Dispersion due to special causes.

Common causes are sources of variation by chance, always present to varying degrees in different processes. Statistics make it possible to study these phenomena. It is possible to model the behavior of hazards and consequently predict the performance of a process subject to common causes of dispersion. These common causes together form the intrinsic variability of the process. When the magnitude of the causes acting on the processes is constant, the characteristic of a state must follow a distribution according to the normal law. The aim of this statistical approach is to allow only dispersion due to common causes. This would be referred to as effectivity in law that is "under control".

Special causes are identifiable, irregular and unstable causes of dispersion, and are therefore difficult to predict. The appearance of a special cause requires intervention in the processes of implementation of the law. Unlike common causes, special causes are generally few in number. Where they are present, this would describe effectivity in law that is "out of control".

Effectivity "under control" means a set of processes in the stages of implementation of the law in which only common causes remain. According to the normal law, the distribution is centered on the target.

Effectivity that is "out of control" is subject to the presence of special causes. The distribution can be off-center with respect to the target.

Controlling variability therefore consists of putting "under control" the effectivity in law; this objective must be met before proceeding with aggregations.

1. Aggregations by legal topic (questionnaire)

The various aggregations have well-defined boundaries for determining effectivity:

1. The effectivity of each criterion;
2. The effectivity of each family of criteria for its own effectivity;
3. The distribution of effectivity of the families of legal criteria in the legal topic;
4. The overall effectivity of the legal topic.

a) Effectivity of each criterion

The specific effectivity for each criterion corresponds to the ratio of the scoring from the response and the maximum scoring. This effectivity is expressed as a percentage. The higher the percentage, the more effective the criterion is.

b) Effectivity of each family of criteria

The specific effectivity of each family of criteria corresponds to the ratio of the sum of the scorings obtained for each criterion over the sum of the maximum scorings for the criteria. This effectivity is expressed as a percentage. The higher the percentage, the more effective the family of criteria is.

c) Distribution of effectivity of the families of criteria within the legal topic

The distribution of effectivity of the families of criteria is obtained by combining, for each family of criteria, the product of its own effectivity with the ratio of its predominance in the legal topic. This distribution is expressed as a percentage. The higher the percentage, the more effective that family is within the effectivity of the topic.

d) Overall effectivity of the legal topic

The overall effectivity of the legal topic corresponds to the sum of the distribution rates of the six families of legal criteria.

2. Aggregation of the area of measurement

This aggregation is only possible if several targets are expressed within the area of measurement, and therefore as many legal topics.

The overall effectivity of the area of measurement corresponds to the sum of the products by legal topic of their rate of effectivity with their predominance in the legal topic.

3. Global aggregation of environmental law

This aggregation is only possible if several areas of measurement have been identified. It uses the predominance of the areas of application of the law of each area of measurement.

Within each area of measurement, a correlation is made between each area and the related questions.

The overall effectivity of the law is obtained by calculating the following for each area:

1. The ratio of the sum of scorings obtained for each criterion over the sum of the maximum scorings for the criteria;
2. Adjustment on a basis of 100 for each ratio by dividing it by the sum of the ratios;
3. The sum of the adjusted ratios to obtain the global rate.

This effectivity is expressed as a percentage. The higher the percentage, the more effective the family of criteria is.

D. Statistical monitoring of effectivity progress within the area of measurement

Statistical monitoring meets two different requirements: to monitor the evolution of effectivity over time within a constant area of measurement, and to do so at the lowest possible cost. This implies:

1. Using the same area of measurement;
2. Using the same questionnaire;
3. Respecting the same principles for the panel structure (although individuals interviewed and supervisors may vary);
4. Applying the same aggregations.

The purpose of statistical monitoring is to:

1. Simplify the survey process by selecting a sample of questions, chosen from each family of criteria for their predominance in the representativeness of effectivity control in the legal topic;
2. Ensure a level of confidence in the results;
3. Significantly reduce the costs of monitoring progress in effectivity compared to the original survey.

1. Principles

Statistical monitoring makes it possible to determine the principles applicable to the management of effectivity measurement in order to guarantee its representativeness over time, that is, confidence and progress in effectivity measurement. This is distinct from the work on representativeness of the panel and the control of data collation which defines the target of the respondents.

For a measurement to be under control, three parameters must be met:

1. The form of dispersion of the effectivity measurement, that is, controlling the sources of variation, distinguishing between what is predictable (common causes), and what is unpredictable (special causes). The control of variability is measured using a statistical approach (the normal law) to see if the effectivity measurement is centered on its target. If the distribution of this measurement is always centered on this target over the course of the surveys, then this measurement is "under control", and only the common causes remain. If the distribution is off-center, then the measurement is referred to as being "out-of-control", or subject to the presence of special causes;
2. The ability to measure effectivity, that is, to control the measurement within its natural limits. When the results of this measurement are within such natural limits, it is called an "able" measurement. If the results are outside these natural limits, the measurement is invalid;
3. The control of effectivity measurement, that is, setting up a measurement control chart, first of all to:

   - Identify the critical parameters of the measurement;
   - Observe the measurement;
   - Analyze the variability of the measurement;
   - Analyze the sources of variability;
   - Optimize the measurement.

To propose standardization of the control at a second stage by:

- Getting the measurement "on track";
- Reducing the frequency of controls.

2. Aims

Instead of repeating the entire questionnaire(s), a sample of questions is used. This has a significant impact on the costs of a survey.

With each effectivity measurement cycle, it will be possible to measure more quickly the progress or regression of effectivity levels, in each area of application of the law.

This makes it possible to represent, in the form of curves compared over time, the progress associated with the rate of change registered in the latest measurement.

E. Graphical representation

Graphical representation is the key to effective measurement. It is applied to all the indicators, and includes criteria appropriate to its intended use:

1. Radar charts allow for data comparison within a comparable data set to visualize the scope of commitments in relation to objectives;
2. Bar charts are used to show the distribution of data in a specific context;
3. Ring diagrams are used to measure the overall achievement of an objective;
4. Curve charts are used to compare a series of data points related to the same measurement, in order to visualize trends.

Graphical representation is of good quality when it quickly and clearly explains a situation in a format that is easy to understand.

1. Forms of representation

a) Radar chart showing effectivity of each criterion

Goal: to highlight high levels of effectivity and those in need of improvement under each criteria in the area of measurement.
Interpretation: immediately identify sources of improved effectivity, for each criterion.

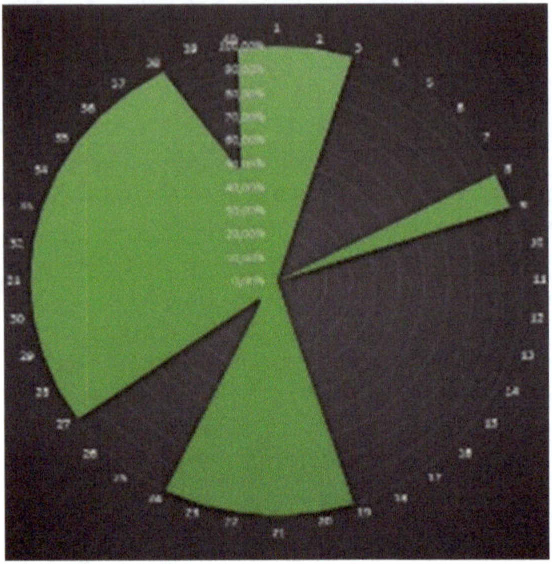

b) Radar chart showing effectivity of each family of criteria

Goal: to highlight high levels of effectivity and those in need of improvement in each family of criteria in the area of measurement.
Interpretation: immediately identify priorities for improved effectivity, whether that be for:

1. Environment in the area of application of the law (family of existential criteria);
2. Material in the area of application of the law (family of applicability criteria);
3. Method in the area of application of the law (family of substantive criteria);
4. Manner in the area of application of the law (family of organic criteria);
5. Means in the area of application of the law (family of enforcement criteria);
6. External environment in the area of application of the law (family of non-legal criteria).

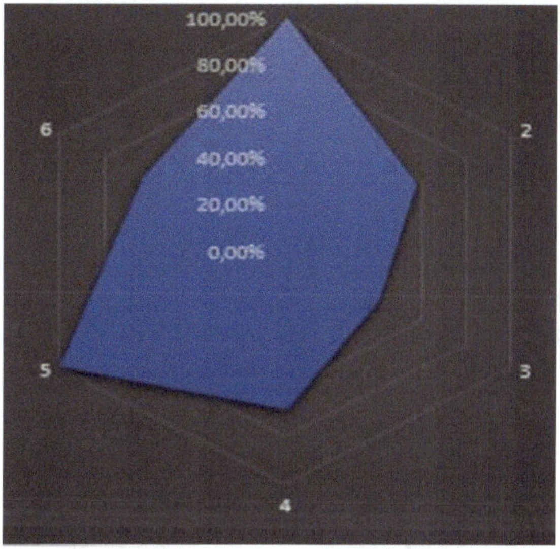

c) Bar chart showing the distribution of effectivity of the families of criteria within the legal topic

Goal: to outline the urgency of action on effectivity for each family of criteria within the area of measurement.

Interpretation: to identify the priorities for action to improve the effectivity of the law for each family of criteria. The higher the percentage in a family of criteria, the greater its influence on effectivity. If the effectivity of each family of criteria (previous chart) is low, but there is a high level of influence, it is an obvious source of rapid improvement in the overall effectivity rate.

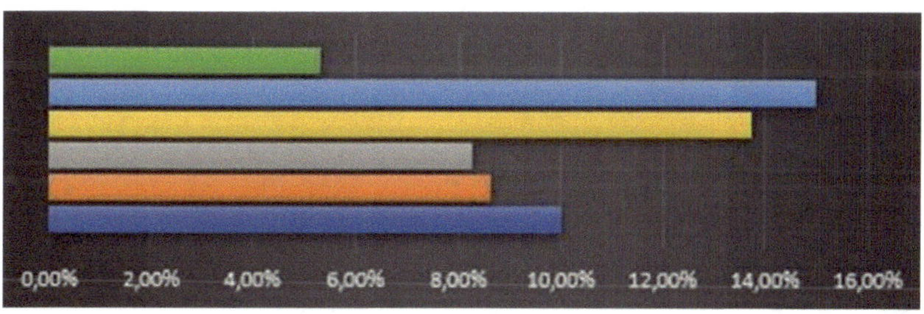

d) Ring diagram showing effectivity of the legal topic

Goal: to highlight the acceptance or nonacceptance of the level of effectivity of the legal topic.
Interpretation: to decide whether or not to take action to improve the effectivity of the legal topic.

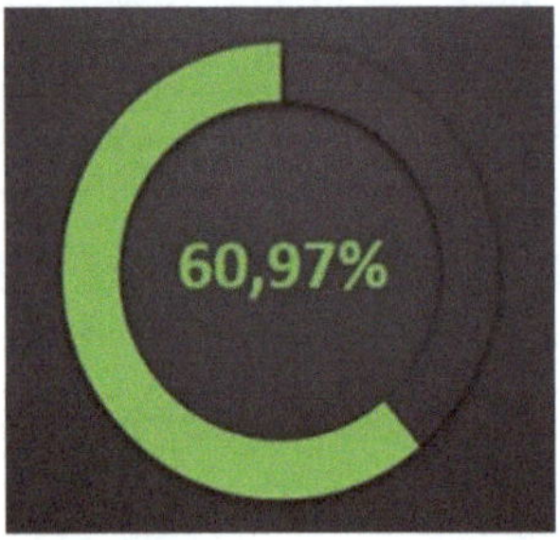

e) Radar chart showing the overall effectivity of the area of measurement or of the law

Goal: to highlight the acceptance or nonacceptance of the overall level of effectivity of the law, as well as high levels of effectivity and those in need of improvement in relation to governance objectives.
Interpretation: to improve governance in the application of the law, when effectivity in a legal topic is deemed insufficient, by setting new objectives and commitments.

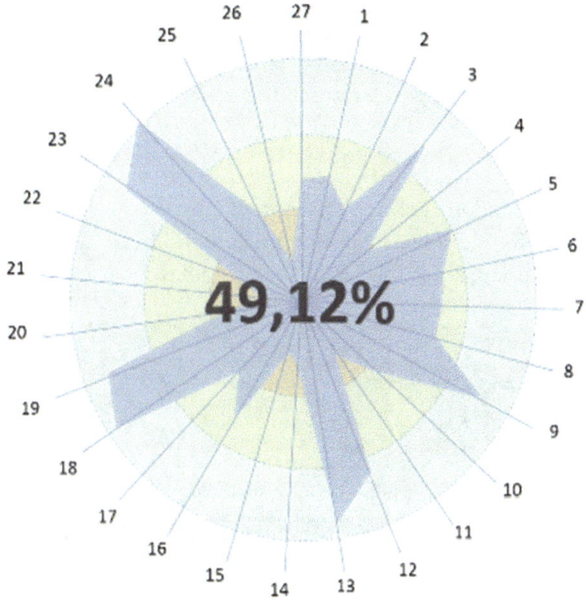

f) Time series showing the evolution of effectivity within the area of measurement

Goal: to show the progression or regression of effectivity in each area of application of the law over time.
Interpretation: manage the improvement of effectivity; in the case of progress, validate the results of actions for improvement; in the case of regression, adjust these actions.

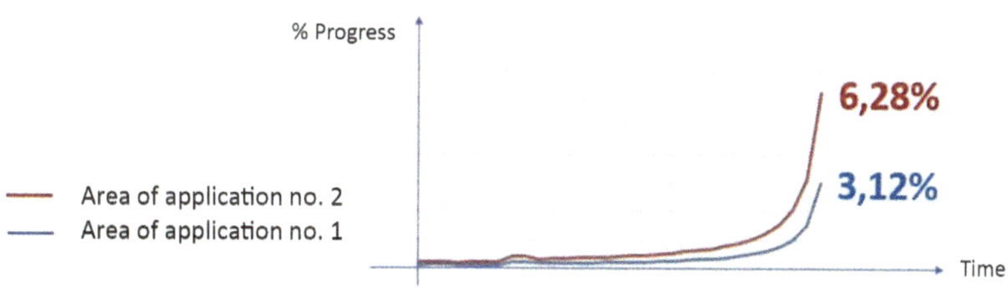

2. Using the graphical representations

The use of graphical representations depends on their correct interpretation. The quicker and simpler they are to interpret, the easier it is to make a decision.

a) Interpretation

Graphical representations are not accompanied by explanations. It is therefore important to clarify the subject through meaningful headings and to represent them in groups, as far as possible in the form of a dashboard.

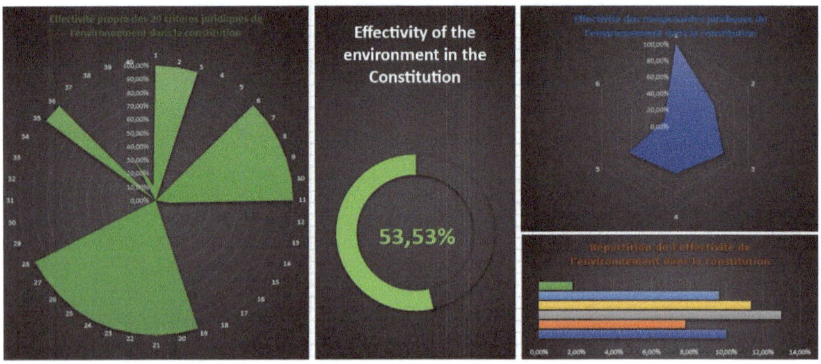

b) Aid to decision-making

In the dashboard, it is easy to identify the areas of non-compliance that characterize non-effectivity of the criterion specific to the legal topic.

Even if the overall effectivity rate of the legal topic appears to be acceptable, gaps by family of criteria and for each criterion are easily identified. These are the causes of non-effectivity that need to be addressed.

This provides a precise identification of the points that need to be improved in order to achieve a satisfactory application of the legal rules. This will directly allow for informed improvement and change to one or more specific points in the stages of implementation of the law.

Conclusion: Strengths and weaknesses of legal indicators

There is unanimous acknowledgment that environmental law is either applied insufficiently or not at all. But what is the solution? Create further laws? Increase sanctions? Intensify controls? Reform governance?

Perhaps legal indicators are the innovation that provide the answer?

Legal indicators are not strictly speaking governance indicators to help to better manage the effective application of the law. Rather, like all indicators, they are decision-making tools. They are the driving force behind proposals for improvements to the proper functioning of the law, rather than tools for identifying satisfactory or inappropriate governance. If they do contribute to governance, they have their limits.

1. Contribution of legal indicators to governance

Legal indicators accurately reflect the life of the law through the stages of its implementation in a given country. They remain State-specific and do not allow for comparisons between States.

They are built uniquely to promote change, to detect barriers and regressions, and to help identify levers for progress. In summary, they make it possible to clarify a situation that has become confused as a result of intervention from a number of public, private, collective and individual actors. Legal indicators provide hope that responsibilities may be identified based on a description of the causal chain of non-effectivity.

By the same token, legal indicators enrich governance data by highlighting the social function of the law and identifying legal, institutional, cultural and other obstacles to the application of environmental law.

It is unreasonable to expect full effectivity of the law owing to legal indicators and inappropriate to think that, alone, they can guarantee its complete effectivity.

However, they do respond to the need to inform public decision-making when implementing public policies. It is well known that when these policies concern the environment in particular, there are often trade-offs between conflicting interests.

Yet, the law itself consists not only of rules that prohibit or authorize, but also of a complex set of procedures, institutions and concepts. Its effectivity therefore depends on the coordination of these various constituent elements, which can be evaluated and monitored through the use of well-constructed indicators.

2. The limits of legal indicators

Legal indicators of effectivity do not make it possible to govern by numbers, nor to stop environmental degradation, and nor to better protect the environment in the immediate future. They are only a partial information tool. This is especially true given that "effectivity is always relative and there are a multitude of intermediate states between a statement and its social translations"[341]. While they offer insights into where inadequacies lie, the percentage of effectivity attributed to an environmental law is less important than the discovery of what is proving to be a constraint or obstacle. This is essential in helping to create understanding of the fact that an ineffective law may as well not exist at all.

Legal indicators reveal the causes for non-application of environmental law and inform about differing levels of effectivity. They raise awareness of the fact that it is not enough just to pass laws or sign treaties in order to protect the environment. The biggest challenge is to engage all stakeholders in the implementation of enacted laws.

As these laws are now the result of both international law and European law, as well as the fulfillment of the Sustainable Development Goals, the legal processes of implementation involve coordination between a multitude of stakeholders and concern a multitude of norms. We realize therefore that legal indicators can be used to hold these numerous stakeholders accountable by highlighting contradictions between moral commitments and legal achievements.

Of course, as they are only indicators, the guidance and teachings that is drawn from them depends on their appraisal or interpretation. This explains why the same indicators are capable of leading to opposite conclusions. Any environmental policy involves decision-making based on values. Legal indicators cannot in any way make disappear such values, nor are they intended to conceal them.

In other words, while legal indicators alone are not enough to save the planet, they can help in the future to improve the outcomes of the law, to warn of abuses, to identify possible resistance and obstacles, to propose solutions, and ultimately to get back on track.

---

341 P. Lascoumes, "Conclusion: l'effectivité, indicateur de la place du droit dans les rapports sociaux", in V. Champeil-Desplats and D. Lochak (eds.), *À la recherche de l'effectivité des droits de l'homme* (Paris, Presses universitaires de Paris Nanterre, 2008), p. 265.

Bibliography

African Union. *First Continental Report on the Implementation of Agenda 2063*, February 2020.

African Union Commission. *Agenda 2063. The Africa We Want. A Shared Strategic Framework for Inclusive Growth and Sustainable Development. First Ten-Year Implementation Plan 2014–2023*, September 2015.

Aiken, J. H. and Wizner, S. "Measuring Justice". *Wisconsin Law Review*, 2013 (pp. 79–99).

Allen, M. J. and Yen, W. M. *Introduction to Measurement Theory*. Long Grove: Waveland Press, 2002.

Arndt, Ch. *Governance Indicators*. Dissertation, Maastricht University, 2009.

Arndt, Ch. and Oman, Ch. *Uses and Abuses of Governance Indicators*. OECD Development Centre. Paris: OECD, 2006.

Auvergnon, Ph. "Une approche comparative de la question de l'effectivité du droit du travail". In *L'effectivité du droit du travail, à quelles conditions?* Bordeaux: Presses universitaires de Bordeaux, 2008.

Ayong Le Kama, A., Lagarenne, C., and Le Lourd, P. *Indicateurs nationaux du développement durable: lesquels retenir?* Rapport du groupe de travail interministériel sur les indicateurs à la Commission des comptes et de l'économie de l'environnement. Paris: La Documentation française, 2004.

Barendrechts, M. "Rule of Law, Measuring and Accountability: Problems to Be Solved Bottom Up". *Hague Journal on the Rule of Law*, 3/2011 (pp. 282–304).

Barreira, A. *Environmental Rule of Law: An Analysis of Data Availability*. Green Growth Knowledge Platform, 2019.

Bartlett, R. "Evaluating Environmental Policy Success and Failure". In N. Vig and M. Kraft (eds). *Environmental Policy in the 1990s: Towards a New Agenda*. Washington, D.C.: CQ Press, 1994.

Beer-Gabel, J. and Labat, B. *La protection internationale de la faune et de la flore sauvages*. Brussels: Bruyant and University of Brussels, 1999.

Bergeret, F. and Mercier, S. *Maîtrise statistique des procédés. Principes et cas industriels*. Paris: Dunod, L'Usine Nouvelle, 2011.

Bertelsmann Stiftung and SDSN. *SDG Index and Dashboards Report 2017. Global Responsibilities, International Spillover in Achieving the Goals*. July 2017.

Bertelsmann Stiftung and SDSN. *SDG Index and Dashboards Report 2018. Global Responsibilities, Implementing the Goals*. July 2018.

Bertelsmann Stiftung and SDSN. *Africa SDG Index and Dashboards Report 2018.* July 2018.

Bertelsmann Stiftung and SDSN. *Sustainable Development Report 2019. Transformations to achieve the Sustainable Development Goals.* June 2019.

Besançon, M. *Good Governance Rankings: The Art of Measurement.* Somerville: World Peace Foundation, 2003.

Bétaille, J. *Les conditions juridiques de l'effectivité de la norme en droit public interne: illustrations en droit de l'urbanisme et en droit de l'environnement.* Law thesis, Limoges, 2012.

Bétaille, J. (ed.). *Le droit d'accès à la justice environnementale.* Toulouse: Presses de l'université de Toulouse, 2016.

Bétaille, J. "L'effectivité en droit de l'environnement". In S. Brimo and Ch. Pauti (eds). *L'effectivité des droits. Regards en droit administratif.* Paris: Mare et Martin, 2019.

Beurier, J. P. *Droit international de l'environnement*, 5th ed. Paris: Pedone, 2017.

Bizikova, L. and Pinter, L. *Indicator Preferences in National Reporting of Progress Toward the Sustainable Development Goals.* IISD, June 2017.

Boskovic, O. *L'efficacité du droit de l'environnement. Mise en œuvre et sanctions.* Paris: Dalloz, 2010.

Botero, J. and Ponce, A. *Measuring the Law.* Working Paper Series 1. World Justice Project, 2011.

Botero, J. C., Nelson, R. L., and Pratt, Ch. "Indices and Indicators of Justice, Governance, and the Rule of Law: An Overview". *Hague Journal on the Rule of Law*, Vol. 3/2, 2011 (pp. 153–169).

Breitmeir, H., Young, O. R., and Zurn, M. *Analyzing International Environmental Regimes: From Study to Database.* Cambridge: MIT Press, 2006.

Brimo, S. and Pauti, Ch. (eds.). *L'effectivité des droits. Regards en droit administratif.* Paris: Mare et Martin, 2019.

Brosset Briand, M. and others. *Le nombre et le droit.* Paris: L'Harmattan, 2020.

Burhenne-Guilmin, F. *Environmental Law in Developing Countries: Selected Issues*, Vol. 2. Environmental Policy and Law Paper No. 43. Gland: IUCN, 2004.

Canadian Bar Association. *Access to Justice Metrics: A Discussion Paper.* Ottawa, 2013.

Canadian Council for International Co-operation. *Progressing National SDGs Implementation: An Independent Assessment of the Voluntary National Review Reports Submitted to the United Nations High-Level Political Forum on Sustainable Development in 2018.* Ottawa, 2019.

Cato Institute. *The Human Freedom Index 2019. A Global Measurement of Personal, Civil, and Economic Freedom*. Washington, D.C., 2019.

Caveng, R. "La production des enquêtes quantitatives". *Revue d'anthropologie des connaissances*, Vol. 6, No. 1, 2012 (pp. 65–88). https://www.cairn.info/revue-anthropologie-des-connaissances-2012-1-page-65.htm.

Cling, J. P., Razafindrakoto, M., and Roubaud, F. "L'ODD 16 sur la gouvernance et sa mesure. L'Afrique en tête". *Afrique contemporaine*, No. 258, 2/2016.

Core Humanitarian Standard. *Core Humanitarian Standard Guide and Indicators*. CHS Alliance, Sphere project and Groupe URD, 2016.

Cooter, R. and Ulen, T. *Law and Economics*, 6th ed. Boston: Addison Wesley Longman, 2012.

Council of Europe. *Rule of Law Checklist*. Strasbourg, 2016.

Couveinhes-Matsumoto, F. *L'effectivité en droit international*. Brussels: Bruylant, 2014.

COWI and Eunomia. *Study: The Costs of Not Implementing EU Environmental Law. Final Report*. Brussels: European Commission, 2019.

Crabbe, A. and Leroy, P. *The Handbook of Environmental Policy Evaluation*. London: Earthscan, 2008.

Craig, S. and Maggiotto, M. "Measuring Political Efficacy". *Political Methodology*, Vol. 8, No. 3, 1982 (pp. 85–109).

Dandurand, Y. and Jahn, J. *Access to Justice Measurement Framework*. Abbotsford, 2015.

Davis, K. E. "Legal Indicators: The Power of Quantitative Measures of Law". *Annual Review of Law and Social Science*, Vol. 10, 2014 (pp. 37–52).

Davis, K., Fisher, A., Kingsbury, B., and Merry, S. E. *Governance by Indicators: Global Power Through Quantification and Rankings*. Oxford: Oxford University Press, 2012.

Delmas, A. *Perspectives pour la révision de la stratégie Europe 2020*. Paris: Conseil économique, social et environnemental, 2015.

DESA. *Synthesis of Voluntary National Reviews 2016*. New York, 2016.

Doumbé-Billé, S. "La mise en œuvre et le suivi du droit international de l'environnement. Rapport général". In M. Prieur (ed.). *La mise en œuvre nationale du droit international de l'environnement dans les pays francophones*. Limoges: PULIM, 2003 (pp. 491–501).

Duclos, E. *La maîtrise statistique des procédés MSP/SPC*. Doussard: Emmanuel Duclos Conseil, 2008.

Dupuy, P. M. and Kerbrat, Y. *Droit international public*, 14th ed. Paris: Dalloz, 2018.

Dworkin, R. *Taking Rights Seriously.* Massachusetts: Harvard University Press, 1977.

Ebbeson, J. *Access to Justice in Environmental Matters in the EU.* Groningen: Kluwer Law International, 2002.

ECA. *Report on Institutional and Strategic Frameworks for Sustainable Development in Africa.* Addis Ababa, 2012.

ECA. *Africa Regional Report on the SDGs.* Addis Ababa, 2015.

Economic and Social Council, Economic Commission for Africa. *Report of the Seminar for Lawyers on Development of Environmental Protection Legislation in the ECA Region.* E/CN.14/784. 21 October 1980.

Environmental Protection Agency. *Principles of Environmental Enforcement.* Washington, D.C., 1992.

EPI. *Global Metrics for the Environment.* 2016. https://epi.envirocenter.yale.edu.

EPI. *Environmental Performance Index, 2018 Release.* https://sedac.ciesin.columbia.edu/data/set/epi-environmental-performance-index-2018.

EPI. *Environmental Performance Index 2020. Global Metrics for the Environment: Ranking Country Performance on Sustainability Issues.* https://epi.yale.edu/downloads/epipolicymakersummaryr9.pdf.

Ercmann, S. *Enforcement of Environmental Law in National and International Law.* 5th Colloquy on Environmental Protection Law, Prague. Strasbourg: Council of Europe, 1995.

European Commission for the Efficiency of Justice. *European Judicial System: Efficiency and Quality of Justice.* CEPEL Studies 11. Strasbourg: Council of Europe, 2008.

European Environment Agency. *The European Environment – State and Outlook 2020.*

European Environment Agency. *Environmental Indicators Report,* No 19. 2018.

European Environment Agency. *Digest of Environmental European Agency Indicators.* Technical Report No. 8. 2014.

Eurostat. "Links Between Statistics and European Union Policy. Euro-Indicators. Structural Indicators. Sustainable Development Indicators". *Europe in Figures,* 2006–2007 (pp. 318–323).

Eurostat. *Smarter, Greener, More Inclusive? Indicators to Support the Europe 2020 Strategy,* 2019 edition. European Union, September 2019.

Eurostat. *EU SDG Indicators Set 2020. Result of the Review in Preparation of the 2020 Edition of the EU SDG Monitoring Report.* European Commission, Final version of 16 January 2020.

FAO. *Improving Governance of Pastoral Lands.* Governance of Tenure Technical Guide 6. Rome, 2016.

FAO. *FAO and the SDGs. Indicators: Measuring Up to the 2030 Agenda for Sustainable Development.* Rome, 2017.

FAO. *Realizing Women's Rights to Land in the Law. A Guide for Reporting on SDG Indicator 5.a.2.* Rome, 2018.

FAO. *The State of World Fisheries and Aquaculture 2018 – Meeting the Sustainable Development Goals.* Rome, 2018.

FAO. *Incorporating Environmental Flows Into "water stress" Indicator 6.4.2 – Guidelines for a Minimum Standard Method for Global Reporting.* Rome, 2019.

FAO. *Tracking Progress on Food and Agriculture Related SDG Indicators. A Report on the Indicators Under FAO Custodianship.* Rome, 2019.

Faure, M. *Analyse économique du droit de l'environnement.* Preface by Michel Prieur. Brussels: Bruylant, 2006.

Ferchichi, W. *La protection de l'environnement en droit tunisien.* Preface by M. Prieur. Tunis: Centre d'études juridiques et judiciaires, 2013.

Fukuda-Parr, S. and McNeil, D. "Knowledge and Politics in Setting and Measuring the SDGs". *Global Policy*, Vol. 10, 2019 (pp. 5–15).

Fundamental Rights Agency. *Developing indicators for the protection, respect and promotion of the rights of the child in the European Union.* Vienna, 2010.

Fundamental Rights Agency. *The Right to Political Participation for Persons with Disabilities: Human Rights Indicators.* Vienna, 2014.

Frydman, B. and Van Waeyenberge, A. *Gouverner par les standards et les indicateurs: de Hume aux* rankings. Brussels: Bruylant, 2014.

Gennari, P. and Kalamvrezos Navarro, D. *A bold call for action needed on measuring SDG indicators.* IISD, 28 April 2020.

Ginsburg, T. "Pitfalls of Measuring the Rule of Law". *Hague Journal on the Rule of Law*, Vol. 3/2, 2011 (pp. 269–280).

Goggin, M. L. and others. *Implementation Theory and Practice: Toward a Third Generation.* Glenview: Scott Foresman, 1990.

Gross Cunha, L., Luci de Oliveira, F. and Glezer, R. E. "Brazilian Justice Confidence Index. Measuring Public Perception on Judicial Performance in Brazil". *Revista Colombiana de Derecho Internacional*, No. 25, 2014 (pp. 445–472).

Gramatikov, A. and others. *A Handbook for Measuring the Cost and Quality of Access to Justice.* Antwerp: Maklu and Tilburg Institute for Interdisciplinary Studies of Civil Law and Conflict Resolution Systems, 2009.

Granier, L. (ed.). *Aspects contemporains du droit de l'environnement en Afrique de l'Ouest et centrale*, IUCN, UNEP, Droit et politique de l'environnement No. 69, Gland, 2008.

Gündling, L. *Legal obstacles to the application of nature conservation legislation.* Nature and environment No. 89. Strasbourg: Council of Europe, 1997.

Gupta, D. K. and others. "Creating a Composite Index for Assessing Country Performance in the Field of Human Rights: Proposal for a New Methodology". *Human Rights Quarterly*, Vol. 16, 1994 (pp. 131–162).

Hopper, J. S. *A Mixed-Methods Approach to Analyzing Environmental Enforcement in the American States.* SAGE Research Methods Cases, 2019.

HLPF. *2017 Voluntary National Reviews Synthesis Report.* New York: DESA, 2017.

HLPF. *2018 Voluntary National Reviews Synthesis Report.* New York: DESA, 2018.

HLPF. *2019 Voluntary National Reviews Synthesis Report.* New York: DESA, 2019.

HLPF. *Handbook for the Preparation of Voluntary National Reviews. The 2020 Edition.* New York, 2019.

Hsu, A. and others. *The 2016 Environmental Performance Index.* New Haven: Yale Center for Environmental Law and Policy, 2016.

ICCWC. *Indicator Framework for Combating Wildlife and Forest Crime. A Self-Assessment Framework for National Use. Assessment Template.* July 2016.

ILO. *Decent Work Indicators: Guidelines for Producers and Users of Statistical and Legal Framework Indicators.* ILO Manual, Second version. Geneva, 2013.

ILO. *Programme and Budget for the Biennium 2018–19.* Geneva, 2017.

IMPEL. *Challenges in the Practical Implementation of European Union Environmental Law and How IMPEL Could Help Overcome Them*, 2015

INECE. *Performance Measurement Guidance for Compliance and Enforcement Practitioners*, 2nd ed., 2008.

INECE-OECD. *Workshop on Environmental Compliance and Enforcement Indicators: Measuring What Matters.* Paris, 2004.

Institut français de l'environnement. "45 indicateurs de développement durable: une contribution de l'IFEN". *Études et travaux*, No. 41, 2003.

Institute for Economics & Peace. *SDG16+ Progress Report 2019. A Comprehensive Global Audit of Progress on Available SDG16 Indicators*, March 2019.

Inter-American Commission on Human Rights. *Guidelines for Preparation of Progress Indicators in the Area of Economic, Social and Cultural Rights.* 19 July 2008. OEA/SER.L/V/II.132.

Inter-American Development Bank and World Justice Project. *Environmental Governance Indicators for Latin America and the Caribbean. A Cross-Country*

Assessment of Environmental Governance in Practice in Argentina, Bolivia, Brazil, Colombia, Costa Rica, the Dominican Republic, El Salvador, Jamaica, Peru & Uruguay, 2020.

International Conference on Environmental Enforcement. Budapest, 1992.

International Council on Human Rights Policy and Office of the United Nations High Commissioner for Human Rights. *Assessing the Effectiveness of National Human Rights Institutions.* Geneva, 2005.

Inter-Parliamentary Union. *Parliaments and the Sustainable Development Goals: A Self-Assessment Toolkit.* Geneva, 2016.

IUCN. *Introduction to the African Convention on the Conservation of Nature and Natural Resources*, 2nd ed. Gland, 2006.

Jeammaud, A. *Le concept d'impact des normes sociales européennes, quels indicateurs?* CRDS (IETL), Université de Lyon 2, 2005.

Jeammaud, A. "Le concept d'effectivité en droit". In Ph. Auvergnon (ed.). *L'effectivité du droit du travail, à quelles conditions?* Bordeaux: Presses universitaires de Bordeaux, 2008.

Kamto, M. *Droit de l'environnement en Afrique.* Paris: EDICEF-AUPELF, 1996.

Kaufmann, D. and Kraay, A. "Two Comments on 'Governance Indicators: Where Are We, Where Should We Be Going?' ". *The World Bank Research Observer*, Vol. 23, No. 1 (2008), pp. 31–36.

Kaufman, D., Kraay, A. and Mastruzzi, M. *The Worldwide Governance Indicators: Methodology and Analytical Issues.* Policy Research Working Paper, No. 5430. Washington, D.C.: World Bank, 2010.

Krever, T. "Quantifying Law: Legal Indicator Projects and the Reproduction of Neoliberal Common Sense". *Third World Quarterly*, Vol. 34, No. 1, 2013 (pp. 131–150).

Lavieille, J.-M., Delzangles, H. and Le Bris, C. *Droit international de l'environnement*, 4th ed. Paris: Ellipses, 2018.

Lavieille, J.-M. (ed.). *Conventions de protection de l'environnement. Secrétariats, conférences des parties, comités d'experts.* Limoges: PULIM, 1999.

Leroy, Y. *L'effectivité du droit au travers d'un questionnement en droit du travail.* Paris: LGDJ, 2011.

Lévy-Bruhl, H. "Note sur la statistique et le droit". In *La statistique, ses applications, les problèmes qu'elle soulève.* Paris: Presses universitaires de France, 1935 (pp. 141–147).

Maggino, F. (ed.). *Complexity in Society: From Indicators Construction to Their Synthesis.* New York: Springer, 2017.

Marais du, B. (ed.). *Des indicateurs pour mesurer le droit? Les limites méthodologiques des rapports*, Doing Business. Paris: La Documentation française, 2006.

Martel, J.-P. *Les œuvres complètes de Marguerite T. De Bané*. Montreal: Cercle du Livre de France, 1973.

Martin, P., Boer, B., and Slobodian, L. (eds.). *Framework for Assessing and Improving Law for Sustainability. A Legal Component of a Natural Resource Governance Framework*. Environmental Policy and Law Paper, No. 87. Gland: IUCN, 2016 (pp. 124–125).

Martinand, Cl. *Environnement et développement durable. L'indispensable mobilisation des acteurs économiques et sociaux*. Paris: Conseil économique et social, Opinion No. 8, 12 March 2003.

Mauerhofer, V. "A Bottom Up 'Convention-Check' to Improve Top-Down Global Protected Area Governance". *Land Use Policy*, Vol. 28/4, 2011 (pp. 877–886).

May, J. and Daly, E. *Judicial Handbook on Environmental Constitutionalism*. Nairobi: UNEP, 2017.

McDonald, S. *Development of an Access to Justice Index for Canada's Federal Administrative Bodies in Canada*. 2017. www.justice.gc.ca.

McGrath, C. *Does Environmental Law Work? How to Evaluate the Effectiveness of an Environmental Legal System*. Riga: Lambert Academic Publishing, 2010.

McGrath, C. *How to Evaluate the Effectiveness of an Environmental Legal System*, PhD Thesis. University of Queensland, 2007.

Merry, S. E., Davis, K. E., and Kingsburg, B. (eds.). *The Quiet Power of Indicators: Measuring Governance, Corruption and Rule of Law*. Cambridge: Cambridge University Press, 2015.

Mickwitz, P. "A Framework for Evaluating Environmental Policy Instruments: Context and Key Concepts". *Evaluation*, Vol. 9/4, 2003 (pp. 415–436).

Mo Ibrahim Foundation. *African Governance Report 2019. Agendas 2063 and 2030: Is Africa on Track?* 2019

Navarro, G. "Diseño de un Sistema de Indicadores para Programa Estratégico Regional para el Manejo de los Ecosistemas Forestales (PERFOR). Región de América Central y República Dominicana". *Jornadas de Análisis Estadístico*, Universidad de Costa Rica, 2016.

OECD. *Environmental Indicators*. Paris, 1991.

OECD. *Environmental Indicators for Agriculture. Concepts and Framework for Analysis*, Vol. 1. Paris, 1999.

OECD. *Environmental Indicators for Agriculture. Key Issues and Design.* The York Seminar, Vol. 2, 1999.

OECD. *Environmental Indicators for Agriculture. Methods and Results.* Paris, 2001.

OECD. *Key Environmental Indicators.* Paris, 2008

OECD. *Ensuring Environmental Compliance. Trends and Good Practices.* Paris, 2009.

OECD. *OECD Environmental Outlook to 2050: The Consequences of Inaction.* Paris, 2012.

OECD. *Green Growth Indicators for Agriculture.* Paris, 2015.

OECD. *Comment va la vie? Mesurer le bien-être.* Paris, 2017.

OECD. *Outcome Performance Measures of Environmental Compliance Assurance: Current Practices, Constraints and Ways Forward.* Paris, 2010.

OECD. *Environmental Enforcement in Decentralised Governance Systems: Towards a Nationwide Level Playing Field.* Paris, 2011.

OECD. *Green Growth Indicators.* Paris, 2014.

OECD. *Environment at a Glance: OECD Indicators.* Paris, 2015.

OECD. *How's Life? 2020. Measuring Well-Being.* Paris, 2020.

OECD. Joint Research Centre of the European Commission. *Handbook on Constructing Composite Indicators. Methodology and User Guide.* Paris: OECD, 2008.

OECD. Open Society Foundations. *Legal Needs Surveys and Access to Justice.* Paris: OECD, 2019.

Office of the High Commissioner for Human Rights. *Human Rights Indicators. Guide to Measurement and Implementation.* Geneva, 2012.

Office of the High Commissioner for Human Rights. *A Human Rights-Based Approach to Data. Leaving No One Behind in the 2030 Agenda for Sustainable Development.* Geneva, 2018.

Organization of American States. *Progress Indicators for Measuring Rights Under the Protocol of San Salvador.* OEA/Ser.L/XXV.2.1, GT/PSS/doc9/13, 2013.

Pariente-Butterlin, I. *Le droit, la norme et le réel.* Paris: PUF, coll. Quadrige, 2005.

Parsons, J. "Developing Clusters of Indicators: An Alternative Approach to Measuring the Provision of Justice". *Hague Journal on the Rule of Law*, Vol. 3, 2011 (pp. 170–185).

Parsons, J. and others. *Developing Indicators to Measure the Rule of Law: A Global Approach.* Vera Institute of Justice and Altus Global Alliance, 2008.

Pillet, M. *Appliquer la maîtrise statistique des processus MSP/SPC*, 6th ed. Paris: Eyrolles, 2005.

Pleasence, P. and Balmer, N. "Measuring the Accessibility and Equality of Civil Justice". *Hague Journal on the Rule of Law*, Vol. 10, 2018 (pp. 255–294).

Praia City Group. *Handbook on Governance Statistics*, 2020. https://paris21.org/news-center/news/new-praia-city-group-handbook-governance-statistics.

Prieur, M. (ed.). *Vers un nouveau droit de l'environnement? Réunion mondiale des juristes et associations de droit de l'environnement*. Limoges: CIDCE, 2003.

Prieur, M. (ed.). *La mise en œuvre nationale du droit international de l'environnement dans les pays francophones*. Limoges: PULIM, 2003.

Prieur, M. *Droit de l'environnement, droit durable*. Brussels: Bruylant, 2014.

Prieur, M. *Les indicateurs juridiques, outils d'évaluation de l'effectivité du droit de l'environnement*. Québec: IFDD, 2018.

Prieur, M. "Pour des indicateurs juridiques des objectifs de développement durable et de la biodiversité". *Humanité et Biodiversité*, No. 5, 2018–2019 (pp. 218–222).

Prieur, M. "The Principle of Non Regression". In L. Krämer and E. Orlando (eds.). *Principles of Environmental Law*. Elgar Encyclopaedia of Environmental Law Series. Cheltenham: Edward Elgar Publishing, Vol. VI, 2018.

Prieur, M. and others. *Droit de l'environnement*, 8th ed. Paris: Dalloz, 2019.

Prieur, M. and Doumbé-Billé, S. *Recueil francophone des traités et textes internationaux en droit de l'environnement*, 2nd ed. Brussels: Bruylant, AUPELF-UREF, 2012.

Prieur, M. and Mekouar, M. A. "Measuring the Effectivity of Environmental Law Through Legal Indicators in the Context of Francophone Africa". In P. Kameri-Mbote and C. Odote (eds.). *Blazing the Trail. Professor Charles Okidi's Enduring Legacy in the Development of Environmental Law*. University of Nairobi, School of Law, 2019 (pp. 238–256).

Prieur, M. and Sozzo, G. (eds.). *La non régression en droit de l'environnement*. Brussels: Bruylant, 2012.

Quiroga Martínez, R. *Guía metodológica para desarrollar indicadores ambientales y de desarrollo sostenible en países de América Latina y el Caribe*. Santiago de Chile: CEPAL, 2009.

Rangeon, F. "Réflexions sur l'effectivité du droit". In CURAPP, *Les usages sociaux du droit*. Paris: PUF, 1989.

Richard, V. *Le droit et l'effectivité, contribution à l'étude d'une notion*, thèse de droit, Paris II, 2003.

Rosga, A. and Satterthwaite M. L. "The Trust in Indicators: Measuring Human Rights". *Berkeley Journal of International Law*, Vol. 27/2, 2009 (pp. 253–315).

Rowe, G. and Frewer, L. J. "Evaluating Public Participation Exercises: A Research Agenda". *Science, Technology and Human Values*, Vol. 29/4, 2004 (pp. 512–556).

Sadeleer de, N. *Les principes du pollueur-payeur, de prévention et de précaution*. Brussels: Bruylant-AUF, 1999.

Sand, P. H. *The Effectiveness of International Environmental Agreements. A Survey of Existing Legal Instruments*. Cambridge: Grotius, 1992.

Sand, P. H. "The Effectiveness of Multinational Environmental Agreements: Theory and Practice". In M. Lewis, T. Honkonen and S. Romppanen (eds.). *International Environmental Law-making and Diplomacy Review 2016*. Joensuu, University of Eastern Finland Law School. UNEP Course Series 16, 2017 (pp. 1–25).

SDSN. *Assessing Gaps in Indicators Availability and Coverage*, July 2014.

SDSN. *Indicators and a Monitoring Framework: Launching a Data Revolution for the Sustainable Development Goals*, 12 June 2015.

Siems, M. M. "Measuring the Immeasurable: How to Turn Law into Numbers". In M. Faure and J. Smits (eds.). *Does Law Matter? On Law and Economic Growth*. Cambridge: Intersentia, 2011 (pp. 115–136).

Siems, M. M. "Numerical Comparative Law: Do We Need Statistical Evidence in Order to Reduce Complexity?". *Cardozo Journal of International and Comparative Law*, Vol. 13, 2005 (pp. 521–40).

Social Indicators Research (International and interdisciplinary journal for quality-of-life measurement published by Springer since 1974).

Social Indicators Research Book Series, 73 volumes, 1997–2020 (Springer).

Solidarity Water Programme. *Sustainable Development Goals for Water and Sanitation Services. Interpreting the Targets and Indicators*. Paris, 2018.

Supiot, A. *La gouvernance par les nombres*. Paris: Fayard, 2015.

Theys, J. "À la recherche du développement durable: un détour par les indicateurs ». In M. Jolivet (ed.). *Le développement durable, de l'utopie au concept. De nouveaux chantiers pour la recherche*. Paris: Elsevier and NSS, 2001 (pp. 269–285).

Tonou, G. (ed.). *Indicators of Quality of Life in Latin America*. New York: Springer, 2016.

UN Habitat. *Proposed Global Land Indicators. Status Report on GLII Indicator Formulation, Disaggregation, Data Sources and Methodology*. GLII Working Paper No. 3. Nairobi, 2015.

UN Habitat. *Sourcebook for Operationalisation of Global Land Indicators*. GLII Working Paper No. 4. Nairobi, 2016.

UN Habitat. *A Multi-Country Capacity Assessment of National Statistical Offices Preparedness to Report on SDG Indicator 1.4.2.* GLII, Working Paper No. 7. Nairobi, 2017.

UNDP. *Access to Justice Assessments in the Asia Pacific: A Review of Experiences and Tools from the Region.* Bangkok, 2012.

UNDP. *Human Development Report 2004. Cultural Liberty in Today's Diverse World.* New York, 2004.

UNDP. *Human Development Report 2011. Sustainability and Equity: A Better Future for All.* New York, 2011.

UNDP. *Human Development Report 2014. Sustaining Human Progress: Reducing Vulnerabilities and Building Resilience.* New York, 2014.

UNDP. *Human Development Report 2016. Human Development for All.* New York, 2016.

UNDP. *Human Development Indices and Indicators: 2018 Statistical Update.* New York, 2018.

UNDP. *Human Development Report 2019. Beyond Income, Beyond Averages, Beyond Today: Inequalities in Human Development in the 21st Century.* New York, 2019.

UNDP. *Africa Human Development Report 2016. Accelerating Gender Equality and Women's Empowerment in Africa.* New York, 2016.

UNEP. *Africa Environmental Outlook: Past, Present and Future Prospects.* Nairobi, 2002.

UNEP. *Towards a Green Economy: Pathways to Sustainable Development and Poverty Eradication.* Nairobi, 2011.

UNEP. *Review of Institutional Capacity Building for Environmental Law and Institutions of Africa*, 2nd ed. Nairobi, 2000.

UNEP. *Measuring Progress Towards an Inclusive Green Economy.* Nairobi, 2012.

UNEP. Intersessional Meeting of the Forum of Ministers of Environment for Latin America and the Caribbean. *Working Group on Environmental Indicators of the Forum of Ministers of Environment of Latin America and the Caribbean.* UNEP/LAC-IC.1.2015/7. 17–19 November 2015.

UNEP. *Environmental Rule of Law. First Global Report.* Nairobi, 2019.

UNEP-ILAC. *Regional Indicators Revision 2011.* Latin American and Caribbean Initiative for Sustainable Development, www.geodatos.org.

UNEP-UNDP. *Compendium of Environmental Laws of African Countries. Sectoral Environmental Laws and Regulations*, Vol. 1–7, 1996–2002.

UNESCO. *Culture Indicators 2030.* Paris, 2019.

UNESCO. *Highlights from the 2019 UNESCO Monitoring and Reporting of SDG Indicator 16.10.2 – Access to Information*. Paris, 2019.

United Nations Department of Economic and Social Affairs. *Public Governance Indicators: A Literature Review*. ST/ESA/PAD/SER.E/100. New York, 2007.

UN-Water. *Sustainable Development Goal 6 Synthesis. Report 2018 on Water and Sanitation*. New York, 2018.

Victor, D. G., Raustiala, K., and Skolnikoff, E. B. (eds.). *The Implementation and Effectiveness of International Environmental Commitments: Theory and Practice*. Cambridge: MIT Press, 1998.

Vladimirova, K. and Le Blanc, D. *How Well Are the Links Between Education and Other Sustainable Development Goals Covered in UN Flagship Reports? A Contribution to the Study of the Science-Policy Interface on Education in the UN System Department of Economic & Social Affairs*. DESA Working Paper No. 146. New York, October 2015.

Voigt, S. "How to Measure the Rule of Law?". *Kyklos*, Vol. 65/2, 2012 (pp. 262–284).

Werker, J. and Silva de, L. *The Environmental Democracy Index*. Technical Note. World Resources Institute, 2015.

WHO. *Stronger Collaboration, Better Health. Global Action Plan for Healthy Lives and Well-Being for All: Strengthening Collaboration Among Multilateral Organizations to Accelerate Country Progress on the Health-Related Sustainable Development Goals*. Geneva, 2019.

Winograd, M. *Indicadores ambientales para Latinoamérica y el Caribe: hacia la sustentabilidad en el uso de tierras*. San José: IICA, 1995.

Winter, G. *Assessing Law as a Factor Towards the Aichi Biodiversity Targets*. 2014. https://www.iucn.org/sites/dev/files/assessing_law_as_a_factor_toward_the_aichi_biodiversity_targets_0.pdf.

WJP Rule of Law Index 2020. https://worldjusticeproject.org/our-work/research-and-data/wjp-rule-law-index-2020.

WMO-GWP. *Handbook on Drought Indicators and Indices*. Integrated Drought Management Programme. Geneva, 2016.

Wolfrum, R. "Means of Ensuring Compliance with and Enforcement of International Environmental Law". *Recueil des cours de l'Académie de droit international*, Vol. 272, 1999.

Wood, C. *Environmental Impact Assessment: A Comparative Review*. London: Prentice Hall, 1995.

Woodruff, C. "Measuring Institutions". In S. Rose-Ackerman (ed.). *International Handbook on the Economics of Corruption*. Northampton: Edward Elgar, 2006 (pp. 105–124).

World Bank. *World Development Report 2020. Trade for Development in an Era of Global Value Chains.* Washington, D.C., 2020.

World Bank. *Atlas of Sustainable Development Goals 2018. World Development Indicators.* Washington, D.C., 2018.

World Bank. *A Decade of Measuring the Quality of Governance: Governance Matters 2007. Worldwide Governance Indicators 1996–2007.* Washington, D.C., 2007.

World Bank. *World Development Indicators.* 2015–2020. https://databank.banquemondiale.org/source/world-development-indicators.

World Bank. *Atlas of Sustainable Development Goals 2017. World Development Indicators.* Washington, D.C., 2017.

World Bank. *World Development Report. Governance and the Law.* Washington, D.C., 2017.

World Bank. *World Development Report 2020. Trading for Development in the Age of Global Value Chains.* Washington, D.C., 2020.

World Health Organization and Secretariat of the Convention on Biological Diversity. *Connecting Global Priorities: Biodiversity and Human Health. A State of Knowledge Review.* Geneva-Montreal, 2015.

Worldwide Governance Indicators 2019. https://info.worldbank.org/gouvernance/wgi.

*Online indicators**

World Bank Worldwide Governance Indicators. http://info.worldbank.org/governance/wgi/index.aspx#faq

UNDP Governance Assessment Portal. http://www.gaportal.org/areas-of-governance

Transparency International Corruption Perception Index. http://www.transparency.org/research/cpi/overview

CBD Biodiversity Indicators Partnership. http://www.bipindicators.net

Yale Environmental Performance Index. http://www.epi.yale.edu

International Property Rights Index. http://internationalpropertyrightsindex.org

World Bank Indicators. http://data.worldbank.org/indicator/all

Global Integrity Index Data. https://www.globalintegrity.org/downloads

World Commodity Indexes. http://www.indexmundi.com/commodities

CIA World Factbook. https://www.cia.gov/library/publications/the-world-factbook/rankorder/rankorderguide.html

Inclusive Wealth Report. http://www.ihdp.unu.edu/article/iwr

World Bank Country Datasets. http://data.worldbank.org/country

Country Property Rights Index. http://www.internationalpropertyrightsindex.org/ranking

Index Mundi – Gini Coefficient by Country. http://www.indexmundi.com/facts/indicators/SI.POV.GINI/compare?country=au#country=dz:ar:au:bb:bz:s3

FAO Statistics – by Country. http://faostat3.fao.org/faostat-gateway/go/to/browse/I/*/E

Global Development Information. http://www.eldis.org

UN Public Administration Portal – Country Profiles. http://www.unpan.org/DPADM/ProductsServices/ThematicPortals/PublicAdministrationCountryProfiles/tabid/677/Default.aspx

Worldwide Governance Indicators. http://info.worldbank.org/governance/wgi/index.aspx#home

Index of Economic Freedom. http://www.heritage.org/index/explore?view=by-variables

* *Source*: Martin, P., Boer, B., and Slobodian, L. (eds.). *Framework for Assessing and Improving Law for Sustainability. A Legal Component of a Natural Resource Governance Framework.* Environmental Policy and Law Paper No. 87. Gland: IUCN, 2016 (pp. 124–125).

Annexes

1. Effectivity and effectiveness
2. Extracts from texts on the effectiveness of environmental law
3. UNEP, *Environmental Rule of Law. First Global Report* (2019), Figure 6.1: Environmental Rule of Law and the Sustainable Development Goals
4. UNEP, *Environmental Rule of Law. First Global Report* (2019), Box 6.1: Indicator Framework for Environmental Rule of Law
5. Article 2.4 of the Decree of 3 December 2019 on the organization of the Department for Legislation and Quality of Law at the General Secretariat of the Government, (*organisation du service de législation et de la qualité du droit au secrétariat général du Gouvernement*), JORF No 0282 (5 December 2019)
6. Article 6.8 of the Regional Agreement on Access to Information, Public Participation and Justice in Environmental Matters in Latin America and the Caribbean, Escazú, 4 March 2018
7. Draft motion presented by the International Centre for Comparative Environmental Law and adopted as a resolution by the IUCN World Conservation Congress, Marseille, 7–15 January 2021, on: "Measuring the effectivity of environmental law thanks to legal indicators"

Annex 1 Effectivity and effectiveness

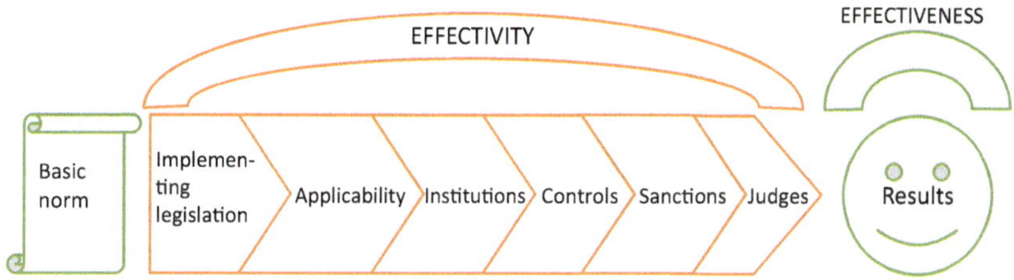

Annex 2 Extracts from texts on the effectiveness of environmental law and indicators

1. Rio Declaration, 1992
   Principle 11: "States shall enact *effective* environmental legislation".
2. Rio Agenda 21, 1992
   "Making laws and regulations more *effective*" (para. 8.16.a).
3. Madrid Protocol on Integrated Coastal Zone Management in the Mediterranean, 2008
   "The Parties shall define appropriate *indicators* in order to evaluate the *effectiveness* of integrated coastal zone management strategies, plans and programmes as well as the progress of implementation of the Protocol." (art. 18.4).
4. Report of the Secretary-General of the United Nations, "Delivering justice: programme of action to strengthen the rule of law at the national and international levels", 16 March 2012 (A/66/749, para. 56)
   "Member States may also wish to consider how progress in the attainment of rule of law goals, once agreed upon, can be *effectively monitored*."
5. UNEP Governing Council decision 27/9 on advancing justice, governance and law for environmental sustainability, 2013
   (4) "combat the noncompliance with environmental laws, including measures to increase the *effectiveness* of administrative, civil and criminal enforcement mechanisms".
6. Mid-term review of the fourth Montevideo Programme, second session of the United Nations Environment Assembly, Nairobi, May 2016 (UNEP/EA.2/13) [same spelling as in para. 13 below]
   "Developing criteria to assist States in assessing the *effectiveness* of environmental law".
7. UNEP medium-term strategy 2018–2021, May 2016 (UNEP/EA.2/15)
   "*Indicator*-based reporting and assessment to keep the environment under review".
8. G7 – Bologna, June 2017
   "...develop new *indicators*".

9. Recommendation of the Committee of Ministers of the Council of Europe on the Landscape Convention, 27 September 2017 (CM/Rec (2017)7)
   "include the 'landscape', as defined by the Convention, in the *indicators* of sustainable development relating to environmental, social, cultural and economic issues."
10. Ministerial declaration of the United Nations Environment Assembly at its third session, Nairobi, 6 December 2017 (UNEP/EA.3/HLS.1)
    "We will increase research and encourage the development, collation and use of reliable scientific and disaggregated data. This will include providing better *multidisciplinary indicators*" (para. 8.a).
11. *Déclaration des ONG à la 3e Assemblée des Nations Unies pour l'environnement*
    "Les indicateurs existants mesurant la réalisation des objectifs de développement durable 2030 ne tiennent pas compte du rôle du droit de l'environnement dans la réalisation de ces objectifs. Il est désormais nécessaire de combler ce vide et de mettre en place des indicateurs juridiques *qui fourniraient des données pour une meilleure gouvernance des lois sur l'environnement et pour mieux documenter leur effectivité".*
    There is no official English translation of this document, but it reads as follows:
    NGO Statement to the third United Nations Environment Assembly.
    "Existing indicators measuring the achievement of the 2030 sustainable development goals do not take into account the role of environmental law in achieving these goals. There is now a need to fill this gap and to put in place *legal indicators* that would provide data for better governance of environmental laws and to better document their effectivity".
12. Resolution of the 4th session of the United Nations Environment Assembly adopting the fifth Montevideo Environmental Law Programme, Nairobi, 15 March 2019 (UNEP/EA.4/19, Annex 1, para. 4.a)
    "Provide … *model indicators* to countries for the effective and inclusive development and implementation of environmental law".
13. Ministerial declaration of the United Nations Environment Assembly at its 4th session (UNEP/EA.4/HLS.1)
    "We recognize that the *effective* implementation of these actions requires enabling and coherent policy frameworks, good governance and *law enforcement* at the global, regional, national, subnational and local levels, and *effective means of implementation*".
14. Report of the 21st Meeting of the Contracting Parties to the Barcelona Convention for the Protection of the Marine Environment and the Coastal

Region of the Mediterranean and its Protocols, Naples, 5 December 2019 (UNEP/MED IG.24/22)
"Enhanced evaluation of the effectiveness of the Convention and its protocols, which was crucial for the continued relevance of the system, called for the strengthening of *legal and other indicators*, assisted by partners such as the International Centre for Comparative Environmental Law." (para. 90)

15. Decision IG.24/1 of the Compliance Committee at the 21st Meeting of the Contracting Parties to the Barcelona Convention for the Protection of the Marine Environment and the Coastal Region of the Mediterranean and its Protocols, Naples, 5 December 2019
"In this context, the Compliance Committee also discussed the development of *legal environmental indicators* for measuring the effectiveness of the Barcelona Convention and its Protocols as an avenue that should be explored in future."

Annex 3 UNEP, *Environmental Rule of law. First Global Report*, 2019

Figure 6.1: Environmental Rule of Law and the Sustainable Development Goals

Notes: An arrow pointing toward the goal indicates that environmental rule of law supports its achievement, and an arrow pointing from a goal indicates that it supports environmental rule of law. Many are mutually reinforcing. Numbers denote the number of each goal's targets that are considered to support or be supported by environmental rule of law. Because some targets both support environmental rule of law and are in turn supported by it, the numbers for some goals may total more than the number of targets enumerated for the goal.

Annex 4 UNEP, *Environmental Rule of law. First Global Report*, 2019

Box 6.1: Indicator Framework for Environmental Rule of Law

Contextual Factors

1. Demography (distribution of wealth; population density, age structure, urban/rural; education/literacy; gender equity)
2. Economy (contribution of natural resource/extractive sector to the state economy; per capita income; evenness of development)
3. Politics (fragility; corruption perception; rule of law generally)
4. Legal System (type; judicial independence; respect for contracts and property rights)

Laws & Institutions

1. Coverage of laws (national environmental laws covering relevant environmental issues)
2. Procedural mechanisms (transparency and access to information, public participation, independent review and oversight of implementation measures)
3. Right to a healthy environment (explicitly recognized in the constitution, held by a court to be implicit in other constitutional rights, or guaranteed by legislation)
4. Rights of free association and free speech (constitutional)
5. Right of nondiscrimination (constitutional)
6. Rights of marginalized populations (indigenous peoples; women; other)
7. Legal pluralism (recognition of customary norms governing natural resources)
8. Anti-corruption measures (covering the environmental context)

Implementation

1. Information collection, management, and use
2. Permits, licenses, and concessions
3. Criteria for implementation of environmental law
4. Enforcement (number of violations – trafficking, illegal pollution; number of inspections per capita or per regulated entity; number of administrative/civil/criminal cases brought; number of convictions/violations corrected; total fines and prison items)

5. Environmental auditing and institutional review mechanisms
6. Corruption (in the control of natural resources/concessions; in management of natural resource revenues; in the enforcement process)

Civic Engagement

1. Access to information (on laws/regulations/judicial decisions; on the state of the environment; on emission data/reports/audits; on natural resource concessions and revenues; media)
2. Public participation (in developing laws and regulations; in permitting/licensing/awarding concessions; in environmental impact assessment; community-based natural resource management; in monitoring and enforcement)
3. Environmental defenders (number of land or environmental defenders attacked/killed; number of attacks/murders prosecuted and convicted)

Dispute Resolution and Access to Justice

1. Effective dispute resolution bodies (courts and tribunals, administrative environmental tribunals, alternative dispute resolution, customary courts)
2. Access to justice (standing; costs, geographic accessibility; timeliness; availability of counsel and advocacy nongovernmental organizations)
3. Remedies

Environmental Outcomes and Current Status

1. Environmental health
2. Environmental compliance by sector
3. Natural resource stewardship

Annex 5 *Article 2.4 de l'arrêté du 3 décembre 2019 relatif à l'organisation du service de législation et de la qualité du droit au secrétariat général du Gouvernement (JORF n° 0282 du 5 décembre 2019)*

Article 2 – *Le service de la législation et de la qualité du droit est chargé, à titre principal, des missions suivantes: …*

4 – *Il suit les mesures d'application des lois et renseigne les* indicateurs *de performances correspondants.*

There is no official English translation of this document, but it reads as follows:

Article 2.4 of the Decree of 3 December 2019 on the organisation of the [French] Department for Legislation and Quality of Law at the General Secretariat of the Government (JORF No. 0282, 5 December 2019)

Article 2 - The Department for Legislation and Quality of Law has the following principal tasks: …

4 – It monitors application of the law and reports on the corresponding performance *indicators.*

Annex 6 Article 6.8 of the Regional Agreement on Access to Information, Public Participation and Justice in Environmental Matters in Latin America and the Caribbean, Escazú, 4 March 2018

Article 6.8: Each Party shall encourage independent environmental performance reviews that take into account nationally or internationally agreed criteria and guides and common *indicators*, with a view to evaluating the efficacy, effectiveness and progress of its national environmental policies in fulfillment of their national and international commitments. The reviews shall include participation by the various stakeholders.

Annex 7 Draft motion presented by the International Centre for Comparative Environmental Law and adopted as a resolution by the IUCN World Conservation Congress, Marseille, 7–15 January 2021, on: "Measuring the effectivity of environmental law thanks to legal indicators".

CONSIDERING that nature conservation requires the effective application of international, regional, national and local environmental rules;

AWARE that the implementation of these rules is often unsatisfactory, and that their application involves all the stakeholders, following a complex legal process: administrations, economic actors, legal professions, environmental associations;

OBSERVING that the reports on the state of the environment only assess policies through scientific or economic indicators, omitting to appreciate their legal effectiveness;

REGRETTING that the indicators regarding the Sustainable Development Goals are rarely aimed at the contribution of the law and lack qualitative data allowing for the assessment of the effectiveness of rules, thereby omitting the contribution of the law to the success or failure of environmental policies;

DELIGHTED AT the emerging interest in more representative indicators of the difficulties of applying environmental law, as revealed by the European Union's 7th Environment Action Plan, demanding specific indicators to control environmental legislation or the Ministerial declaration on the third session of the United Nations Environment Assembly encouraging the development of multidisciplinary indicators;

NOTING that the Escazú Regional Agreement on Access to Information, Public Participation and Justice in Environmental Matters in Latin America and the Caribbean provides for indicators to assess the efficacy, effectiveness and progress of environmental policies;

NOTING the promotion by IUCN, the United Nations Environment Programme, the Institute of La Francophonie for Sustainable Development-International Organisation of La Francophonie (IFDD-OIF) and the ECOWAS

of an innovative methodology designed by the International Centre for Comparative Environmental Law for the creation of legal indicators during the at the Symposium on the effectiveness of environmental law in French-speaking Africa (Yaoundé, 2018);

CONVINCED that the legal indicators will make it possible to measure the effective application of environmental law by using qualitative and quantitative data, on the basis of questionnaires relating to the existence and content of the rules, and the procedures for their implementation and their control; and

PERSUADED that the legal indicators will increase the visibility and legitimacy of environmental law, allowing for a greater understanding of the reasons why it is poorly or insufficiently applied;

The IUCN World Conservation Congress, at its session in Marseille, France, 7–15 January 2021:

1. CALLS ON the World Commission on Environmental Law and its members, supported by the IUCN Environmental Law Programme, to develop experiments and training in the creation of legal indicators on nature conservation, with the participation of law professors, lawyers, judges, prosecutors and the administrative services responsible for the enforcement of environmental law;
2. REQUESTS the IUCN Secretariat to invite the United Nations system and other international and regional organizations to add legal indicators to the existing indicators on the Sustainable Development Goals;
3. REQUESTS the States Parties and the European Union Party to regional and global conventions on the environment to also introduce legal indicators to measure the effectivity of such conventions through the implementation reports required by the same conventions;
4. INVITES all governments and NGOs members of IUCN to take voluntary initiatives to test and promote the creation of legal indicators under their domestic environmental law, in particular in the area of nature protection; and
5. URGES all the governments and secretariats of international and regional organizations to introduce legal indicators in their periodic reports on the state of the environment at the global, regional, national et local level.

Table of Contents

Series published titles

Vol. 1 Émilie Gaillard and David M. Forman (eds.), *Legal Actions for Future Generations*, 2020.

Vol. 2 Michel Prieur et Christophe Bastin (dir.) (avec la coll. de Mohamed Ali Mekouar), *Mesurer l'effectivité du droit de l'environnement. Des indicateurs juridiques au service du développement durable*, 2021.

Vol. 3 Michel Prieur and Christophe Bastin (eds.) (in coop. with Mohamed Ali Mekouar), *Measuring the Effectivity of Environmental Law. Legal Indicators for Sustainable Development*, 2021.

Vol. 4 Michel Prieur y Christophe Bastin (eds.) (con la colaboración de Mohamed Ali Mekouar), *Midiendo la efectividad de la Legislación Ambiental. Indicadores jurídicos al servicio del desarrollo sostenible*, 2021.

Vol. 5 Émilie Gaillard et Amandine Cayol (dir.), *Regards croisés sur le(s) transhumanisme(s)*, 2021.

Printed by
CPI books GmbH, Leck